Unsolved Texas Mysteries

Wallace O. Chariton

C. F. Eckhardt   Kevin R. Young

Republic of Texas Press

Library of Congress Cataloging-in-Publication Data

Chariton, Wallace O.
    Unsolved Texas mysteries / Wallace O. Chariton.
        p.   cm.
    Includes index.
    ISBN 1-55622-256-4
    1. Texas—History—Miscellanea. 2. Curiosities and wonders
—Texas. I. Title.
F386.5.C46   1990
976.4—dc20   90-12933
                                   CIP

2320 Los Rios Boulevard
Plano, Texas 75074

ISBN 1-55622-256-4
10 9 8 7 6
A9010

All inquiries for volume purchases of this book should be addressed to Wordware
Publishing, Inc., at the above address. Telephone inquiries may be made by calling:

(972) 423-0090

Contents

Acknowledgements

As is always the case when you write a book, remembering to thank all the people who helped along the way is a difficult task. The truth is, a lot of people are generally involved in one way or another with any writing project and it is often extremely hard to remember names or to find the little scraps of paper on which you dutifully recorded those names. With the fond hope that no one has been left out, I would like to thank the following people for their kind assistance.

I owe a large debt to Jerry Coley of the *Dallas Morning News*. Not only did he share his story about the Kennedy assassination, but he allowed me to print it, something he had refused to do for over twenty-five years. Thanks also to Joe Reynolds for introducing me to Mr. Coley.

Next, I would like to thank retired U.S. Marshal Clinton Peoples of Waco. Not only is he one of the most famous lawmen in the entire United States, he is also a generous, caring individual who took time out from his busy schedule to allow me an extensive interview on the Henry Marshall story.

My thanks to Kevin Young of San Antonio, not only for his great story on John Wilkes Booth, but also for being a friend and converted Texan. Mr. Young also sent me on a trail that ended with my sharing a pound of fantastic sausage with Charlie Eckhardt in Seguin. Mr. Eckhardt is a sure enough Texan and a new found friend. He also deserves a fair amount of credit for this book because he not only contributed one story but he also participated heavily in two others. Thanks Charlie and Kevin.

My appreciation goes out to the people of Eastland County for answering my questions one hot day. A special thanks to Roy Lee Smith for taking time out to discuss the most famous horned toad in history and to James Dabney for sharing his views.

Thanks also to Dorothy Vaughan of the *Paris News*. She allowed me some of her time and, more importantly, let me have a peek at some old files that contained information on Camp Maxey. In addition, a lot of people in Lamar County freely offered help and information to a stranger without ever asking his name or offering theirs. That proves, to me at least, that the Texans in that part of the country are among the friendliest in the state.

A very special thank-you goes out to Lt. Colonel Dan Wisely of the Army National Guard who probably broke some rule by allowing me to tour Camp Maxey and take photographs. Thanks also to SFC James H. Baker for acting as my guide, keeping me from being run over by a tank, and providing valuable information.

Another big thank-you goes out to Jo Ann Miller of Granbury. She not only allowed me and Kevin Young into her home, but she also let us copy some interesting and valuable photographs.

As always, I owe much appreciation to the staffs of the Dallas, Houston, Austin, and San Antonio public libraries, to the staff of the Texas State Archives, and the Barker Texas History Center at the University of Texas at Austin. A special thanks to Michael Green of the state archives for talking to me about a most difficult subject and to John Anderson of the state archives for helping find some pictures. Thanks also to Jack Grieder of the state office of the comptroller for providing a valuable photograph.

For the story "From Ford's Theater to the Granbury Opera House," Kevin Young offers the following acknowledgements:

I would like to express my thanks to Jo Ann Miller of Granbury who graciously shared her material and script concerning John St. Helen; to Gill Eastland and Jeff Hunt who encouraged me to pursue this story; to the staff of the library of Trinity University; William Gawltney of the National Park Service; the staff of the Warren-Lincoln Library, Ft. Wayne, Indiana; and to the numerous authors who have spent their careers delving into the story of the Lincoln Assassination. Special thanks to Doug Beach and Fred Bell and my undying gratitude to C. Steve Abolt, who first told me of this story and who has helped my work with encouragement and friendship every step of the way.

Dedication

This entire book is dedicated to Mr. Robert Stack, host; Mr. John Cosgrove, producer; and to the entire staff of the NBC series "Unsolved Mysteries." Their creative efforts have paid off with a successful program that is quality television.

Special Dedication for "From Ford's Theater to the Granbury Opera House" by Kevin R. Young: This story is dedicated to my father, George Righter Young, a Lincoln admirer and historian, from a son who chose to follow the Stars and Bars.

Introduction

Ok, I'll admit it, this book was inspired by a television program. It was not, however, just any old program; it was NBC's popular series "Unsolved Mysteries," hosted by Mr. Robert Stack.

As one who is usually highly critical of television programs, especially the ones that are poorly written or about stupid subjects, I find "Unsolved Mysteries" a pleasant change of pace. For my money, the show is the essence of what television ought to be all about. The program is interesting, well written, entertaining, and the material presented provides a valuable service to mankind. And no, I was not paid to say that, I am not related to Mr. Stack or John Cosgrove the producer, and I do not own stock in NBC. I simply think the program is excellent.

In case you are one of the few who haven't yet tuned in to the show, the format is simple. Each week as many as four unsolved mysteries are presented in capsule form, often featuring a recreation of the events using the actual people who experienced whatever adventure is being chronicled. The subject matter may be escaped criminals, unsolved crimes, lost loved ones, missing persons, UFOs, or even buried treasure. In all cases, viewers with information are invited to call a special 800 number.

Not only is the program entertaining, but it is also helping to solve many of the mysteries presented. There have been numerous cases where information provided by the show led to the arrest of criminals or at least to the solution of a crime. It must be a real shock for some escaped criminal, who has gone to great lengths to establish a new identity, to suddenly see his picture on television and know that a lot of people, perhaps including his neighbors, are watching the same program. There have been some cases where a criminal who had been living a comfortable life for a number of years was suddenly arrested, thanks to a tip from a viewer. Other crooks have had to immediately pull up stakes and flee after their pictures were shown to the world.

Helping capture criminals is a beneficial part of the show, but the most valuable service probably comes from helping people find long-lost loved ones who possibly would not otherwise be found. Thanks to the show, many families have been reunited and many more probably will be in the future.

I have been a fan of the program since it first aired three years ago. Sometime during those first years, I noticed that the program occasionally featured stories about Texas or Texans. That ignited a small spark of an idea. It occurred to me that there have, indeed, been many Texas mysteries that remain unsolved and such information might be the fodder for an interesting book. After a little research and some strenuous reading, I became convinced that there was more than enough material for a book. In fact, it became obvious very quickly that one problem would be to decide which mysteries to write about since there were so many.

In considering the project, I talked to a couple of friends who are known to be devout Texans like myself and who are, coincidentally, writers. Yes, those friends said, they did know of some interesting mysteries but no, they wouldn't just give me the information. They would, however, write the stories and allow me to include them in my collection. For that reason, you will find one story by Kevin Young and one by Charlie Eckhardt. Charlie also assisted on a couple of other stories by providing some valuable information.

Inside this book you will find, I trust, some interesting tales about mysteries that are, as far as is known, unsolved. The subjects range in time from the days when Texas was still part of Mexico, through the days of the Republic and up to the time John Kennedy was killed in Dallas. Some of the stories have never before been published, and even in cases where the tales are old, some new information or at least a new perspective is included. A number of the photographs have never, to our knowledge, been previously published.

The purpose of this book is entertainment — recreational reading if you will — and it is not intended to be serious history. For that reason, cumbersome, often distracting footnotes were omitted. However, an extensive list of all sources used is included so anyone interested in doing so can retrace the tracks of the authors in most cases. In some instances, the material was obtained through first person interviews and thus even the authors could not verify the information. In such cases, which are clearly indicated, you are encouraged to make up your own mind about whether to accept the information as fact or fiction. In most instances, the name of the person providing the information was included. On the other hand, while perhaps frustrating to potential readers, if the person providing information requested anonymity, that request was dutifully honored.

There is another purpose for this book. Since all the subjects are unsolved mysteries, there is the possibility that someone, somewhere may have information relating to one or more of the stories. If you happen to fall into that category and have information, photographs, etc., the authors are most interested in hearing from you. We do not suppose to have anything like the impact of the television show, so we'll be elated if any new information is brought to light because of our efforts. Please write to the authors care of Wordware Publishing, Inc., 1506 Capital Avenue, Plano, Texas 75074. We'll get back to you as soon as possible.

Wallace O. Chariton

Postscript

The original edition of this book contained a most unfortunate mistake. In the chapter "The Pool of Vanishing Blood" former *Dallas Morning News* reporter Mr. Hugh Aynesworth was listed as deceased and his name was misspelled. Although two separate sources confirmed both the supposed death and the spelling, the information was incorrect. When Mr. Kent Biffle, currently of the *Dallas Morning News*, pointed out the errors in one of his columns, I immediately contacted Mr. Aynesworth and offered my apologies, which he graciously accepted. I promised to bring him back to life in the next edition and it has been done.

This book is about certain unsolved mysteries that occurred in the state of Texas. The names, places, dates, and events are all real. Whenever possible, accounts from actual participants were used as supporting evidence. What you are about to read is not historical fiction.

The Best Mystery in Texas

by Wallace O. Chariton

In 1883, Robert E. Ellison and his wife were moving some cattle between Marfa and Alpine in far West Texas. Just before sundown one evening, the couple stopped their wagon on a flat mesa that looked like a perfect place to camp for the night. While his wife unpacked, Ellison tended to the horses and rounded up some wood for a cook fire. The couple planned a quiet evening after a hard day's ride but the plans changed. Instead, the rancher became an early witness to one of the longest running, hardest to explain Texas mysteries of all time.

As Ellison prepared to build his fire, he noticed that some strange lights had suddenly appeared across a valley in the Chinati Mountains. The lights seemed to come and go as if moving. First there was one light, then three, and then two. The sight of unexpected lights alarmed Ellison who immediately assumed the Apaches were on the move and perhaps headed in his direction. He spent the rest of that night sleeping in the dark with one eye open and one hand on his trusty Winchester.

Not long after the Ellison incident, a surveyor named Williams, the grandfather of 1990 Texas gubernatorial candidate Clayton Williams, was working in the mountainous area around Marfa and saw the strange lights. He later recorded in his personal journal that the Indians of the region believed the lights to be the spirit of dead Apache chief Alsate. Ranchers in the 1890s saw the lights and assumed they were Apache campfires but were amazed and bewildered when the area was checked the next day and no sign of any fire could be found.

The Ellison and Williams reports are the earliest known recorded sightings of the mystery lights but it is generally believed that Indians in the area had seen illuminated spirits dancing in the desert for many years before the white man arrived. Some people believe the lights may have been flickering in that portion of Texas for hundreds, even thousands of years or possibly since the beginning of time. No matter how long they have been there, as the old saying goes, the only thing that is certain about the famous Marfa lights is that nothing is certain.

Marfa's mysterious lights are almost as hard to describe as they are to explain. Usually, there are from one to three lights, mostly white in color but often in pastel shades. The lights may appear stationary but usually they have some movement, frequently described as being similar to a fishing cork bobbing up and down in the water of a West Texas stock tank. It is not uncommon for the lights to move fast in any direction and they may even blend together to form a streak of light. Sometimes the lights seem to blink on and off like a light bulb and at other times they fade slowly to blackness and then suddenly brighten up again.

For a lot of years, the mystery lights were largely a West Texas story. Residents of that area grew up with the lights and didn't pay them much attention. Then, during World War I, some army observers in the area saw the lights and immediately jumped to the conclusion that they were some sort of spotlights set up to guide an invasion force into the United States from the south. The army was wrong, fortunately, but word of the lights slowly began to spread far beyond the desert regions of deep Southwest Texas.

The strange lights got a real boost in publicity during World War II when the army established a pilot training base near Marfa. Soldiers from all over the nation were shipped into the area for training and most, if not all, eventually saw the lights during their stay in Texas. It was also during the second world war that strange stories about the lights started circulating. Today, many of those stories survive and some of them are actually stranger than the lights are mysterious.

Many of the Marfa light tales involve the military, and the wildest is about the purported team of army experts that supposedly went out into the desert determined to find out what the lights were or die trying. According to the tale, they did die trying but it's just a legend, or more appropriately a hoax. There is no evidence whatsoever that any team of army personnel died while on a Marfa light expedition. One man later claimed the "expedition" was actually a bunch of soldiers who got drunk and took off after the lights in a jeep. They didn't catch the lights but the driver did hit a boulder and turned the jeep over. To cover up the incident, the soldiers set fire to the wreckage and then tried to blame the lights for the mishap.

There have been many stories of aerial reconnaissance flights made over the mountainous area in an effort to spot the source of the lights. One army officer claimed that each night a squadron of four planes was sent out on a chase mission but each time the lights headed for Mexico and disappeared. Not true. Neither is the story that the army sent out planes to bomb the lights with sacks of flour in an effort to pinpoint the spot from which the lights originated. Some claim the flour sacks were, in fact, dropped but when the site was inspected later, nothing, not even the flour, could be found. The truth is, no reliable evidence has been uncovered to prove that the army has ever done anything concerning the lights. The story about the flour sacks is almost certainly just that, a story.

Fritz Kahl, a flight instructor during the war, did actually try to give chase on one occasion but he didn't have much luck. Although the lights were bobbing on the horizon when he took off, he never did see them from the air and thus he could not give pursuit. The story that the lights actually lead Kahl into a fiery crash on the side of a mountain is, however, false. He survived the war and later operated the Marfa airport. Other pilots, usually in airliners flying over the area, have reported seeing the strange lights, but the rumor that a pilot once mistook the mystery lights for the landing beacon of an airport and crashed when trying to land his plane is false.

The automobile has also played an important role in some of the Marfa light stories. In fact, a lot of people seem to believe that the lights are nothing more than reflections from headlights on automobiles traveling on Highway 67 which runs south from Marfa to Presidio. There are, however, serious problems with that theory. Many reported sightings of the mystery lights occurred long before Highway 67 was built. Some sightings, like those of Ellison and Williams, occurred before automobiles were even invented. Finally, if headlights were the culprit, only cars coming toward Marfa from Presidio could be involved, so the lights would have to move from left to right. While the lights often move in that direction, they are just as apt to move from right to left. This means if cars are the cause, someone is backing up at a high rate of speed, at night, on a dangerous mountain highway. That does not seem even remotely possible.

Some of the best stories of automobiles and lights involve virtual close encounters between drivers and the lights. There have been some reports of drivers trying to give chase without results. Another tale reversed the circumstances and had one maverick light chasing a car, often at speeds approaching 100 miles an hour. Supposedly, after the light finally disappeared, the driver stopped to check his car and found the rear end scorched as if it had been in a fire. It is a good story but there is absolutely no verification or evidence to prove it actually happened.

Most of the automobile stories involve a driver who narrowly missed having an accident because the lights suddenly appeared over the road. The most bizarre versions, frequently told by students at Sul Ross University in nearby Alpine, had the mystery lights luring automobiles into head-on crashes along Highway 67. Local law enforcement agencies advise that they have no record of any such accident reportedly being caused by strange lights. Drunk drivers, yes, but not the Marfa lights. There have been some reported cases of motorists seeing the lights and thinking they were about to crash into another car but in every case, the lights disappeared and no accident resulted.

The news media has always had an interest in the Marfa lights. There isn't a newspaper, television station, or radio station in Southwest Texas that has not done a story at one time or another on the mystery of the ghost lights. Occasionally, news teams have traveled great distances with the hopes of getting a story, and one of those teams actually had a very close encounter with the usually elusive mystery lights — and the news boys got pictures to back up the story they later told.

It happened in 1980 when the *Houston Chronicle* dispatched reporter Stan Redding and photographer Carlos Antonio Rios to "check out this Marfa light thing and see if there is anything to it." They found out there sure was something to the story but neither man knew exactly what.

As they were driving down a dirt road on the high black-brush flats at Paissano Pass east of Marfa, the energetic mystery lights suddenly appeared, almost close enough to reach out and touch. For once, the lights, which usually seemed to just disappear when anyone came close, lingered long enough for Rios to get some pictures. Redding later offered one of the best descriptions ever of the famous lights. He said, "They darted about the ground — red, white and blue orbs, baseball-sized. They would blend into one, then separate. One would zoom high into the air, then plummet down to disappear in the brush, only to pop up an instant later and spin away crazily. Unsupported and unattached, each illuminated the brush over which it hovered." Redding also indicated that it seemed almost like the lights knew somehow that they were being photographed and were intent to put on a show.

Another good description came from a man who saw the lights from a bus passing through the area. He said the lights, which appeared to be 200 or so yards from the road, were about the size of basketballs. He saw several balls of light, in soft pink and pale yellow, that were bobbing up and down; changing colors and size; and disappearing then reappearing quickly only to disappear again.

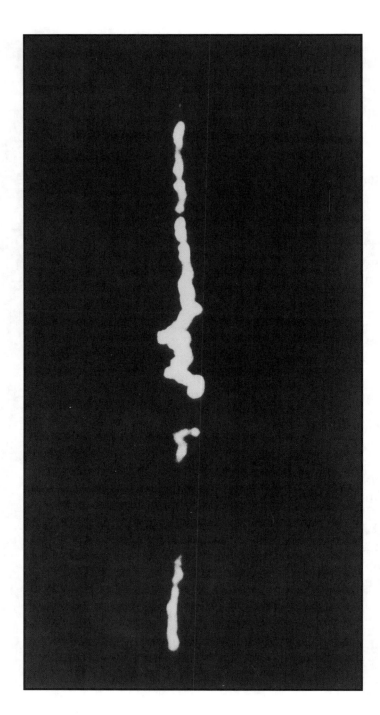

The famous Marfa lights captured on film.

One of the strangest Marfa light tales of all time was collected by Ed Syers for his book *Ghost Stories of Texas*. Syers got the story from Mrs. W. T. Giddens of Sundown, Texas, who said she was given the details by her father, a rancher who had actually lived the adventure.

According to the story, the rancher was up in the Chinati Mountains near old Shafter looking for some stray cattle when a sudden blizzard struck. Ordinarily, the man could have easily found his way home, but darkness was fast approaching and the howling, icy winds and blowing snow reduced visibility to almost nothing. He was forced to feel his way along what he hoped was the right trail. The man tried to hurry because he knew the temperature was dropping quickly and if he did not find shelter soon, his frozen body would be found later by search teams.

As the panicked rancher inched along, he came to a large outcrop of rocks that he would have to find his way around, because it was too dark for any climbing. Being unfamiliar with the territory, he carefully felt his way and started around the rocks. He stopped when suddenly some of the strange mystery lights appeared. Although he never explained exactly how they did it, the rancher claimed the lights "spoke" and advised him that he was three miles south of Chinati Peak, considerably off course, heading in the wrong direction, and dangerously close to a precipice. The lights advised the rancher to follow them or he would surely die.

With no alternative he could think of at the moment, the man did follow the lights and they lead him to a small cave that would provide shelter from the fierce storm. The smaller lights disappeared but the largest one remained in the cave with the rancher, apparently providing much needed heat and some "spirited" conversation.

According to the rancher, the light claimed they were "spirits from elsewhere and long ago." It relayed that they meant him no harm and wanted him to be safe so he could sleep in peace. The next morning, the storm and the light were gone, and as the rancher headed toward home, he passed the outcrop of rocks and discovered that when the lights had intercepted him, he had been on the edge of a sheer cliff several hundred feet high. The man had no doubts — the lights had saved his life.

Mrs. Giddens told Syers that she believed her father, which is perhaps the daughterly thing to do. She also claimed that after the incident, the lights would often appear in their pasture. She concluded, "They're curious and want to investigate things new to them, like the air base was during the war. They're friendly; our animals had no fear of them at all."

As far as is known, Mrs. Gidden's tale is the only one in which the lights actually communicated with real people. Apparently Mrs. Giddens had no explanation for why her particular family would be the only one in history singled out by the lights to be favored with direct communication.

One point from the lady's story that does have a solid ring to it is that the lights are friendly. Despite numerous rumors of aggression and downright devilment on the part of the lights, there is no proof of any aggression or that the lights have actually caused any harm whatsoever. The only things the lights are guilty of is being reasonably consistent in their appearances and always managing to avoid explanation.

There have probably been as many different theories about what causes the lights as there have been strange stories attached to the phenomenon. In the late 1800s, the most popular opinions were that the lights were either current Indian fires or the glow of Indian spirits on some sort of celestial warpath.

In more modern times, some scientists have tackled the problem; but honestly, the theory about Apache fires makes about as much sense as most of the experts. A common explanation for the phenomena is that the lights are the result of swamp gas escaping from underground pockets and igniting. Perhaps that is the answer, but as many people have pointed out, there hasn't been a swamp in that part of Texas for thousands, perhaps millions of years. If it is swamp gas, there must have been a heck of a lot it or perhaps it has just taken a long time to reach the surface.

Another popular theory is that the lights are an electrostatic illumination such as Saint Elmo's Fire. An expert advised that while something like Saint Elmo's Fire might be a plausible explanation for the Marfa lights, it is not probable. The expert claimed that ol' Elmo's Fire only occurs when conditions are absolutely perfect. The Marfa lights, on the other hand, don't appear to depend on anything or any certain prerequisite. The lights are seen year-round, in all kinds of weather and under all sorts of different atmospheric conditions. Although many have tried, no pattern of any sort can be identified for the Marfa light appearances. The fact that the lights are seen in all sorts of conditions, the expert claimed, also makes it doubtful that they are caused by ball lightning.

A few of the scientific deep-thinkers have come up with the theory that tremendous pressure is being exerted on underground faults and the result is that deep underground movement of rocks releases piezoelectric energy which is manifested as light when it reaches the surface. In other words, there are thousands of tiny earthquakes occurring almost constantly in the area and they are the culprits in the light mystery, believe it or not.

There are plenty of other theories. Some people, who can't accept any scientific reasoning, believe the lights are not of this world but rather are UFOs who use that part of Texas as a sort of base. Others believe the lights themselves are not UFOs but rather are some sort of waymarkers used to guide the extra-terrestrial vehicles in for a landing in much the same fashion as modern landing lights at an airport. Other people, who don't believe in UFOs, think the Marfa lights are a sort of spiritual apparition or simply ghost lights.

Another possibility is that the mystery lights are actually a sort of atmospheric distortion similar to a desert mirage. The theory is that reflections from lights on cars, houses, or even nearby communities are somehow bent over the horizon so they appear to be actual lights in the mountains. That theory probably makes as much sense as the explanation that the lights are jackrabbits with glow worms attached to their tails.

My favorite explanation came from Charlie Eckhardt. He believes that whatever is causing the Marfa lights is the same phenomenon that produces tiny sparks in your mouth when you bite into a wintergreen Lifesaver in a dark room while standing in front of a mirror. Knowing Charlie is one who enjoys a good yank on your leg occasionally, an experiment was conducted to determine if such a thing was possible. Standing there in the darkness of my bathroom, looking considerably more foolish than usual, I bit into a Lifesaver. Nothing seemed to happen. I continued until finally I did detect some tiny spark-like lights in my reflection in the mirror. I have no idea if that has one blessed thing to do with the Marfa lights, but I can say the Lifesavers produced sparks. If you want to try it, be sure to use wintergreen because no other flavor works.

The Marfa lights finally made the big time in July of 1989 when a crew from NBC's "Unsolved Mysteries" series brought their cameras to Texas to check into the mystery of the lights. That show turned out to be quite a production.

Many local Marfa residents were interviewed for firsthand reports of the mysterious lights. One man told how his efforts to track down the lights failed because the lights always seemed to stay far ahead, much like a mirage might do. He said because it was so difficult to judge size and distance in the area, that the lights might have been as large as a tire or as small as a cantaloupe. Another witness claimed she was among a group of four people when the lights appeared but that only she and one other member of the party actually saw them; the other two people saw nothing. Very strange.

In an effort to get to the bottom of the mystery, the producers of "Unsolved Mysteries" arranged for three scientists from a nearby observatory and university to conduct some experiments into the cause of the lights. One of the investigators was a chemistry professor, another a geologist, and the third was an astronomer. That group was joined by eleven other technicians, observers, and spotters.

Because of the presence of Highway 67 through the Chinati Mountains, the investigators wanted to be certain that whatever they might see would not be headlights. Special lights were set up on either end of the stretch of the highway that was visible from near Marfa so that if any light was seen outside the markers, the scientists would know they were seeing the ghost lights. Spotters were stationed along the road so that they could note any vehicles in the area if the lights seemed to appear.

Using sophisticated cameras and night viewing equipment, the crew laid in wait for the lights to make an appearance. Early in the evening, the beams of headlights from an automobile were photographed as they passed between the markers and in front of a beacon light on a radio tower. Then at 11:59 p.m. an unknown light appeared outside the markers. Using radio communications the investigators asked a spotter stationed in the mountains to verify that there was no traffic on the road. There was not, which meant the light could not possibly have been from an automobile. True to the advanced billing, a Marfa light had appeared for a performance.

The host of the program, Mr. Robert Stack, described the light as being "ghostly gold" in color. The bright light appeared visible for a few moments, faded from view, and then returned as bright as before. There was no doubt that the light was not man-made but the question remained, what was it? One of the scientists thought it might be refracted starlight; another thought it could be luminous gasses produced by small earth-quakes; no one could say positively what the mysterious light was or what caused it. Although the film crew produced irre-futable evidence that the lights exist, the solution remained as elusive as it had since the earliest recorded sightings.

Since the lights have never been anything but a friendly mystery, the people around Marfa who have grown up with the lights as a part of their daily lives are not necessarily interested in anyone solving the mystery. As one lady said on the tele-vision program, "Let's don't find out what they are. Let's just leave them a mystery. I'm not going to try to solve it. I'm going to be content with ghosts and let the ghosts take care of them."

The best thing about the mystery lights is that they are somewhat predictable. On any given night, they may appear and put on a show for any who care to watch. If you want to see for yourself, a special viewing area has been set up just off Highway 90 about nine miles east of Marfa. Almost any night you'll find cars parked there hoping for a glimpse of history. While most of the sightings have been from the area around the viewing spot, the lights have also been reported at other places in the Chinati, La Cienega, and Dead Horse mountains as well as around Blue Mountain, located between Marfa and Fort Davis. If you do make the trip, be sure to watch for lights that move in ways automobile or ranch lights could not so you will know you are seeing the authentic Marfa lights.

As far as a possible solution is concerned, the chances, much to the delight of most folks in Marfa, are slim that anyone will ever come up with a theory that will be universally accepted. For some who are obsessed with seeking the truth for all things unexplained, the lights will continue to be an enigma. For those of us who appreciate a good mystery and an even better legend, the prospect that the best little Texas mystery of all time will never be solved is not particularly unsettling. After all, life itself would be boring if there weren't a few mysteries around to keep things interesting.

If you have an idea that might explain the Marfa lights and you would care to share it, please send your information to the author at Wordware Publishing, Inc.

The Guns of the 49th Division

by Wallace O. Chariton
Story idea by C. F. Eckhardt

Five months after the Japanese surrender ended World War II, a small detachment of U.S. Army troops spent several weeks completing a special detail at Camp Maxey, eight miles northwest of Paris, Texas. The troops in that detail didn't realize it at the time, but they were creating a mystery destined to live on long after they were gone.

This story actually began in January of 1940, a time when it was becoming apparent to most people that the United States would eventually be dragged into another shooting war. Three Paris businessmen, Jim Caviness, Pat Mayse, and R. Walter Wortham, knew that along with war would come opportunity, so they conceived an idea to propose to the U.S. Army that the military use some of the vast acreage in the gently rolling hills of Lamar County to construct a major training facility. The men knew there was more than enough acreage in the county to build any type of facility that might ultimately be required for any part of the war mobilization effort. And they knew a major military installation would be an economic boom to Paris.

The businessmen proposed their concept to then Paris Mayor J. Morgan Crook. Although he had perhaps the worst possible name for a politician, Mayor Crook had a good head for economic opportunity and he quickly warmed to the idea of having a military installation in the area. Ultimately, Mayor Crook became so involved in the pursuit of the camp that most people would even credit him with having the original idea. Caviness, Mayse, and Wortham didn't particularly care who got the credit as long as Paris got the installation.

There was, however, a potential major problem. Many of the landowners in Lamar County held title to property that had been in their families for generations. In some cases, farmers were plowing ground that their ancestors had worked during the days of the Republic of Texas. It was feared that no cause, regardless of how noble it might be, would inspire those people to be dislodged from the precious ground.

A coalition was formed to take the cause directly to the people. After a couple of months, it was clear the patriotism in that Texas county was stronger than any ties to the land. To a person, the landowners agreed to sell out to the government if a base were to be built. Once that issue was settled, the coalition spent a few more months organizing the logistics of a base in the area to see if the plan made total sense and to determine if there were any major problems that could not be overcome. When everyone was satisfied the plan would work, it was time to call in the troops.

On October 12, 1940, Mayor Crook wrote Major General H. J. Brees, then commander of the 8th Army, and officially requested that representatives of the army visit the area to determine the fitness of Lamar County land for military purposes. As a matter of courtesy and to further his cause, Crook also sent copies of his proposal to U.S. Representative Wright Patman, as well as Senators Tom Connally and Morris Shepard, all from Texas. Although a simple, small town Texas mayor, Crook knew that big political guns would be required if Lamar County was to be successful. And in the early 1940s, there were few political guns bigger than Patman, Connally, and Shepard. It didn't hurt anything that Shepard happened to be chairman of the Senate Military Affairs Committee.

General Brees received the Crook proposal with enthusiasm and set the wheels in motion for a complete review of the possibilities. As the citizens of Paris would quickly learn, however, military wheels move slowly even with significant political prodding. Although correspondence continued between the parties and all the signs seemed favorable, it was several months before army representatives actually visited the county to survey the area and review possible sites.

True to Crook's prediction, the army brass, when they finally did arrive, were favorably impressed with the available land and they informed local Paris officials that a military installation would probably be recommended for the area. The brief excitement that pronouncement caused soon dulled as the wheels of military motion again bogged down in the usual sea of paperwork. Despite almost constant rumors, little progress was seen and it appeared it would be some time before the installation could become a reality.

Then came dawn, December 7, 1941, when hundreds of Japanese planes attacked and virtually destroyed the United States Pacific fleet in Pearl Harbor. The following day President Franklin Roosevelt asked for a declaration of war against Japan, and within a week Adolph Hitler had declared war on the United States. Suddenly, after so many months of anxious anticipation, the inevitable had become reality and America found itself completely immersed in the great war.

The citizens of Paris and Lamar County immediately learned that the military machine which moved so lethargically in peacetime was capable of a much faster pace when the shooting started. On January 20, 1942, forty-four days after Pearl Harbor, Representative Wright Patman sent a telegram to the *Paris News* announcing that the War Department would, indeed, build a major facility in Lamar County. The foresight of the Paris businessmen and the strategic planning of Mayor Crook had paid off with the big jackpot. Within days of the announcement, 30,000 of the eventual 70,000 total required acres had been obtained and bids were out for construction of the facilities. On February 27, 1942, twenty-five months after the idea was spawned, construction began on a twenty-two-million-dollar army training unit just to the northwest of Paris.

Bulldozers and cement trucks rumbled over the Texas prairie and the camp, eventually named in honor of Confederate General Sam Bell Maxey, started taking shape almost overnight. The enormous headquarters building was first to go up and the troop barracks and officers' quarters quickly followed. Then came the various training facilities, the first of three mess halls, a chapel, a field hospital, warehouses, and equipment maintenance buildings. When finally complete, Camp Maxey, one of the largest U.S. wartime installations, contained 1,720 buildings that included seven movie theaters, a bowling alley, several service clubs, a waste treatment plant, five fire houses, a post exchange, a photographic lab, and a complete printing plant. The camp was a self-contained city that, during its peak period of utilization, had an average constant population of 50,000 persons, which was five times the size of Paris, Texas.

Although the primary stated purpose of Camp Maxey was advanced infantry training, Mayor Crook's prediction of site versatility proved totally correct and the camp actually became one of the most diverse facilities in the nation. In addition to the training of two complete infantry divisions, Camp Maxey was also used to train one cavalry reconnaissance group, two groups (eleven battalions) of field artillery, thirteen ammunition companies, six companies of military police, six battalions of quartermaster troops, one salvage company, one photo lab company, one searchlight battalion, and one pigeon company. In total, 194,800 Americans, not counting the pigeons, passed through the gates of Camp Maxey. The total of all troops who passed through the facility would be 200,000 if you were to count the Nazis who came to Lamar County.

As the great American war machine began to mobilize, one part of the strategic planning was to allow for the incarceration of prisoners of war. It was naturally assumed from the very beginning that with the addition of American might, the Allies would ultimately crush the Axis. That would mean prisoners — potentially large numbers of prisoners — would have to be handled. Unfortunately, the American military was woefully short of trained combat troops in 1942 so there weren't any excess men to use as guards in prisoner of war camps. The solution to that dilemma was the decision to bring the prisoners to the United States for imprisonment.

Headquarters building at Camp Maxey.

Inside view of the officers' quarters.

One of the chapels on the base.

Some infantry troops in training at Camp Maxey.

Because of its size, good climate, and location, Camp Maxey was selected as one of many training installations to also be designated as a P.O.W. facility. Location was, surprisingly enough, a critical part of the decision. As a result of the Geneva Convention, it was determined that prisoners could be held in any country in the world as long as the country was at approximately the same latitude as that where the prisoners were captured. The theory was that it would be inhumane to move prisoners captured in a warm climate to a cold area and vice versa.

The theory was perhaps based on sound logic but there were complications. The first prisoners taken by Americans were part of Field Marshal Rommel's Afrika Korps in North Africa. Since many of those Nazis were transported to Camp Maxey, apparently someone believed North Texas was very much like a desert. The irony was, of course, that the German soldiers were accustomed to a much colder climate than they found in either North Africa or North Texas.

In early 1943, the first enemy soldiers were processed into Camp Maxey and most were shocked to find the country intact and the citizens thriving. It seems Hitler's propaganda ministers had assured the German fighting men that America was undergoing widespread devastation similar to that being experienced in Italy, Sicily, and much of Europe. The Nazis, who expected to find famine and destruction, actually found there was plenty to eat and the accommodations were comfortable, almost pleasing.

Seventy-five thousand enemy troops were ultimately sent to Texas and slightly more than 5,000 of Hitler's finest were housed at Camp Maxey. Despite the fact that facilities were anything but fortified prisons, there were relatively few escape attempts and no recorded acts of sabotage were ever attributed to the prisoners. Most of the escape attempts amounted to little more than curious Germans interested in seeing the sights outside the confines of the camp. Of the 100 or so prisoners that did manage to escape, only eight remained at large by early 1945.

One factor that may have contributed to the small number of escape attempts at Camp Maxey was the fact that the army brought in military police trainees from New York and New Jersey, and part of their duties were to guard prisoners. Since rule number one in the P.O.W. escape manual is to bribe the guards for information on local surroundings, that effort proved futile for the Nazis since the guards did not know much more about Texas than the prisoners. In fact, the guards were so ignorant on Texas at first that they could not help the Germans identify the strange little creatures that seemed to be everywhere. Without proper identification, the Germans referred to the creatures as panzer swine — armored pigs. Eventually, everyone learned the creatures were really just harmless armadillos.

As the prisoner population of Camp Maxey began to swell, a sort of independent society developed among the internees. Inadvertently, the most powerful positions in the society fell into the hands of the most fanatical Nazis. Although those leaders did attempt to organize sophisticated intelligence gathering networks among the various prison camps, they were not particularly successful in the attempt. The pro-Nazis did succeed, however, in frightening and controlling the anti-Nazi Germans to the extent one former prisoner reported after the war that if it hadn't been for the Americans on guard, he and other anti-Hitler prisoners like him would have been killed while they slept.

The German soldiers (other than officers) were pressed into service to build their own facilities and perform various other labor intensive jobs around the camp, such as meat packing, farming, carpentry, and mechanic work. Some prisoners were actually rented out to farmers in the surrounding counties to perform menial labor. Although many of the elite German troops felt cotton-picking was beneath them, they quickly adapted and some actually became accomplished farm hands; others never did seem to learn the difference between a cotton stalk and a cocklebur plant.

To reward the prisoners for their labor, the United States, unlike Germany and Japan, decided to abide by the Geneva Convention provision that called for P.O.W.s to be paid when pressed into the labor force. Accordingly, Germans brought to

America were paid about $21.00 per month or roughly the equivalent of a U.S. army private. A special prisoner-run post exchange was set up to allow the Germans to spend their earnings on things like cigarettes, candy, electric razors, soft drinks, and even beer. The prisoners were also allowed to subscribe to magazines and newspapers and to own radios. It's hard to imagine the reaction of those Germans when they began to hear reports on their radios of how their beloved homeland was being devastated the way they had planned to devastate the world.

The presence of Germans did not prevent a strong bond from developing between the camp and the civilians in Lamar County. The Texans welcomed the army with open arms and the army reciprocated by employing as many as 10,000 locals to assist in the camp operations. The local citizens who weren't directly employed often volunteered to do whatever they could. The ladies of Paris baked special treats for the men and frequently packed up their sewing machines and headed to the camp to mend the soldier's clothes and sew on chevrons. Soldiers on passes were welcomed into the town and into the homes of many Paris residents. Some sort of special celebration or church social seemed to be on the agenda almost every weekend. Clearly, the attitude of Paris residents was simply that they couldn't do enough for the brave young men who would one day risk their lives to keep America, and Paris, Texas, free.

One of the busiest volunteers was Mrs. Dorothy Hubbard. On July 8, 1942, she organized the Maxey Command, a special hostess corps comprised of 150 local Texas girls dedicated to being friends to the young and often lonely boys being trained at the camp. Members of the hostess corps escorted soldiers to dances, wiener roasts, barbecues, hayrides, and to special holiday events. When gas rationing was implemented, the girls and their chaperones would gather together and ride special buses out to the camp and entertain the boys in the service clubs. Of course, being a member of the hostess corps did have special rewards, the best of which was frequently being invited to see the latest movies at the camp, often six or eight weeks before the same film was available in Paris theaters.

While life on Camp Maxey was, for the most part, very pleasant, no one ever forgot the purpose at hand, which was to train American fighting men. Some of the first men trained at Maxey participated in the fighting in North Africa, Sicily, and many were in the historic Allied landing at Normandy. A few Maxey trained troops that were shipped overseas to fight later actually returned to North Texas as special escorts for captured Germans.

The first full infantry division trained at Maxey was the 102nd Division of the 9th Army. That particular division was activated September 15, 1942 and saw its first action near Geilenkirchen, Germany on October 26, 1944. As part of the spearhead racing through Europe, elements of the 102nd captured a total of 86 towns and more than 145,000 prisoners, some of which ended up back in Lamar County, Texas while the 102nd continued fighting. The other major division trained at Maxey was the 99th, which was rushed through Maxey and on to Europe to combat the Nazi resurgence that came to be known as the Battle of the Bulge. In addition to the 99th, Maxey was also one camp that specialized in retraining air force troops that volunteered for infantry duty when it appeared Hitler was anything but beaten and a severe shortage of ground troops was anticipated.

As it turned out, Hitler's last gasp Battle of the Bulge was just that, a last gasp. The Allies, including Maxey trained troops, proved the undoing of the 1,000-year German empire, and on May 8, 1945 hostilities in Europe officially ended. But there still remained the dangerous war of the Pacific. From all appearances, the empire of Japan was determined to fight to the last man. With Europe reduced to a mopping-up action, the military minds turned their attention to the land of the rising sun and began preparing to invade the Japanese homeland with a Normandy-like operation. Privately, many generals were predicting the war might drag on for two or three more years and that perhaps millions of Americans and as much as 90 percent of the population of Japan would be killed before the last shot was fired.

Part of the Japanese invasion plans called for a new division, the 49th Armored, to be activated and trained at Camp Maxey. The 49th had originally been one of the non-existent phantom divisions that was supposedly attached to General Patton's force that was, the Germans were led to believe, to invade Europe at some point other than Normandy. It was one of the classic military ruses of all time so it was decided to bring some of the ghost divisions to life for the real invasion of Japan.

Even before the fall of Hitler's Germany, plans were under way to activate the 49th at Camp Maxey. As early as February, 1945, supply trains were rolling into Camp Maxey loaded with new tanks, trucks, jeeps, half tracks, personnel carriers, and field artillery pieces. More trains came in carrying M1 rifles, Browning Automatic rifles, automatic pistols, Thompson machine guns, hand grenades, bayonets, bazookas, mortars, radios, and case after case of ammunition in all sizes and descriptions. Special truck convoys arrived loaded with uniforms, packs, canteens, ammunition belts, shovels, helmets, and boots. By the time Europe was secure, the staging areas, warehouses, and armories at Camp Maxey were bulging at the seams with everything needed to outfit an entire armored division. By the middle of summer, 1945, the men that would ultimately use all that equipment began to arrive in North Texas and it was anticipated the division would be at full strength, fully trained, and ready to ship out by February or March of 1946.

While most of the U.S. armed forces were planning to invade Japan, there was a small, select group of scientists working almost round the clock on the Manhattan project trying to develop nuclear weapons that would make the invasion unnecessary. At 8:15 on the morning of August 6, 1945, the first atomic bomb was dropped on Hiroshima, Japan. Two days later the U.S.S.R. declared war on Japan and the following day, August 9, Nagasaki was demolished by a second atomic bomb. The spirit of the Japanese was finally broken and on August 10, their government issued a statement offering to accept a conditional surrender. On September 2, 1945, General Douglas MacArthur formally accepted the Japanese surrender terms and the war was finally, mercifully, at an end.

Once the war — the entire war — was over and done, the United States government found it had a serious problem that was almost totally unexpected because of the swiftness with which the atomic bombs had brought about the end of the fighting. Since there had been so many uncertainties surrounding the future of the nuclear project, the military preparedness departments had continued stockpiling arms and munitions at a full tilt pace virtually up until the surrender was accepted. Then, incredibly, the fighting was finished and instantly those huge stockpiles were no longer needed. U.S. government officials found themselves saddled with a tremendous surplus disposal problem, and because of a dangerous old precedent that dated back to the Civil War, it wasn't an easy problem to resolve.

Following the war between the states, almost one hundred years earlier, the United States government had faced a similar surplus problem. There was suddenly an enormous surplus of firearms that would not be needed in the foreseeable future. In essence, the government officials had three choices: they could store the guns for possible future use but that would mean maintaining guards and security; they could simply destroy the guns but that would be a terrible waste; or they could sell the weapons at bargain prices. The U.S. Army, in its infinite wisdom, opted for a gigantic sale and they promptly disposed of their surplus problem and deposited some cash to help replenish a much depleted treasury.

Unfortunately, in solving its own problem, the government inadvertently created utter chaos in the civilian firearms market. With army pistols and rifles available for pennies on the dollar, the weapons manufacturers could not compete. Eventually only the largest and most financially sound gun companies were able to continue operations. The remaining smaller companies were literally forced out of business and into bankruptcy.

At the close of World War II, the surplus of military materials was even more dramatic than following the Civil War. Not only were there vast stores of weapons to be dealt with, there were also thousands of automobiles, trucks, and jeeps that could have been sold quickly to transportation- starved citizens of the

United States. The only problem was that the major automobile companies that suddenly were without their lucrative government contracts would depend on normal retail sales for continued existence. Therefore, if the armed forces dumped their surplus vehicles on the market, the auto makers might have gone the way of the Civil War arms companies. And if the surplus guns were placed on the market, the modern arms companies would almost certainly go under. The government quite simply could not risk putting several large employers out of business at a time when so many ex-servicemen would be looking for jobs.

To resolve the vehicle problems, many cars and trucks were just left in Europe either to be used in the post war administration or to help replenish the decimated equipment inventories of the Allies. When vehicles still remained, a tremendous number of them were loaded on ships, sailed out into the Atlantic Ocean, and pushed overboard. The bottom of the Atlantic also became the final resting place of untold tanks, cannons, and guns of all descriptions from the European theater. But there still remained the problem of what to do with the stateside war munitions that were housed at inland bases and thus could not be hauled out to sea and dumped.

At Camp Maxey, the surplus problem came to the forefront in mid-September, 1945, when Congressman Wright Patman officially notified both the camp officials and the Paris Chamber of Commerce that, as of October 1, the camp would be deactivated. Even though the economic impact on Lamar County and the city of Paris would be dramatic, the move was not altogether unexpected thanks to the inevitable rumors that had been circulating for weeks, virtually since the moment the war ended.

The U.S. Army Surplus Administration moved to dismantle the camp almost as quickly as the War Department had moved to build it four years earlier. A "For Sale" sign was hung out over most of the land and many of the original owners actually bought back their property for what was reported to be bargain prices. The city of Paris obtained the sewage treatment plant, the water tower, and some fire engines. Although many of the buildings were sold with the understanding they would be moved, some were sold in place with the land. The DeKalb Hybrid Seed Company of DeKalb, Illinois purchased most of the troop barracks with the intention of turning them into one of the world's largest chicken farms to help satisfy the staggering demand for fresh poultry products.

As the land was sold and the buildings were moved or torn down for scrap lumber, there still remained the large problem of what to do with enough brand new weapons to outfit an entire armored division. The guns could not be sold, given away, drowned, or destroyed. There appeared only one viable alternative: the guns of the 49th Division had to be buried so everyone could rest in peace. Since most of the troops and all the German prisoners had been transferred out, the remaining soldiers were assigned to the burial detail.

Once again, in early 1946, the bulldozers rumbled over the Texas prairie. This time they were digging large, deep trenches big enough to accommodate everything from small arms to an entire Sherman tank. As the trenches were completed, the tanks and other vehicles were driven into the ground. The small arms were carefully packed into metal drums filled with Cosmoline brand petroleum as a preservative and rolled into the ditches. Once all the arms and vehicles were interred, the bulldozers rolled for the last time and every trace of the gun graves was obliterated.

Eventually, Camp Maxey was reduced to a few thousand acres reserved for a Texas National Guard unit, and today what is left of the camp is home for the 49th Armored Division. Although many people know of the guns and more than a few have searched for the final resting place, as far as is known, a large quantity of brand new, never-fired, vintage World War II firearms lie today, undetected, beneath the rolling hills of Lamar County.

Although no one knows for sure (and the government certainly isn't talking) it appears likely the buried Maxey guns include M1 rifles, 30-caliber carbines, Browning Automatic rifles, Colt 45-caliber automatic pistols, Thompson machine guns, 30- and 50-caliber machine guns, deadly "grease guns," flame throwers, bazookas, mortars, and probably much more.

Ruins of a large mess hall at Camp Maxey.

A smoke stack that may have been at one of the Maxey kitchens.

The stockade building at Camp Maxey that was used to hold American soldiers gone astray of military law. German prisoners were held in other facilities.

The foundation of one of the officers' quarters at the base.

All that remains of the largest Camp Maxey recreational hall.

The remains of a bunker-type structure that served as the base paymaster's office.

Bunker-type buildings that have no windows and may have been some sort of secure area. When the base was closed, the buildings were filled with dirt and sealed with concrete slabs. They have never been opened.

All that remains of a German officer's quarters.

The foundation of a small arms warehouse.

The remains of one of Camp Maxey's theaters. Today, the troops at the base use the sunken part of the structure to raise fish.

One of the modern tanks stationed at Camp Maxey.

National Guard troops who receive weekend training at the camp.

By today's military standards, such weapons would be obsolete, but as collectors items these guns are highly sought after and are often very valuable, especially if unfired.

Perhaps the most intriguing part of the story of the buried guns is that some, possibly most, of the weapons could still be in virtually perfect condition despite having been buried for almost fifty years. By all accounts, the small arms were carefully packed in Cosmoline, a petroleum derivative used to preserve metal. Cosmoline effectively seals weapons in a protective coating that prevents air and water from contaminating the metal parts. There have been numerous instances of guns preserved for more than fifty years when packed carefully in Cosmoline, so there is every reason to believe the Maxey guns may still be in almost perfect condition, even if the metal packing barrels have long since rusted away. If a large number of vintage World War II weapons could be found in perfect condition, they would be worth a small fortune.

Naturally, before the condition of any of the guns could be checked, the burial site would have to be located. No one knows, or will admit to knowing, where the trenches were dug, but there have been isolated reports indicating that at least some of the weapons may have been found. In the late 1950s and early 1960s, game wardens in and around Lamar County occasionally would report hearing what sounded like machine gun fire deep in the woods. The speculation was that someone had found a few of the 49th's guns and were either taking target practice or using the automatic weapons as a decided edge against the large deer population of the area.

Charlie Eckhardt from Seguin was given a clandestine guided tour of the National Guard reservation in the late 1950s and he saw the front end of a buried Sherman tank sticking out of the bank of dry creek bed. Unfortunately, Charlie was unfamiliar with the terrain and has no idea where the tank was located. His guide for the excursion, who claimed to have considerable knowledge of the buried weapons, was lost in Vietnam. However, another acquaintance of Charlie's actually retrieved a large wad of Cosmoline and found it contained several new Colt 45-caliber automatic pistols.

Local residents of Lamar County who now live on land that was once part of the camp report that occasionally a stray grenade will be found, and one man claimed that when he did excavation work to enlarge his stock tank, a cache of unfired ammunition was found. The current residents acknowledge they have heard of the missing guns but if any have actually found one or two, they aren't willing to admit it, perhaps because unregistered ownership of a machine gun is highly frowned on by the folks in the Bureau of Alcohol, Tobacco and Firearms.

The likelihood that any quantity of the guns of the 49th Division will ever be found seems remote at best. Almost certainly the guns are buried beneath land that was retained by the National Guard and the troops of the 49th would take a very dim view of anyone digging up their post looking for lost guns. It seems equally unlikely that the government would ever give anyone official permission to search for the weapons because, in addition to guns, the burial detail also planted large caliber ammunition, grenades, mortar rounds, and land mines. These explosive devices were not packed in Cosmoline so they have undergone chemical breakdown and are, more than likely, extremely volatile and very dangerous. Anyone silly enough to start sticking shovels into the ground at Camp Maxey would probably be killed by an explosion long before any guns were found. The government is apparently sufficiently leery of any such search that officials routinely reject all requests from Camp Maxey for mine sweeping equipment that could also be used as metal detectors.

If the threat of death by explosion and the fact that trespassing on a military reservation is a federal offense aren't sufficient deterrents to potential treasure hunters, there are other considerations. On almost any given weekend, you can stand outside the fence surrounding the camp and easily hear the unmistakable sound of machine gun fire as the troops are put through training exercises. And remember, Camp Maxey is home of the 49th *Armored* Division. Armored means tanks — big, fast, powerful, modern tanks with an effective kill range of three miles. Even though the mystery of where the weapons are buried might be solved quickly with some powerful metal detectors, the associated risks in making the search would appear to make it much more prudent to simply allow the guns of the 49th Armored Division to rest in peace.

If you have any details about the guns of the 49th Division that you would care to share, please send your information to the author at Wordware Publishing, Inc.

The Pool of Vanishing Blood

by Wallace O. Chariton

Perhaps the darkest day in the history of Texas was November 22, 1963, the day John F. Kennedy was gunned down on a Dallas street. The entire world was shocked by the sudden death of a vibrant, exciting leader with so much promise. Nowhere was the pain of that loss felt more personally than among the people of the Lone Star State.

The young president that so many Texans had welcomed with open, loving arms was suddenly gone. While the people of Texas wept for the loss of their leader, the jaundiced eye of public opinion was cast suspiciously upon the land of oilmen and cowboys. The world's perception of an "old west" mentality in Texas was heightened. Although it was never said in so many words, the feeling that every Texan would have to shoulder some of the blame was almost inescapable. The whisper in many circles was simply that JFK would have lived had he not come to Texas. Never mind that anyone bent on assassination could pick virtually any city in the world for performance of the deed; the fact was the assassin chose Dallas, and it seemed inevitable that the history of the city and the state would be forever marred by a giant black mark.

A wise man once said that time heals all wounds. In most cases, that may be true, but the assassination of John Kennedy was a wound of a different kind. In the weeks and months following the tragedy, questions began to crop up about the events that unfolded in Dallas that fateful day. As the months became years, still the mysteries lingered and no succinct answers were forthcoming.

Was Lee Harvey Oswald the triggerman? Did Oswald act alone or in concert with conspirators who were on the now famous grassy knoll? Was the mafia, the Cubans, or, worse yet, the CIA, instrumental in staging the assassination? Was the Warren commission a whitewash orchestrated by Lyndon Johnson? Was Johnson himself involved in the assassination plot? Did someone tamper with the president's body after it was taken to Washington, D.C.? Exploring the possibilities became an infatuation with many and an obsession with some. Despite years of intensive study and research that continues to this day, most of the answers to the questions remain elusive and a matter of opinion. However, researchers continue to uncover more and more evidence, so perhaps one day at least some of the mysteries will be solved. That process is aided by people who were once afraid to speak out coming forward to finally tell their stories.

The assassination of John Kennedy is often singled out as the event most responsible for establishing the real value of a medium that was still in its infancy in 1963 — television broadcast news. For one of the first times ever, Americans could sit in their living rooms and see historic events as they actually unfolded. And for the very first time ever, Americans saw the live broadcast of a man killed when Jack Ruby burst through Dallas police lines and shot Oswald. The coverage of events surrounding the death of JFK and Oswald signaled a new era in news reporting that continues to be refined and defined today.

With that new era came another phenomenon — a more enlightened public. No longer did people have to hear about events secondhand, they could see for themselves firsthand and draw their own conclusions. In the case of JFK's untimely death, many of the conclusions drawn by the public didn't square with official positions. It seemed the more people knew about the assassination, the more they wanted to know, and that cause was helped along by some dramatic home movies taken by a Dallas businessman named Abraham Zapruder.

Like so many other Dallasites, Zapruder left work early that fateful morning so he could get a good spot from which to watch the motorcade. And like most people in the crowd, Zapruder took along his camera, a Browning home movie camera, with which he hoped to catch the historic event on film. Little did he know that having that camera would secure his place in history.

Zapruder selected a spot near the top of the grassy knoll, north of Elm Street and just a block or so from the Texas Schoolbook Depository. As the motorcade drew near, Zapruder realized he would have a better view from the top of a small concrete block near the top of the stairs that lead down to Elm Street. He mounted the block and started filming as soon as the president's car came into view. When the shooting started, he kept filming until the president's car disappeared under the triple underpass and sped away toward Parkland Hospital. Those thirty seconds of film are now among the most famous in all history.

Without hesitation, Zapruder jumped down from the block and hurried to notify authorities that he had the shooting on film. A few minutes later, the police arrived and they quickly arranged to have the film developed at the *Dallas Morning News* lab. An original and one copy was made to assure the film would be preserved. In a matter of days, the dramatic pictures were being shown and re-shown on television. People around the world could see the gruesome images of a president being killed. A lot of people also thought they could see something that was destined to become a major controversy about the assassination.

Zapruder's movie clearly showed the president's head snapping backwards violently, a clear indication to many that at least one shot had been fired from the front, probably from the grassy knoll. The only problem was that government officials were adamantly maintaining that all the shots had been fired from the Texas Schoolbook Depository to the rear. Incredibly, the government stuck to their story even though so many eyewitnesses claimed they heard shots from the knoll and there were actually other pictures which clearly showed spectators pointing frantically toward the knoll immediately after the assassination. The matter of where the shots actually came from continues to be debated.

The disagreement over which direction the shots came from was one of the first Kennedy controversies but it was nowhere near the last. Investigators poured over every scrap of information searching for clues — and there were a lot of clues. It seemed the more that was learned, the less that was known. For instance, when the FBI released some Kennedy files in the mid-1970s, they included a report that the shell casings found in the schoolbook depository had been traced to a small manufacturer in Philadelphia. Supposedly, the company had manufactured four million rounds of the bullets and sold them to the United States Marines. Since Oswald had been a marine, it would have been logical to assume that he had obtained the shells while in the Corps. Unfortunately, there was a problem. The United States Marines had never had rifles that fired that particular caliber of shell. The speculation then became that the sale to the marines had been a front for an actual sale to the CIA. Presto, more controversy.

One of the more perplexing aspects of the assassination is actually not what we know but rather what we don't know. There has always been a suspicion that there is a lot of information out there somewhere that, for one reason or another, has never been made public. Today, many witnesses are finally coming forward to tell what they know or what they saw, and many report that they have remained silent for so many years simply because they feared for their lives. Jerry Coley, a long-time employee of the *Dallas Morning News*, is one of those persons who has come forward, and his account of a pool of vanishing blood, which has never before been published, may one day offer valuable clues.

On the morning of Friday, November 22, 1963, thirty-year-old Jerry Coley was hard at work in the advertising department of the *Dallas Morning News*. Like so many other *Morning News* employees, he planned to be present when the presidential motorcade passed through downtown Dallas so he would have a chance to see Kennedy, Vice President Johnson, and Governor Connally. To make sure he would have plenty of time for the parade, Coley, who sold food and drug advertising in those days, grabbed a couple of cups of coffee and left on his normal downtown rounds an hour or so earlier than usual.

Coley returned to the *Morning News* offices about 10:30 and walked into the cafeteria for another cup of coffee. The room was not crowded but several people, John Newman, and Don Campbell were lounging about. At another table sat three men, two of whom Coley did not recognize. The third man, a character well known to Coley and the staff of the *Dallas Morning News*, was Jack Rubenstein, better known as Jack Ruby, a longtime customer of the newspaper.

Ruby owned the infamous Carousel Club, a seedy strip joint in downtown Dallas, and on Fridays he was in the habit of dropping by the *Morning News* for a late breakfast and then working on his advertisements for the weekend. He would often lounge around the cafeteria for some time, bragging about his tough-guy image and telling stories to anyone who would listen. Because Ruby's stories were generally interesting and often entertaining, people always seemed to listen. Ruby, a character well-known by police, talked of his exploits with women, particularly those who worked in his club, and he never failed to find a way to flash the large roll of bills he always carried.

On November 22, 1963, Ruby followed his regular routine with some slight variations. Some witnesses remembered he arrived earlier than usual that day and, as events began to happen, he stayed considerably longer than ever before. Jerry Coley and Don Campbell sat with Ruby for a few moments listening to his stories and drinking a couple more cups of coffee. In anticipation of large crowds forming early, Jerry Coley, along with friend Charlie Mulkey, walked out of the *Morning News* building sometime before 11:30 a.m. and headed toward Dealey Plaza with plenty of time to find a good vantage point from which to watch the parade. Coley said so long to

Ruby because he didn't expect to see the nightclub owner again that particular day. He was wrong about that prediction.

Jack Ruby hung around the cafeteria for a few more minutes and finally paid his tab with a large bill peeled off the roll "big enough to choke a horse." He then walked over to the classified advertising desk and began composing his weekend ad. John Newman would later remember the time was 12:10 p.m. because, as usual, Ruby was running late and the deadline for weekend ads had supposedly passed at high noon. Knowing Ruby was habitually late but was also a good customer, Newman, who handled his account, decided to extend the deadline and wait for the advertisement to be completed.

Jerry Coley and Charlie Mulkey chatted idly while walking the four blocks over to the motorcade route, which had been published in the paper. The publicity about the president's arrival had worked, and the crowds were larger than either man expected, so they took up a position near the entrance of the old county jail on Houston Street a short distance from the schoolbook depository. To get the best possible view, Coley climbed up on the concrete base of one of the portable stop signs that had been erected to help control traffic along the parade route.

When the big black Lincoln convertible limousine passed by right on schedule, Coley clung to his perch and waved madly. He had a clear view of President and Mrs. Kennedy and that made fighting the crowd worth the effort. As he climbed down from the stop sign, the motorcade turned left onto Elm Street and proceeded in front of the schoolbook depository heading for the triple underpass.

Shortly after the motorcade turned, Jerry Coley and Charlie Mulkey heard some noise, lots of noise. Neither man knew — or even considered — that what they heard might be gunfire, but it was apparent that something had happened because people were running in the direction of the schoolbook depository, which was just down the street to the north. The two men crossed Houston Street to have a look but the Dealey Plaza wall blocked their view. They then hurried around the wall and saw motorcycle policemen throwing down their cycles and running, with guns drawn, toward the fence that was then on the top of the grassy knoll. There was no longer any doubt; something had happened but *what* remained in question.

Coley and Mulkey, with their inherent news instincts kicking in, quickly ran down the street toward the depository, hoping to turn onto Elm Street and go see what had happened. As they ran past one bystander, he screamed that the president had been shot. By the time the two men reached the corner of Houston and Elm, the Dallas police were already beginning to control the crowds. A uniformed Dallas police officer appeared carrying a shotgun and looking very determined. The police-man demanded, in no uncertain terms, that the two *Dallas Morning News* employees "get the hell out of here."

Not to be denied, the pair circled around behind the depos-itory, where there was then very little activity, and crossed a dirt field that is now part of the West End Marketplace parking lot. Considering the excitement of the moment, both men were surprised to find little activity on the top of the knoll. Everyone, it seemed, was concentrating on the schoolbook building. As Coley and Mulkey emerged from behind the top of the knoll and started down the hill, they noticed a large pool — more than a pint — of a dark red substance on the steps that led down to Elm Street.

"What do ya' suppose that is?" Coley asked.

"Maybe somebody spilled a cold drink," Charlie answered as he bent over and dipped a finger into the liquid. He changed his mind when he tasted the strange liquid. "My God, Jerry," he exclaimed, "that's blood."

The presence of such a large quantity of blood alarmed Coley and he suggested they get back to the offices as quickly as possible. Mulkey agreed and the pair trotted across Elm Street, up Dealey Plaza, and on down Main Street to the *Morning News* offices. When they arrived, someone else had just come in with the news that President Kennedy had been shot. As Jerry walked through the lobby, he noticed Jack Ruby in a corner office, sobbing as he tried to talk on the telephone. It would be some time before Coley would realize that from the office where Jack was standing it was possible to look out the window and have a full view of the schoolbook depository.

Jerry Coley frantically searched for Jim Hood, a photographer assigned to the advertising department, who would be able to return to the scene and make a photograph of the mysterious and unexplained bloodstain. As he searched, reports began to come in on the television in the *News* offices indicating that the rumors were true; President John Kennedy had been shot in Dallas.

Jim Hood was in a back office watching television reports of the shooting when Coley found him. "Jim," he said, "I've found some strange bloodstains over by Elm Street that I think we need to get on film." That was all Jim needed to hear. He grabbed his camera and the two men hurried back to the scene. As they approached the grassy knoll, people were still running around but most of the action had, by then, shifted to the schoolbook depository. Almost incredibly, Jerry and Jim were able to walk right up the knoll without being stopped, questioned, or having to identify themselves.

The pool of blood was still there but it had begun to coagulate. Jim carefully focused his camera and took several pictures from different angles. "Ok, I got 'em," Jim announced, "what next?"

Jerry Coley quickly looked around but saw no other evidence of any kind that might require photographing. He also saw that activity around the depository was increasing quickly and the police were cordoning off the area. "Lets get back to the office so we can find out what's going on and so you can develop those pictures," Coley suggested. Hood agreed and they quickly left the area without being detained or questioned. When Coley walked back into the *News* offices for the third time at about 12:45 p.m., Jack Ruby was still on the phone, still crying, and still watching the depository.

After finally hanging up the phone, Ruby, with reddened eyes, walked back over to the classified desk and resumed work on his ad. Because of the dramatic developments, many people were calling in to cancel their ads out of respect for Kennedy. Ruby heard John Newman take several such cancellation calls and he decided he ought to change his ad for the Carousel Club. Ruby crumpled up his old ad and threw it away and then

The schoolbook depository, as seen from the position of President Kennedy's car at about the time the first shot was fired. The large tree above the sign has been trimmed back to allow easy viewing of the famous sixth floor window from which some of the shots were fired.

The steps leading from Elm Street up the grassy knoll. The pool of blood was found near the top, opposite the spot behind the fence from which many people believe at least one shot was fired. The large concrete block in the right side of the picture is where Abraham Zapruder was standing when he took his famous assassination film.

instructed Newman to run the simple ad in bold print: Closed Friday Sat. and Sunday. Out of respect for his president, Jack Ruby had decided to shut down his strip joint. In the excitement of the moment, no one noticed or particularly cared when Jack Ruby finally did leave that day.

Jim Hood hurried up to the *Morning News* photo lab and quickly developed the pictures. He returned to the main floor and handed Jerry a copy of the finished photo that clearly showed a pool of blood on the steps. However, because information was coming in so quickly by then, neither man had time to speculate as to where the blood might have come from.

Later that afternoon, as events continued to unfold, Hugh Aynesworth, an investigative reporter for the *Morning News*, interviewed Coley and listened to his story of where he had been when the shooting occurred and what he had seen. Jerry told Aynesworth the entire story and showed him the photograph. Aynesworth took some notes but did not ask for a copy of the photograph.

Aynesworth, who still resides in the Dallas area, was contacted and asked to comment on the story. He did confirm that Jerry Coley told him of the suspicious pool of liquid on the grassy knoll steps but he also indicated he did not place much importance on the information. While he could not recall the specific time, Aynesworth did say that some time later, perhaps a day or two after the shooting, he examined the concrete steps and found no pool of blood. He did, however, discover the remains of what appeared to be a broken soft drink bottle. Based on that evidence, he concluded that the pool of liquid seen by Coley and Mulkey was nothing more than spilled soda pop. Perhaps Aynesworth's theory is absolutely correct but if so, how is it possible that Charlie Mulkey could have tasted the mysterious liquid and instantly pronounced it to be blood? Is it possible the blood had been cleaned up by the time Aynesworth went to the scene and thus he made a perfectly logical deduction based only on the broken bottle evidence? We'll probably never know.

Despite numerous eyewitnesses claiming that at least some of the shots had come from behind a wood fence on top of the grassy knoll, the attention of the world had shifted to the now famous schoolbook depository by late on the afternoon of November 22, 1963. Investigators had located a "sniper's nest" on the sixth floor of the depository and recovered a rifle plus several spent cartridges. The Dallas police had an employee from the depository, Lee Harvey Oswald, in custody for questioning about the murder of Kennedy. By the time the first of many Hugh Aynesworth assassination stories appeared in the November 23 edition of the *Dallas Morning News*, it was already being assumed by most people that Oswald had fired the fatal shots from the sixth floor window of the depository. The Aynesworth story of November 23 contained no mention of Coley or the pool of liquid, and the photograph was not printed.

The weekend following the assassination was one of the busiest in history for the media in Dallas. Television crews were everywhere and reporters clamored for more information and new angles to cover. At the *Morning News*, everyone was at work whether they had been asked to come in or not. Even advertising men like Jerry Coley showed up to do whatever they could.

On Sunday, November 24, Coley stayed home with his family and they, like most of the people in the world, were watching the live television coverage when Lee Harvey Oswald was gunned down by a man wearing a trench coat and hat. Unlike most of the people in the world, Jerry Coley recognized the stranger as none other than Jack Ruby. Sensing his association with Ruby might be valuable, Coley immediately went to the office where he was again interviewed by Aynesworth. He confirmed that he knew Ruby and relayed what he knew about Ruby's movements at about the time of the assassination of John Kennedy. In Aynesworth's story of November 25, Coley's name was mentioned several times, but there was again no reference to the possible pool of blood. Neither Coley nor the blood was ever mentioned again by any reporter, Aynesworth included, and because of that, the story was almost lost for all time.

Shortly after Coley's name appeared in the *Morning News* story of the 25th, Mrs. Coley started receiving strange and threatening phone calls at home. Some unknown callers demanded to know if she or her husband were part of a plot to kill the president. There were threats of violence against Jerry and his wife but, more importantly, there were threats of harm to the Coley children.

When Coley's wife called him to report the strange calls, he immediately went home to be with his family. For the next two days, perhaps 20 more wild, strange, and frightening calls were received at the Coley household. One caller went so far as to say, "If you have little children, you'll never see them again." Other callers continued to suggest that Coley had been part of an assassination plot. Like other aspects of the strange story, it would be some time before Jerry realized that the callers were talking about a possible conspiracy when most people were being told the assassin was a single gunman acting alone.

Coley, naturally alarmed by the threatening calls, finally telephoned his boss, Cy Wagoner, head of the advertising department, and reported the problem. Wagoner, concerned for the safety of the Coley family, suggested to Jerry that he send his wife and children out of town for a few days. On Tuesday, Mrs. Coley and the kids headed for East Texas to escape the turmoil in Dallas, and Jerry went back to work resolved not to talk about his small involvement and certainly not about the blood. Before reporting to the office, Coley walked over to the grassy knoll. Somehow he wasn't surprised to find that not a trace of the bloodstain remained.

On Wednesday, November 27, a *Time Magazine* reporter suddenly appeared at Coley's desk wanting to interview him and take photos for the magazine. Coley, alarmed at the prospect of more publicity, went back to Cy Wagoner for help. Wagoner, a crusty veteran of the newspaper game, promptly threw the *Time* reporter out of the office with specific instructions for him not to return. Cy then suggested that perhaps Jerry should also get out of town for a while until things began to settle down. It was not a suggestion that Coley had to hear twice, and he headed for East Texas to join his family.

A little over a week later, the atmosphere in Dallas had begun to calm down so Jerry Coley returned to work. The following day, two men appeared at Coley's desk, identified themselves as FBI agents, and said they wanted to talk to him and Jim Hood, the photographer. Jerry again turned to Wagoner for advice and help. Of course, there is a big difference between a *Time Magazine* reporter and an agent of the Federal Bureau of Investigation. After Wagoner talked to the agents for a moment, he was convinced they were for real and told his two employees to answer their questions.

The four men went into a conference room for privacy and the agents lost no time in getting to the point. "Tell us what you saw," one of agents said matter-of-factly.

Jerry and Jim began their story. They told of standing near the jail, seeing the president pass by, and then hearing the shots. One of the agents cut short the story. "Tell us about this photograph you have," he said.

For a moment, Coley was startled. Neither he nor Jim Hood had, as yet, mentioned the pool of blood or the photograph. The question that went through Jerry's mind was simply how could these guys know about that? Despite some apprehension, Coley produced his copy of the photo and handed it to one of the agents. "What do you suppose that is?" Jerry asked innocently enough.

The shorter of the two agents replied curtly, "Mister, we're here to ask questions not answer them. Tell us whose camera you used."

"It's mine," Hood replied.

"Ok," the agent replied, "we'd like to see the camera, any negatives you have, and all the prints."

Jim Hood shrugged and left the room to get what was requested. He returned in a moment and handed the items to the agents.

The short agent took the photos and negatives and placed them in an envelope. "All right, gentlemen, that's the end of the interview, the end of the story, and the end of the blood."

"What do you mean the end of the blood?" asked Coley.

"For your benefit," the agent replied, "it never happened. You didn't see it. Someone got hurt and it's ridiculous to carry this thing any further. Someone just fell and got hurt and if you continue, you're just going to cause yourself a lot of problems. Just forget this entire incident; it never happened."

Coley stared at the agents for a moment. He wanted to argue; he wanted to ask how someone who had simply fallen down could possibly have lost so much blood so quickly; he wanted to point out that if someone had fallen down with such a force as to lose a pint of blood so rapidly, that almost certainly the person would have been knocked unconscious and thus still been present when he and Hood arrived. Coley wanted to ask how in the world the agents had heard the story in the first place. But Jerry Coley didn't argue or even comment. The agents obviously meant business and they were in no frame of mind for arguments or even logic.

Without saying anything more, the FBI agents took the photo file and the camera and walked out, never to be seen or heard from again. Jerry, with the memories of the threatening phone calls still fresh in his mind, made a quick decision. He decided to follow the advice of the FBI guys and never again speak of the pool of vanishing blood. Coley didn't believe the story that someone had fallen but he did believe that silence would be the best course to insure the health and well-being of his family. He got no arguments from Mrs. Coley.

For more than twenty years, Jerry Coley and everyone else who knew about the blood pool maintained their silence. Coley never forgot the blood but he never talked about it either. As the years began to add up, one by one the other witnesses who had personal knowledge of the mysterious pool of blood began to die. Today, more than twenty-five years after the assassination, most of the original witnesses who could corroborate Coley's story are gone. Jim Hood, Charlie Mulkey and Cy Wagoner are all deceased. Hugh Aynesworth, while very much alive, still believes the mysterious pool of liquid was nothing but spilled soda pop. Jerry Coley, however, remains certain the pool of liquid that Charlie Mulkey tasted was definitely blood.

In 1988, when a film crew approached Jerry for an interview about Jack Ruby to be used on a television special on the assassination, he decided on a new course of action. The Coley children were grown by then and the assassination of John

Kennedy, while still very much in the public eye, was nowhere near the headline-breaking story it had been in 1963. Perhaps, Jerry thought, it was time to share the whole story with the world. Accordingly, when the television crew showed up for what was to be a routine interview, they were handed a new and provocative story on the proverbial silver platter.

As Coley began to talk, the crew became more and more interested. What was to be a simple interview turned into three days of talking and filming. Coley showed the crew where the bloodstain had been found, and they shot footage of every possible angle in an effort to determine the spot from which a shot might have been fired that could have resulted in someone being hit and bleeding in that exact spot.

The film crew, excited about their discovery, hurried off to Los Angeles intent on including the new story in their film, but it never happened. Three days later, the reporter on the film crew called Jerry Coley with what he perceived to be bad news. It seemed that while the reporter desperately wanted to use the story, the director had killed it because so many who could corroborate the facts were dead. The newsman expected something more than the "that's fine" he got from Jerry Coley.

"That's fine?" the reporter asked, "What do you mean that's fine? You do understand that we're not going to run your story?"

"I understand and it's fine with me if you don't use the story," Coley replied. "The truth is my wife wasn't all that happy about the interview. She's probably afraid the crank calls would start again." With that Jerry hung up and the mystery of the pool of vanishing blood was once again put to bed without ever being taken public.

Unlike that Hollywood producer. I know, trust, and believe Jerry Coley. I sought him out for permission to tell the story because I believe there are questions that need to be asked and answered, if that's possible at this late date.

Perhaps the number one question is how did the FBI men know about the photos and that Jerry Coley was involved? Both Jim Hood and Coley did talk about the blood, but only to close friends and associates. Did one of them leak the information, or did the FBI have other sources for their information? And what about the Hugh Aynesworth theory that the liquid was only spilled soda pop? If that theory is correct, then why did the FBI agents even bother with confiscating the photographs? And why did the FBI agents seem to confirm that the liquid was blood with their "someone fell down" excuse? If it was nothing more than spilled soda pop, why didn't the agents just say that and put an end to the story? We will probably never get the answer to any of the questions that remain.

And what about the blood itself? Where did it come from? Did someone fall down as the FBI agent suggested, or was someone caught in a deadly crossfire? If it was a crossfire and the blood came from an accidental gunshot wound, does that mean the assassination was the product of a conspiracy and one of the shooters was in the area of the grassy knoll? How did the blood manage to completely disappear in four or five days without leaving any trace unless someone cleaned it up? But who, and why, and when was the blood cleaned off the steps?

If the blood did come from a bullet wound, what happened to the victim? Better yet, who was the victim, innocent by-stander or conspirator? It's far too late to try to trace old missing persons reports or to determine if a hospital treated a strange bullet wound back in November of 1963.

What if the victim was a conspirator who was then shot himself to protect the identity of his employers? Why didn't anyone report seeing something on the steps of the grassy knoll? Even if someone did fall down, why wasn't it ever reported? Unless the person who lost the blood was one of the conspirators, how did the person manage to escape detection since so many policemen ran immediately to the knoll? On the other hand, if the victim was a conspirator, how did he manage to escape after losing so much blood?

What happened to the photos and negatives confiscated by the FBI? If, as the agents claimed, there was nothing to the blood story, then why hasn't the Bureau released the files? A lot of other seemingly more sensitive information has been released but nothing on the pool of blood. Does the failure to release the files perhaps suggest that the information is still considered too sensitive to be shown to the public?

And what about Jack Ruby? Why did he remain in the *Dallas Morning News* offices so long that morning? Was he, in fact, watching the schoolbook depository before it was generally known that at least some of the shots came from that location?

As for Jerry Coley, he doesn't have any answers. "I don't know where the blood came from or why it was there," he said. "All I know is that it was there and then it was gone." And does he think Jack Ruby might have been involved in the assassination? "I don't know for sure," he replied, "but I think it is a possibility. And if he was involved, he sure built himself a perfect alibi." Mr. Coley also added a personal observation: "After Jack killed Oswald, he claimed he did it because he loved John Kennedy so much. Well, if Jack Ruby had so much affection for Kennedy, why didn't he stop drinking coffee long enough to walk three or four blocks to see his president in person? Jack could have easily placed his ads in plenty of time to have walked over to the parade with me or any number of other people. Instead, Jack Ruby just ordered more coffee. I have wondered why he did that for more than twenty-five years and I still don't have a reasonable explanation."

There are, of course, hundreds of unanswered questions concerning the assassination of John F. Kennedy. The mystery of the pool of vanishing blood is just one more on the list and one more that may never be solved. There will doubtless be people who question the validity of Jerry Coley's story, but you can bet that there will be no doubters among the hundreds of people who know Jerry Coley as an honest, forthright, respected businessman who would have no possible motive for concocting such a tale. Others may question why he waited so long to come forward. The truth is, Jerry Coley did not come forward. He would have been content to live out his life and never tell the story. What he did was simply to allow a friend to tell the story because the friend believed it needed telling.

An exerted effort was made to find anyone else who might have had knowledge of the blood. Although it was not anticipated that any would be found, there was a sort of confirmation. When U.S. Marshal Clinton Peoples was interviewed for another story in this book, it was learned that he has a deep interest in the Kennedy Assassination and has actually worked privately on the case since November of 1963. When asked if he knew of the pool of blood and if it was involved in the assassination, he simply replied, "It most definitely was involved." He declined to elaborate.

One of the strangest aspects of the blood story is that whatever happened was almost captured on film. Abraham Zapruder was standing on a concrete block immediately to the east of where the blood was found. Had Zapruder had a wide-angle lens, his camera might have captured the action that resulted in the bloodstain. Of course, with a wide-angle lens, Zapruder might have also photographed conspirators making a getaway on the grassy knoll. If that had happened, the one man, one gun theory might have been totally discredited before it ever began. We might then know of a conspiracy and know what happened to cause a pool of blood to suddenly appear. Without that evidence, the explanation for the pool of vanishing blood remains an unsolved Texas mystery.

Perhaps you or someone you know has specific knowledge of the mysterious pool of blood. It is almost certain that other people saw something that would help clear up the mystery but they, like Jerry Coley, may have been intimidated into silence. If that's the case, the cat is now out of the bag, as we say in Texas, and it is perhaps time for others to come forward. Anyone with any information to contribute to this mystery is encouraged to write the author at Wordware Publishing.

The Ghost of Love

by Wallace O. Chariton

The chronicles of Texas legends contain many references to mysterious apparitions that are supposed to be the ghosts of Texans past. Texas ghosts, it seems, come in all varieties, sizes, and shapes. There are old cowboys, old Indians, old dogs, some unknown "things," and plenty of eerie young women supposedly haunting various parts of Texas from the Panhandle to the Rio Grande. Some of the stories are fascinating, some ridiculous, but most are at least interesting. And some Texas ghosts have become virtual celebrities in their own right.

Perhaps the most famous Texas ghost is the so-called "Lady of White Rock Lake." Even though the mystery lady hasn't been seen lately, her legend lives on whenever folks get around to discussing ghosts. Some people refuse to believe the story, saying it is just another "lady from a lake" tale that is duplicated almost verbatim around the nation and even in other parts of the state. But those who have seen the White Rock Lady swear she is as real as you and I except that she is a bit more transparent.

Although there are many variations to the story, the best one involved a young couple, both employees of the famous Neiman Marcus department store, who were driving north on Garland Road in Dallas back in the 1930s. As they were passing

White Rock Lake, a young lady suddenly appeared on the side of the road. The headlights of the car clearly showed the young woman was dressed in a fine gown and that she was soaked from head to foot.

The couple stopped and asked if the stranger needed help. The young lady replied that she did; that there had been a terrible accident and she had ended up in the lake. She asked to be taken to a certain address in a fashionable part of East Dallas. As the mysterious hitchhiker got into the back seat, the lady in the front noticed that the passenger had good taste because she was wearing a gown that only recently had been sold at Neiman's. In fact, the lady in the car had actually used the very gown in a special window display.

As the soaking wet passenger settled into the back seat, the man put the car into gear and drove off. His wife, naturally concerned about the poor young girl, asked if there was anything else she could do for her. When the mystery girl didn't answer, the lady turned to find that the girl had vanished leaving only a very wet spot on the back seat.

The man and his wife were naturally concerned about what had happened so they decided to drive to the address supplied by the girl and see if they could gather any more information. An older man answered the bell at the house and, when told of the experience, explained that his only daughter had drowned sometime earlier in White Rock Lake. He also said three other people had supposedly picked her up in the previous three weeks and had come to his door seeking more information. When asked by the lady, the grief stricken father said yes, his daughter did buy all her clothes at Neiman Marcus.

What separates this ghost lady from most of the others is that she doesn't always try to hitchhike home. On many occasions she simply walks up to the front door of one of the houses that ring the lake and asks to use the phone. She usually says there has been an accident and that she wants to call her father. Naturally most people agree but when they turn away for a second, the girl vanishes leaving only a small puddle of water on the porch.

The lady has also been seen just walking around the lake. When friend Charlie Ekhardt was in the business of upholding the law in Dallas, his partner Steve Wester claimed, and Charlie believed him, that he saw the mysterious lady walking near some wet marshes along the edge of the lake. And how did Wester know she was a ghost? She was walking over ground that was wet and sticky enough to bog down a small kitten and yet the lady left absolutely no tracks.

Whether real or imagined, fact or fiction, the Lady of White Rock Lake has achieved a sort of celebrity status among Texas apparitions. Thanks to publicity over the years, the lady has become the queen of Texas spooks. Other ghosts, however, have never received much publicity at all and thus are just drifting around out there somewhere doing whatever it is that ghosts do. The ghost of Love is a perfect example.

At ten o'clock on the morning of June 30, 1903, Colonel R. M. Love, comptroller for public accounts for the state of Texas, was in his office at the capitol building chatting with Reverend M. F. Cowden of Bonham. The friendly conversation was abruptly interrupted when W. G. Hill, a former state employee whom Love had dismissed, barged into the small office. The colonel, ever a gentleman, rose to greet Hill, shook his hand and then introduced him to the minister. The three then took their seats and engaged in some small talk, mostly about Hill and his family.

After a few moments the minister decided to leave but as he walked toward the door, Hill jumped from his seat and produced a two-page note which he demanded Love read immediately. The colonel took the papers and began to read the curious words:

> Dear sir - Public office is a public trust. Public offices are created for the service of the people and not for the aggrandizement of a few individuals.
>
> The practice of bartering department clerkships for private gain is a disgrace to the public service and in the nefarious traffic you are a "record breaker."

You have robbed the state's employees, and your incompetent administration has permitted others to rob the state.

The man who, claiming to be a Christian, deprives others of employment without cause is a base hypocrite and a tyrant.

If the host of democratic spoilsmen-politicians of this state, of the McGaughey-Love-Robbins-Sebastian-Rountree type had such a thing about them as a conscience, in a healthy state of activity, they could not look a republican in the face without blushing.

The greatest mind that ever gave its wisdom to the world; the mind of all others most capable of "umpiring the mutiny between right and wrong," said: "You take my life when you do take from me the means by which I live."

If that be true you are a murderer of the deepest crimson hue.

Although I can not help myself, before laying life's burden down, I shall strike a blow - feeble though it be - for the good of my deserving fellowman.

"For the right against the wrong
For the weak against the strong."

Yours truly, W. G. Hill

Obviously, Mr. Hill blamed Colonel Love for all of what must have been a significant number of problems that stemmed from his unemployment. The carefully worded note seemed a clear indication that Hill wasn't intent on asking Love over to Sunday dinner. The words appear to indicate a premeditated plot to rid the state of its comptroller, and Love might have become instantly alarmed if he had had the chance to finish reading all the words. Hill did not give the colonel that chance.

As Love read, the preacher brushed against Hill on his way into the adjoining office of Miss Allie Stanfield, Love's private stenographer. With no apparent warning, other than the note, Hill drew a 38-caliber Smith and Wessen revolver, that he had borrowed from his son, from his pocket. With careful aim, he pointed the gun at Love and fired once, hitting the comptroller in the chest.

The Honorable R. M. Love who was assassinated in the state capitol in 1903.
Some say his ghost still roams the halls of the capitol.

The Texas state capitol as it appeared about the time R. M. Love was assassinated.

J. W. Stephens, chief bookkeeper for the state, was at his desk just inside a small office that adjoined Love's. When Stephens heard the shot, he dashed into the comptroller's office to come to the aid of Love. As Stephens charged, Hill squeezed off another round and shot Love a second time, also in the chest. As Love collapsed to the floor gasping for air, Hill spun on his heels and tried to point the gun at Stephens. The bookkeeper reacted instinctively and ducked down low under Hill's arm and below the gun. As he reached the gunman, Stephens rose up, grabbed the gun with one hand and Hill with the other. The force of the attack sent both men sprawling backwards toward the door and onto the floor. As the pair rolled on the polished hardwood, each grappling for the gun, a third shot rang out.

Reverend Cowden came back into the room when he heard the shots. He saw the two men lying on the floor but he was unsure which one had been hit by the third bullet. There was a moment of suspense that would warm the heart of any Hollywood director while both men just lay on the floor. After a few seconds, Stephens struggled to his feet leaving Hill lying in a quickly expanding pool of his own blood. The assassin, realizing he was mortally wounded and destined to suffer an agonizing death, reached a trembling hand into his vest pocket and pulled out a small phial of laudanum, then thought to be a deadly poison. "Let me take this and die easy," Hill pleaded, but Stephens wouldn't hear of it. He snatched the bottle from Hill's hand and left the killer to suffer. It was later speculated that Hill had intended to take his own life after killing Love.

As soon as the brief scuffle was over, Colonel Love struggled to his feet and tried to walk. He exclaimed, "I've been shot," and collapsed back to the floor. Reverend Cowden hurried to his friend's side and slipped a pillow under his head. According to the minister, Love looked up and said, "I am shot but it is well with me. God bless you and God bless him." Apparently, even though he probably knew the end was near, Colonel Love held no particular grudge for his assailant.

Virtual pandemonium broke out in the capitol. Several people rushed to the scene to do what they could for their fallen friend. A leather chair was used to extend the couch beside Love's desk and he was gently raised onto the makeshift bed and made as comfortable as possible while everyone awaited the arrival of a doctor. Aides scurried off to get blankets, pillows, water, whiskey, anything they could think of that might make the suffering easier. Hill, on the other hand, was roughly carried to the south side of the capitol rotunda and placed on a cot where he was left to wait, virtually without attention, for doctors to arrive.

As Love lay on his couch clutching one hand against the wounds to hold down the flow of blood, it quickly became clear to all present that the assassin had done his evil deed well. It was, everyone speculated, but a matter of a few moments before Love would be gone. That sentiment was echoed by the state health officer who arrived shortly after the shooting and examined Colonel Love. When informed that he was dying, the colonel asked for his stenographer so she could take down his last statement. Miss Stanfield complied although she was on the verge of a breakdown. Love, speaking in a hushed voice, explained briefly what had happened and then concluded "I have no idea why he shot me. May the Lord bless him and forgive him. I can say no more."

News of the shooting spread quickly and Love's wife, son, and sisters hurried to the capitol to be with their beloved in the final moments. All arrived in time for Love to offer the prayer that they go in peace and that God protect them. Governor Latham also arrived on the scene in time for a final plea from Love, "I have but one request to make before the bullet of the assassin rushes me into the presence of God. Appoint Mr. Stephens to take charge of my official family." The kindness of the gentleman was evident to everyone and not an eye in the room, including the governor's, was dry.

At about 11:05 a.m., Colonel Love seemed for a moment to get better but then he took a turn for the worse. A reporter for the *Austin American Statesman* described what happened next: "One slight movement of the hand, one muscular twitch of the lips, one unsuccessful effort to give to the world and those around him a last parting word, and the soul of R. M. Love plumed its snowy pinions and sailed away to the pearly portals of Paradise . . . ."

As for Hill, although his wound was diagnosed as being fatal, his end did not come quite so quickly. He lived long enough to be transported to the Austin sanitarium. Despite repeated requests for a statement to explain his actions, Hill refused to say other than, "He didn't treat me right." Just before three that afternoon, Mr. Hill's wound finally took its toll and he expired.

The brutal assassination of a high ranking state official naturally sparked quite a controversy. Immediately, security was increased and there was some call that the capitol should be declared off limits to anyone not having official business. One state employee even suggested that everyone entering the building ought to be frisked for guns or knives. Another suggestion was that no one would be admitted to the capitol without an appointment, but that failed when it was pointed out that in all probability, Love would have granted an appointment to Hill.

As is always the case, the Love killing eventually slipped out of the category of current news and into the pages of Texas history. Unless something drastic happens, Colonel Love may be destined to enjoy the dubious distinction of being the only person assassinated in the state capitol. There is also some scant evidence that perhaps the colonel's spirit has yet to vacate the premises.

Although some ghost hunters may claim otherwise, there never has been any specific criteria established to identify the exact conditions under which a person's ghost will be tied to the place of mortal death. In Love's case, however, there are circumstances which often seem to be justification for a spirit to remain. He was killed instantly and unexpectedly, which means he left behind some unfinished business. Since Love also never had the chance to read the fatal note, perhaps his spirit is still wandering around looking for the document so he can finally understand why he was killed. Of course, it is also possible that some of Hill's charges hit closer to home than most imagined and that Love's ghost is still in the capitol trying to undo any wrong that was done.

The best evidence of a ghost's presence has to be eyewitness testimony from people who claim to have actually seen the apparition. In the case of Colonel Love, there have been sightings but they have been few and far between. One such sighting was made by Bill Thornton of Dallas. While he will be the first to say he doesn't know exactly what he saw, Thornton will also swear he saw something that cannot be explained.

It happened several years ago when the Thornton family was in Austin doing some sightseeing. During a late evening tour of the capitol, Bill's daughter became separated from the group and he went looking for her. A short distance down the East wing, near the office that had been occupied by Colonel Love, Bill encountered what he thought was either an employee or another tourist. The man was fairly short, about five foot eight or nine and of slightly stocky build. He had dark hair and a large bushy mustache. He was dressed in a white shirt with tie and odd looking trousers and shoes that seemed out of style.

Without ever saying a word, the mystery man politely stepped aside, when Thornton came close, and let him pass. Once by the man, Bill turned to look back down the corridor for any sign of his daughter and he noticed the man had simply vanished into thin air. There were no doors or hallways into which the man could have escaped and the hall was completely empty. The strange appearance startled Bill and he reported immediately to the capitol police. The man on duty at the time sort of laughed and informed Bill he had probably seen Colonel R. M. Love, the ghost of the capitol. Somewhat shaken, Bill gathered up his family and they left, determined to continue the capitol tour at a later date and in the daylight.

Thornton's account of the supernatural sighting set the wheels of investigation into motion. Unfortunately, the trail of Love's ghost proved almost as elusive as the spirit itself. Not one of the current employees in the state capital recalled ever seeing a ghost or even of hearing that one existed. Many of the younger capitol employees said they weren't even aware that an assassination had taken place. Efforts to locate the guard that had given the information to Bill Thornton proved futile. A few longtime residents of Austin remembered hearing rumors "many years ago" that there was supposed to be a ghost in the capitol. Unfortunately, none recalled that it was supposed to be the ghost of Love and no one could remember any specific details.

It appeared the trail was dead-ended but then a tip lead to a man who had worked in the capitol for many years before moving on to a railroad job. The man, who preferred that his name not be used, claimed that he often worked late in the capitol and did, on rare occasions, see something strange. He said that what appeared to be a man would occasionally be seen walking the East corridor at about the same spot where Bill Thornton had his close encounter. The witness said he had always heard that the man was the ghost of Colonel Love but that whenever he tried to talk about it, his co-workers always seemed to laugh and make fun. Finally the man decided to simply keep his mouth shut. He also decided, whenever possible, to avoid the East wing at night like a hog might avoid an electric fence. Although the supposed ghost never said or did anything frightening, the man concluded, "I never did see no future in taking unnecessary chances."

A former Austin resident did claim he had heard of a capitol ghost but he believed it was Representative Louis Franke and not Colonel Love. As the story goes, Franke had been drinking one day down at a saloon on Congress Avenue. After paying his tab with a large bill and pocketing the change, the representative headed back to the capitol about 7:30 in the evening. As he walked up the steps of the capitol toward the front door, he was accosted by two hoodlums who beat him severely, stole his wallet, and tossed him down the steps. Within two hours, Franke had died. Despite an intensive search supported by eyewitness testimony, the killers were never brought to justice.

While it is true that Franke was the only other person ever killed at the capitol, there is a large complication. Franke was killed on February 19, 1873, fifteen years before the present capitol building was opened. Since the capitol at the time of Franke's death later burned, any possible ghost would not only have had to endure the flames but then would have to lay in wait for a new building to be constructed, which took several years. It seems much more logical to assume that if there is a ghost, it is Love and not Franke. The witness, however, countered that legend has it the ghost of Franke is going to hang around the vicinity of where the killing took place, which would be the present capitol, until the murder is finally solved. Since the murder cannot possibly be solved at this late date, the ghost is destined to linger around the capitol for all eternity.

The search for additional evidence continued with very few results. Several persons who have studied Texas history and folklore with a passion for many years recalled hearing something about ghosts in the capitol but none could recall any specific references. In his excellent book *Ghost Stories of Texas*, Ed Syers did not include any mention of a capitol ghost. In fact, no written reference of any kind could be found to a possible ghost in the state house.

So what is the truth? Does the ghost of R. M. Love still haunt the capitol? Or is the ghost that of Louis Franke? In either case, the ghost is perhaps the shiest in recorded history. If there is no ghost lurking in the halls of the capitol, then what did Bill Thornton and the former capitol employee see? Whatever the truth is, the possible ghost of the capital is certainly one of the strangest stories and best kept secrets in all of Texas.

If you or someone you know has seen something strange in the state capitol at Austin or has any other pertinent information that might help solve this mystery, please contact the author at Wordware Publishing.

Old Rip — Fact or Fiction?

by Wallace O. Chariton

One of the best Texas stories of all time began on February 18, 1928, when the cornerstone of the old courthouse in Eastland County was opened after having been sealed for thirty-one years. Inside was a very flat, dirty, but very much alive horned toad, also known as horned frog in parts of Texas. A legend was instantly born that lives on to this day, but the question remains: did it really happen or was the whole thing just a well-planned hoax? There are still a lot of people around, especially in Eastland County, that believe very strongly one way or the other. Whether fact or fiction, the legend of the famous horned toad is an unsolved mystery.

Like a lot of Texas legends, the tale of the Eastland County horned toad undoubtedly has some stretched truths or even outright fiction intertwined among the strands of truth. There are several versions about what supposedly transpired, but the story that follows is the one generally accepted as being closest to what really happened.

The seed for the great adventure was supposedly planted back in 1897 when the *Dallas Morning News* ran a story about the possibility that horned toads might be able to live for extended periods — perhaps as long as one hundred years —

without food, water, or air. The theory was that the horned toads, which are actually lizards, could put themselves into a state of suspended animation or prolonged hibernation and thus avoid the necessity of having to eat or breathe. Surprisingly enough, the story was not thought to be too far-fetched because a lot of oldtime Texans already believed that the horned, spiked-back little creatures could live long periods in the desert without the normal necessities of life. There was also an Indian legend that some lizards could live forever.

Timing is, of course, critical in any legend. It just so happened that the *Morning News* story appeared not long before the folks in Eastland County were ready to complete a brand-new brick courthouse to replace the old stone structure which had served them since about 1875. A large local celebration was scheduled for July 29, 1897, the day the cornerstone of the new building was to be leveled. Speeches were planned about the bright future for the area and the town band was scheduled to play a number of selections.

Around noon on the day of the leveling, Ernest E. Wood, the county clerk and a cornetist in the band, hurried home for a quick lunch and to pick up his instrument. Since it is customary to put all sorts of odd items in cornerstones before they are sealed, Wood wished he had something to contribute but could not decide what that might be. Then, as he was leaving home to rush back for the festivities, he noticed his four-year-old son Will playing with a horned toad in the dusty front yard. The *Dallas Morning News* story came to mind and Ernest Wood instantly decided the cornerstone would provide the perfect test to see if horned toads could indeed survive without food and water. He snatched the critter from his son and headed back downtown and into history.

Wood arrived at the town square and found that the stone was about to be sealed. The clerk took the horned toad from his pocket and handed it to a friend with the suggestion that the little lizard ought to be slipped inside the stone. Even though the friend failed to see how entombing a horned toad could possibly contribute to posterity, as items inside cornerstones were supposed to do, he nevertheless dropped the animal inside the small opening on top of the cornerstone before it was covered with a sheet of galvanized iron, tapped into place, and sealed with mortar. As the story goes, the only other thing inside the cornerstone was a small Bible.

Thirty-one years later, Eastland County commissioners again faced problems with their courthouse. The 1897 structure was in a sad state and in need of expensive repair work. The biggest problem, however, was that Eastland County was the site of considerable oil activity. There had been major strikes at Ranger and at Hogtown, which was renamed Desdemona. With oil came oil leases, and where there were leases, the lawyers were never far behind. The old courthouse was literally bulging at the seams.

After giving the matter some thought, the county commissioners decided the smart thing to do would be to tear down the existing building and construct a new, more modern facility on the same site. When word began to circulate that the old courthouse was coming down, Ernest Wood, who was still very much alive and kicking, realized the cornerstone would be opened. He quietly began to remind people that when the stone was opened, there would be a horned toad inside and it would be his property. The story eventually reached a man named Boyce House and a certifiable media event was launched.

Boyce House was editor for the *Eastland Argus Tribune* and he wrote a syndicated column entitled "I Give You Texas." He enjoyed a strong reputation for being a staunch Texan and firm believer in West Texas and was a frequent speaker on the value and fun of life in Texas. He eventually published several humorous books on the Lone Star State that have become classic somewhat. When the producers of the movie *Boom Town*, a tale of oil wildcatting based on the famous 1918 strike at Ranger, needed an expert on both Texas and Ranger, Boyce House was selected. He later wrote a book about his experience working in Hollywood with a cast that included Clark Gable and Claudette Colbert.

In 1928, Boyce House was still a newspaper man and he quickly realized the potential value of the horned toad tale. He wrote the first of many stories about the possibility of there being a toad inside the stone. The story aroused the curiosity of the folks in Eastland County and excitement began to build. There are some who believe Boyce House also did more than just write the stories.

As the day drew closer for the opening of the cornerstone, the media interest created a credibility problem for Eastland County officials. No one really knew for sure if there was a horned toad inside the stone but it occurred to some that the whole thing might be a hoax. It was decided, for the good of the local reputation, that a few of the community's best citizens ought to be tapped to act as sort of judges to insure that there was no attempt to salt the stone with an impostor lizard like old-timers once salted gold mines with imported gold. County Judge Ed. S. Pritchard was asked to officiate at the opening ceremonies. He was to be assisted by Brother H. W. Wrye of the Church of Christ, Reverend H. M. Sell, pastor of the Church of God, and Reverend F. E. Singleton, a Methodist minister of unquestioned veracity, who was asked to be the first to peer into the tomb and determine if, in fact, a horned toad was inside.

On opening day, a crowd variously estimated at between 1,500 and 3,000 was on hand. Media representatives from as far away as Dallas and Fort Worth were present and so was the Associated Press. If there was a horned toad inside the stone, the world would know soon enough. Ironically, one person who was not there was Boyce House. According to one story, he was so nervous about the opening and the prospect that there wouldn't be a horned toad inside the stone that he couldn't bear to watch. Instead, he waited for news down at the bank building.

In preparation for the ceremony, the demolition crew in charge of tearing down the old courthouse had left in place an eight foot section of wall surrounding the cornerstone. When the moment of truth arrived, an oil field chain was looped around the remaining wall of jagged bricks and then connected to a nearby tractor. The driver slipped the tractor into gear and accelerated. The chain drew taut, the tires spun, and slowly the last remaining wall of the old courthouse gave way. Amid a cloud of dust and cheers from the spectators, the bricks fell leaving only the cornerstone in place.

Workmen stepped forward with picks and in a moment the mortar around the top of the stone had been chipped away. Carefully, under the supervision of Judge Pritchard, the piece of galvanized iron was loosened and then removed; the stone was finally opened. Ernest Wood, who was watching with his now grown son Will, called out, "If there's a horned toad inside, it's mine." Reverend Singleton smiled, stepped forward, and peered cautiously into the blackness. He squinted to get a better view and after several moments of hushed anticipation, he said he could see the toad. A small cheer went up from the crowd. Just to be sure, the other preachers each took their turn looking into the vault to see the creature. All were satisfied there was, indeed, a horned toad inside.

Eugene Day, destined to become one of the most famous Texas oilmen of all time, then reached into the vault and retrieved the horned toad that was said to be flat as a match, crusted over in dirt, and either fast asleep or stone cold dead. Day, holding the creature carefully by one leg, handed it to Singleton who in turn handed it to County Judge Ed Pritchard. The judge held up the horned toad for the crowd to see and everyone pushed closer for a better view. Suddenly, unexpectedly, one of the frog's legs twitched and then moved; he inhaled a gulp of air and he puffed up to almost normal size. A woman screamed, others yelled "it's alive" and a loud roar of applause went up. The great adventure had begun.

Several people took turns briefly holding the scared little creature. One was a young coach from Ranger named Blair Cherry, who eventually became head football coach at the University of Texas. Someone suggested that the horned toad ought to be named in honor of Rip Van Winkle who, according to legend, had slept for twenty years and the crowd agreed. Old Rip, as the horned toad came to be called, was then placed carefully into a Roi Tan cigar box that could be used as a temporary cage. It was suggested the toad ought to be given a medical checkup, so patrolman Bob Hammitt took the cigar box and gave Rip a motorcycle ride down to the clinic. Beta Maxey took some X rays which revealed a broken leg and assorted other minor injuries but overall the prognosis was that Rip was

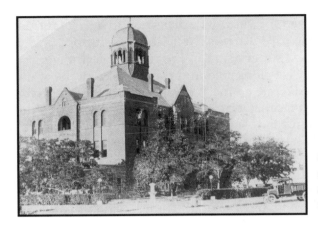

The courthouse where Old Rip allegedly slept for thirty-one years.

The scene at the opening of the cornerstone. The man standing on the ledge (circled) is E. S. Pritchard. The man standing on the ground just below Pritchard is holding Old Rip up for the camera.

The cornerstone that may have been a prison for a harmless horned toad.

in fine condition. One of the doctors present sent Rip's official report to a medical magazine for publication. That medical checkup, which gave Rip a clean bill of health, also sent him on his way to being a legitimate celebrity, the only horned toad ever so honored.

Old Rip was placed in a goldfish bowl partially filled with sand and put on display in the window of a local store. Boyce House, who had hurried to the scene when Harry H. Johnson burst into the bank with the news, wrote the details and it became his first story ever picked up by United Press. Newsreel companies that had ignored the opening, quickly came to town to catch Rip on film. Robert L. Ripley, whose "Believe it or Not" column was perhaps the most widely read at the time, included a story of the now famous horned toad. Local Eastland residents lined up to press their faces against the glass window for a closer look at the phenomenon. Street vendors reaped large rewards selling postcards depicting Rip and telling the story. As for Rip, he wasn't all that impressed with what was happening around him. For several weeks he did not eat or even move around much; the extent of his activity was simply to blink occasionally at the curious faces pressed against the window glass.

The publicity surrounding the event was almost beyond belief. Various newspapers around the nation, with a combined subscriber base of more than fifty million people, carried pictures of Rip. One picture showed a close-up of Rip and the other showed Judge Pritchard and Patrolman Hammitt. The *Chicago Tribune* carried the pictures and two sub-headlines. The first claimed the horned toad had been "flat as a silver dollar when found." The second proclaimed, "Well, you would be too if you'd had a courthouse on your chest for 31 years." Arthur Brisbane, a columnist for the Hearst papers, said that Will Wood had speculated the toad had gotten its strength from the Bible that he had shared space with for all those years. At Memphis, Tennessee, a minister mentioned Old Rip in his sermon at the Central Baptist Church.

Extensive publicity may have almost spelled the end of Old Rip. A couple of days after the opening, C. F. Sheppard took Rip out of the fish bowl and quickly left town, intending to take the horned toad to California and display it, for a fee, while the story was still hot. He made it as far as El Paso where he was apprehended because of an alert sent out from Eastland. The crook and his victim were returned; Sheppard was ultimately released and, by some accounts, barely avoided a date with a lynch mob. Although Rip was rescued, it wasn't the last time he would find himself in the middle of a controversy.

While almost everyone in West Texas seemed to find their way to Eastland for a look at the famous toad, people in other places began to clamor for a firsthand view of the famous little reptile. Hundreds of letters arrived, some addressed simply to "Old Rip" or to "Home of the 31-year-old Toad, Texas." All the letters were eventually delivered to Eastland and, apparently, read. Will Wood was approached by a promoter named Dick Penney who wanted to put the toad on display in Dallas for ten days. Although the details have been lost, Wood must have begun to realize the promotion possibilities of the famous toad and some sort of deal was struck. Penney, along with Wood, gathered up Old Rip and headed toward Big D for what turned out to be a short stay.

Although Rip was gone, hundreds of spectators continued to pour into Eastland expecting to see the famous horned toad. They all went home disappointed and the good people of Eastland became quickly embarrassed — so much so that Judge Pritchard finally ordered Will Wood to return the reptile. The only problem was, Dick Penney claimed he had a contract to show the toad in Dallas for ten days and that returning Rip would constitute breach of contract. He promptly sued for $6,295.25 and tried to get a writ of attachment preventing the reptile from being removed. A Dallas judge set bond in the case at $10,000 which the members of the Dallas Chamber of Commerce posted. Will Wood, with Rip secreted away in a brown paper sack, quickly departed Dallas and went back home. A hearing was held and Judge Prichard finally ruled that Will Wood should have custody of the horned toad since he had been the original owner back in 1897. The Penny lawsuit was never settled.

Publicity and controversy continued to swirl around the tale of Old Rip. Leading scientists, including members of the Smithsonian Institution; Dr. William M. Mann, director of the National Zoological Park; Dr. Raymond L. Ditmars of the New York Zoological Gardens; Dr. D. W. Hamlett of Indiana University; and doctors D. B. Casteel and J. T. Patterson of the University of Texas, among many others, all went on record as doubting the story. They claimed that it was impossible for a horned toad to live such a time without food or air.

There were just as many believers. E. E. Wood, Eugene Day, and Judge Pritchard all swore the toad was in the stone when opened. H. A. Parks and Roy Whatley of the Christy Dolph Construction company that was handling the demolition swore that they opened the stone and that it absolutely had not been tampered with in any way before the mortar was chipped away. Both men steadfastly maintained that there was no way anything could have been placed inside that cornerstone except before it was sealed. As many as twenty representatives of Texas Christian University, whose mascot is the horned toad, ventured to Eastland to make scientific tests to try to determine how the toad managed to live so long under such conditions.

The most interesting part of the controversy was the numerous reports of other horned toads that had been discovered under somewhat similar situations. Elam Dudley wrote to say that in the late 1870s he had found a live toad buried forty-five feet underground near Onion Creek, not far from Austin. In the 1880s, a man in Nacogdoches County claimed he found a live toad in an air-tight chamber thirty-five feet below the surface. Another man maintained that in 1906 he and some friends from an Eastern college were searching rock formations along White Rock Creek in Dallas. One forty-pound boulder was broken open and inside they found a flat but very much alive horned toad. Another 1906 story, which was printed in the *Home and Farm Magazine*, claimed a man had found a toad sealed in some limestone south of Dallas.

This Old Rip cartoon appeared in the Dallas Morning News *on February 28, 1928.*

While such testimony might be considered suspect, some scientists, including Prentiss F. Reid, head of the biology department at Austin College, also joined the parade of believers. Reid said that while he had no proof, he believed it possible for a horned toad to live such a time in the tomb if it had just a slight bit of natural moisture. Given the circumstance of the tomb, the chances were excellent, he believed, that there was some natural moisture in minute quantities. Dr. William T. Hornaday, former director of the New York Zoological Gardens, was another who said he believed the story. He also claimed to have found a live, entombed toad while digging for ancient elephant tusks in Ceylon.

As the publicity continued to spread, other people came forward to claim direct knowledge of the events, and the strangest reports came out of Oklahoma of all places. W. H. Day, a Tulsa barber and brother of Eugene Day, the oilman who retrieved the toad, claimed that a group of four boys, including he and his brother plus John White and Henry Cobb of Wichita Falls, were responsible for putting the toad in the stone. The barber claimed that he had been working on the courthouse and when it came time to close the cornerstone, a crowd of boys gathered round and one of them found a horned toad which they slipped inside the stone just before it was closed. Although Eugene Day never did confirm the story, two other people did. Mrs. Harry W. Clegern, who had been a little girl in 1897, said she watched the boys put the toad in the stone. Charles U. Connellee also said he watched the others do the deed. Connellee even offered an explanation for all the doubters. "Every loyal Texan," he said, "inherently knows that a Texas horned toad will live for 100 years without food or air if he remains in Texas. It's just jealousy of Texas that is causing these scientific doubts about that toad."

Pressure continued to mount on Will Wood to take the famous horned toad on tour, and he finally relented after most of the people in West Texas had had a chance to view Old Rip. Wood, along with N. M. Day, son of Eugene Day, left on what was to become one of the most unusual publicity tours of all time.

At St. Louis, the zoo offered a $1,000 reward for anyone who could prove the story false and then had to contend with somewhere between 10,000 and 40,000 people who stormed the zoo for a peek at the marvel. So large was the crowd that human blockades were created in several places and special police had to be called in to maintain order. No one — not even the world's best scientists — ever even attempted to claim the reward.

In New York, Rip was such a hit that a movie company actually wanted to make a film of him eating. Unfortunately, red ants are the main staple of a horned frog's diet, and none could be found locally in New York. A professional bug catcher was called in and he supplied ants at fifty cents a bag. The cameras rolled and Old Rip enjoyed a feast. One of the co-stars of the $5,000 film was Henry Ford but, unfortunately, no copy survived. When Rip appeared bored, a hotel sponsored him for a visit to Broadway to see the musical comedy "Here's Howe" and to have his picture taken in the palm of the show's star Irene Delroy. Rip also attended a banquet for Trans-Atlantic Fliers, but Arthur Brisbane, the Hearst columnist, was there and he ruined the evening by claiming the tale of Rip was a hoax.

The crowning achievement of Rip's career was in Washington D.C. It had been arranged that Dr. William T. Hornaday, a believer in Rip, would examine the horned toad, but former senator Earle B. Mayfield of Texas upstaged that event by arranging a personal audience with President Calvin "Silent Cal" Coolidge. Some people claim the president actually canceled several appointments for the chance to see Rip and then was kept waiting for fifteen minutes, something that never happens to a United States president. When the meeting finally got started, the president and Wood had an enjoyable talk while Coolidge sat stroking Rip's back with his horn rim glasses. At one point the president and Rip sat motionless staring at each other for a moment. One newspaper reported, "Silent Cal had met his match." No one seems to know what happened to the photographs taken showing Coolidge holding Old Rip.

Following the White House appearance, Wood, Day, and Rip returned to Texas for the May 30, 1928 dedication of the new courthouse. For Rip, life could not have been better. All he did was rest in his glass house in Wood's parlor and feast on red ants often supplied by neighborhood children in return for a look at the famous horned toad. If Rip could live thirty-one years under the worst of conditions, some thought he might live forever under the best of conditions. Unfortunately for Old Rip, forever turned out to be less than a year.

In January of 1929, Old Rip was peacefully hibernating, as all horned toads do, beneath the sand in his glass house. For some unknown reason, Will Wood decided to place the glass cage outside on a porch railing. The warmth of the afternoon sun, which may have been magnified by the glass, apparently fooled Rip's biological clock and he assumed it was time to awaken from hibernation. In a classic case of poor timing, Old Rip wiggled around and stuck his head out of the sand at about the time a fierce norther struck. In moments, the temperature plummeted, something that is definitely not good for a supposed-to-be-hibernating horned toad. Wood got the fish bowl back inside as quickly as possible but the damage had been done. Rip contracted pneumonia and on January 19, 1929, he passed away quietly. The Texas weather had done something in one brief moment that a tomb sealed for 31 years had not been able to accomplish.

News of Rip's death spread rapidly and sympathy cards started pouring in from around the nation. Even though a lawsuit was still pending in the matter of Old Rip, Judge George L. Davenport granted Will Wood permission to have the body embalmed. Ben Hamner, an Eastland mortician volunteered for the job and then placed the remains in a special miniature, velvet lined, glass covered casket donated by the National Casket Company. For several days, Old Rip laid in state in the window of the Barrow Furniture Company, which was also the offices of Barrow Undertakers. Hundreds of people, most with teary eyes, filed by the window to pay their last respects to the lizard that put Eastland, Texas on the world map. It was the only time in history that a horned toad actually laid in state.

Although he had gone to whatever reward awaits horned toads, Old Rip continued to be an Eastland County celebrity. Through the years, visitors to the area would always find their

The original monument to Old Rip.

The funeral home where the body of Old Rip laid in state for three days.

way to the courthouse for a glimpse of the famed lizard. A small controversy erupted in the early 1960s when John Connally came to town during his campaign for governor. He was handed Old Rip as a publicity stunt and when he handed the critter back, one leg was missing. For a time Connally was branded a horned toad defacer until it was learned that the leg had actually been broken off by Will Wood's daughter while she was showing Rip to a friend. No one knows for sure, but that announcement may have saved the election for Connally. At the very least, it probably saved the Eastland County vote.

The saga of Old Rip took a sinister turn on January 16, 1973, when the remains were "toadnapped." Eastland County officials were shocked and outraged but there wasn't much to do except use an impostor so at least the legend could be kept alive. The use of impostors spurred the toadnappers into action. On March 30, 1974, James Dabney of the *Abilene Reporter-News* printed the following excerpt from an anonymous letter he received, ostensibly from the horned toad thief:

To the public. The purpose of this writing is to clarify the mystery surrounding the disappearance of Old Rip . . . I . . . am the person who removed Old Rip from public display and he definitely remains in my possession as the enclosed photograph should establish beyond any doubt . . . I had planned to remain silent but this attempt to keep "the legend of Old Rip" alive by replacing him with an obvious fake has forced me to tell my story.

I am one of three surviving perpetrators of the hoax which grew into "the legend of Old Rip." One evening some 45 years ago five young men, including myself, decided to place a live horned toad in the cornerstone in the old courthouse which had just been demolished. With a little help from a member of the demolition crew we were able to lift the cornerstone and toss the horned toad inside. The cornerstone was reopened the next day at the ceremony . . . .

The writer, who enclosed a photo of a horned toad sitting on a current issue of a newspaper, went on to claim he had become disheartened by the fact that civic leaders had been exploiting the legend and neglecting other responsibilities so vital to a small town. He was equally dismayed when an impostor was promptly substituted for the original and the exploiting continued unabated. He realized it was futile to continue his game of intrigue and offered to return the original if the impostor were removed. It never happened. The horned toad on display today in the Eastland County courthouse is a stand-in. Whatever happened to the authentic Old Rip has never been discovered.

Old Rip's legend continues to this day, but it is actually a double sided mystery and whichever side is the real mystery remains unsolved. If the legend is true and a horned toad did manage to survive for thirty-one years in a cornerstone, the mystery becomes how did it survive? Conversely, if the legend is a great hoax, the mystery becomes who did it, why did they do it, and, more importantly, how did they do it?

The body of a horned toad on display in the Eastland County courthouse. This is not the real Rip since the original was stolen in the 1970s. This impostor horned toad nevertheless keeps alive the legend.

As to the possibility that the toad did survive his entomb-ment, there are a lot of people — admittedly most of them are in Eastland County — who believe the story is absolutely factual. In a very unscientific poll that was conducted recently, twenty-five people in Eastland were interviewed and twenty said they believed the story. Four said they did not believe it and one person said he had never heard of Old Rip. He turned out to be a salesman just passing through.

Mr. Roy Lee Smith, a lifelong resident of Eastland County and a historian, said he certainly did believe the story as did his father before him. Jim Golden, another longtime resident, believes the story. Although he was unavailable for an inter-view, his beliefs are a matter of record and he even claims that a number of boys, including himself, spent the night before the opening at the courthouse to be sure there was no hanky-panky, and there was none.

On the other side of the coin is Mr. James Dabney, the news-paper man who printed the stories of the toadnapping. He is a longtime resident of Eastland and a disbeliever in the toad story. He stated, in a telephone interview, that members of the demolition crew were staying in his father's home at the time of the opening and that he heard them tell how the deed was done. He said they went down to the site the night before to make sure everything was prepared for the ceremony. Suppos-edly, the men had heard that there was a Bible inside the stone and decided to see if it was true. They opened the stone and found the Bible but then as they were about to reseal it, one of the men discovered a horned toad and pitched it into the stone for a joke. He did not explain how the men managed to open the stone and then close it with out leaving behind any evidence of tampering.

If there was a horned toad in the stone, the mystery is how did it survive for thirty-one years without food, water, and air? Roy Smith claims there actually isn't much of a mystery. He pointed out that the tomb was never actually sealed to be airtight. All the workmen did was lay a sheet of galvanized iron across the top of the stone, slap on some mortar, and finish laying the brick. Smith believes, as a lot of people stated in 1928, that mortar and iron do not constitute an impenetrable barrier to air and insects.

It is Smith's contention that there were enough cracks and crevices in the crude mortar to allow for some air, an occasional bug, and a precious few drops of water to find their way to the hidden tomb of Old Rip. He stated that once, as a boy, he had placed a single drop of water on a flat horned toad and in a few moments, the creature had swelled to normal size. If that theory is correct, and there is not sufficient evidence to prove or disprove it, then the legend of Old Rip is probably no legend at all but hard fact.

Believers in Old Rip continue to point to other evidence that may be applicable. It seems almost certain that the brick wall, and consequently the cornerstone, had not been tampered with in any way. Guards that were on duty swore no one tried to pull a fast one and a number of reliable, trustworthy witnesses swear there was a toad in the stone when it was opened.

The best argument that the legend is real, according to the believers, is the fact that horned toads do hibernate, usually from October until the end of April or the first of May. Members of the pro-Old Rip coalition are always quick to point out that there were no horned toads running around that cold February day and thus it would have been very difficult for anyone to simply find a toad that could be slipped into the stone. Such evidence, coupled with a theory similar to Roy Smith's, is sufficient to cause a lot of people to completely disregard the claims of the scientific community. Old Rip is another case of a Texas legend usurping scientific knowledge.

In the case of Old Rip, there is more to the story. As anyone above the age of 35 who grew up in Texas — especially West Texas — can testify, horned toads are curious, even ominous, creatures. There was a time when they made great pets and just about every little Texan, at one time or another, encountered the creatures while stalking the wilds of his backyard. There was even a provocative rumor that, when excited or in danger, the horned toads could spit blood that rendered you instantly blind if some of the blood got in your eye. The truth is horned toads can expel blood when in danger, but it comes out of their eyes and not their mouth and it will not, under any circumstances, cause blindness.

Another false rumor often associated with horned toads is that the bite of one of the creatures can be fatal to certain animals. Not true, even though Roy Smith said he heard once that a prized bulldog was found dead in South Texas with a horned toad clamped securely to his lip. Horned toads were actually the most ideal pet for boys because, while harmless, they looked frightening as the devil and thus there was nothing better to scare the curls out of a girl's hair.

Since the curious creatures were harmless, there wasn't a kid in Texas that didn't try to keep one (or a drawer full) as a pet and, sadly, the results were almost always disastrous. The creatures actually do not make good pets because their main diet is red ants, which is probably why God invented them in the first place. Without horned toads, West Texas might be one large ant bed. Speaking from experience, efforts to feed horned toads lettuce, bugs, chopped ham, and cat food simply do not work. Attempts at keeping horned toads as pets almost always ended in a somber funeral in the backyard.

So how is it that one toad could possibly have lived for 31 years without even the hint of a juicy red ant? The answer, according to Jim Dunlap, is that the horned toad could not have survived. Dunlap, who is director of the Living Materials Center of the Plano Independent School District, ought to know what he's talking about. He is the author of the new book *They Don't Have to Die*, which concerns keeping small critters alive. He says that the average lifespan of a horned toad is three to five years and considerably less for one trapped inside a sealed cornerstone. He completely discounts the possibility that enough air and nutrients could have reached the horned toad in the center of the stone to sustain his life. There is no way, according to Dunlap, that Old Rip could have possibly survived for any length of time in the Eastland County courthouse cornerstone. A great story, he admits, but a false one nonetheless. How sure is he of his information? "I'd be willing to testify in court," he said, and, as an acknowledged expert, his testimony would be accepted.

That pronouncement complicates the legend of Old Rip. If no horned toad could survive 31 years in a tomb, then the lizard found in the cornerstone must have been a plant. However, that possibility seems remote since all the evidence, based on eyewitness accounts, points to the fact that the cornerstone had not been disturbed in any way before it was opened. If the legend of Old Rip was a monumental gag, the only possible way it could have been carried out was at the time of the opening, which means the story becomes a "whodunit" mystery.

Oddly enough, although the possibility that the story was a fake is not new, all the previous implications have been of tampering before the opening. Most people apparently assumed that since the crowd was so large and that so many leading citizens were involved, that there was no way everyone could have been fooled. However, if the brick wall was not tampered with and no horned toad could have lived that long, then a little sleight of hand at the opening must have occurred. Because of the number of people involved, there was perhaps a conspiracy of fun that day.

Ernest Wood was probably involved, because he started the story well before opening day. What is not known is whether or not he actually did put a horned toad in the vault. If he did, then the plant was simply a hedge against the possibility (or probability) that the original had expired. There is actually some evidence which suggests there may not have even been a horned toad inside the stone in the first place. According to several accounts, when the stone was about to be opened, Wood called out, "If there is a toad in there, it's mine." Why, if he knew there was a horned toad inside, did he use the word "if"? Perhaps he was not sure the friend he originally gave the horned toad to actually did place it in the stone.

Conversely, the chances seem good that there was the body of a horned toad inside the cornerstone. Either that or Reverend F. E. Singleton was in on the gag. Most accounts claim he peered into the stone and announced he could see the creature. Of course, there have been cases of Methodist ministers straying off the path of righteousness, but it seems doubtful Singleton would have strayed off for the sake of a gag and then never admit the truth.

The entire matter might have been resolved if the preacher had actually reached into the tomb and extracted the evidence. Although Singleton had removed his coat and rolled up his sleeves to do just that, it did not happen. Eugene Day, with coat on, stepped forward and actually reached into the opened stone. He pulled the horned toad out and handed it to the preacher. That opens the door to the possibility that Day had a "ringer" horned toad up his sleeve and that is the one he produced.

A complication to that theory is the matter of hibernation. Horned toads do disappear for the winter months, so if a "ringer" was involved, that surely means there was a conspiracy afoot and someone — we'll never know who — actually went out into the prairie and hunted until one of the sleeping toads could be found.

Once the horned toad was lifted out and it began to move, all attention was diverted away from the open cornerstone. There is no record anywhere attesting to the fact that the interior of the stone was searched publicly for the body of another horned toad. Everyone assumed the wiggling reptile that was held up for all to see was the one from the stone. Based on the facts, everyone may have been wrong. No one can swear positively that, while everyone's attention was diverted, one of the possible conspirators did not reach into the vault and secretly remove the body of the real Old Rip. In fact, given all the facts in the case, that may be exactly what happened.

One piece of evidence that might actually shed some light on the mystery is the Bible that, by most accounts, shared the tomb with Old Rip. If the Bible did not have any chew marks or evidence of deterioration caused by moisture, it might be proof that Old Rip was a plant. If there was such evidence, then that might be proof that Rip was in the stone. Unfortunately, no one has any idea what happened to the Bible after the opening.

If the horned toad adventure was a hoax, what might have been the motive? The one that comes quickest to mind is that it was simply a joke which, unexpectedly, got way out of hand. If Ernest Wood, Eugene Day, and anyone else involved did cook up one of the greatest gags of all time, they surely could not have predicted it would reach all the way to the White House. Perhaps the conspirators intended to laugh for a couple of weeks and then tell the truth. On the other hand, since Boyce House was involved, perhaps the gag was well planned to get as much publicity for Eastland County as possible. There were, and still are, some who suspect House was involved right up to the top of his typewriter keys, and some even think he orchestrated the whole charade. It must be said, in House's defense, that not one shred of evidence exists to suggest Boyce House did anything other than report the events, which was his job.

Old legends die hard in Texas so the mystery of Old Rip will probably be around for generations to come. Was it a gigantic hoax or did Old Rip actually beat the scientific odds and manage to live through hell? You decide. Whether he did or didn't, in some respects the Eastland County residents win either way. If it could be proved that all the experts like Jim Dunlap are wrong, then Eastland would be the home of a certifiable scientific phenomenon. If the experts happen to be correct, then Eastlanders can still be proud because their town was the site of the greatest gag ever pulled off in Texas and the only one, as far as is known, that actually fooled a United States president.

There is, however, a sad postscript to the tale of Old Rip. In West Texas, where once millions of the innocent little ant eaters once roamed, today the species is on the endangered list and threatened with extinction. You can now receive a hefty fine and even some jail time for simply having a horned toad in your possession. If that law was retroactive, three-fourths of the people in West Texas, myself included, would be in a lockup somewhere. While it may be stretching a point, Old Rip could have been a contributing factor to the decline.

Immediately after all the publicity surrounding Old Rip broke nationally, the promoters stepped in, as they always seem to do, and tried to take advantage of the situation. Baby horned toads were rounded up by the thousands and shipped north to become pets. A good bet is that not a single one survived.

As late as the mid-1950s, I can recall walking into a five and dime store in Fort Worth and seeing a display of baby horned toads for sale at ten cents apiece. It struck me as odd that anyone would pay the equivalent of two Dr Peppers for something that could be picked up in most backyards. To prove the point to a friend who had just moved to town from somewhere up north and who had never seen a live horned toad, we ventured out into the woods in search of one he could have free. We did not find a horned toad that day and, looking back, I don't ever recall seeing another one in the wild.

Today, there are some of the rare creatures still around but the numbers are dwindling. If you or your children should discover one, please be careful. Observe it, marvel at it, even hold it for a moment. Don't worry about the blood, it will wash out; don't worry about getting bit because they don't even bite. But please, do not attempt to keep the little critter as a pet. The mystery of exactly what happened in Eastland, Texas on February 18, 1928 may never be solved. There is no mystery about what will happen to horned toads if the few that remain are not protected.

If you have any information, family legends, old records, or even photographs concerning Old Rip and you would care to share them with the author, please contact him at Wordware Publishing, Inc.

The Famous Five-Shot Suicide
by Wallace O. Chariton

Texas has had more than its share of sensational death cases. But few, indeed, are the cases that involved two U.S. presidents, a U.S. vice-president soon to become president, a U.S. attorney general who would run for president, a U.S. attorney who would become a federal judge, a Texas attorney general who wanted to become governor, a chairman of the U.S. Department of Agriculture who wanted to be attorney general, the head of the FBI, a Texas Ranger captain who would become a federal marshal, a Pulitzer Prize winning Texas journalist, a future network news anchorman, two former University of Texas student body presidents, assorted senators and congressmen, and the king of the Texas wheeler-dealers.

The investigation into the death of Henry Marshall involved just such a cast, plus hundreds of other lesser known characters. The Marshall case, which involved more twists, turns, and curves than a rain barrel full of pygmy rattlesnakes, also provided the fodder for hundreds of newspaper stories that were almost always printed under sensational headlines. And yet, thirty years later, despite worldwide press coverage and untold thousands of investigative hours, there is no positive proof to explain how and why Henry Marshall died.

Like so many other Texans, Henry Marshall enjoyed having what he called "a little place" in the country where he could go to work the land, raise cattle, and, for a while on weekends, forget the pressure of his job with the Agricultural Stabilization and Conservation (ASC) Committee of the United States Department of Agriculture. Outside of being with his wife and ten-year-old son, there was nothing Marshall liked more than to go out to his place, which was a 1,500-acre ranch eight miles north of Franklin, Texas, and spend the day working, breathing clean air, and letting the rest of the world just sort of go by without him. In fact, Henry was so fond of his ranch and of life in Texas in general that he had turned down a lucrative promotion in the Agriculture Department because acceptance would have meant relocation to Washington, D.C.

Early on the morning of June 3, 1961, Henry and his son Donald climbed into a 1960 Chevrolet pickup and left their home in Bryan for the thirty-mile drive to the ranch. On the way Henry made a quick stop at the house of his wife's brother, L. M. Owens, to drop off young Donald, who was to accompany Owens on his rounds as a Dr Pepper delivery man. Marshall arranged to return by 4:00 p.m. to pick up the boy and then continued on thirteen miles north of Franklin to settle an account with Joe Pruitt for bailing hay. Henry found Pruitt, along with Wylie Grace and Lewis Taylor, loading hay in Pruitt's field. He paid his $36 bill with a check and offered to pay Grace for cutting the hay, but the friend declined to accept.

The four men stood around for a few minutes kicking dirt clods and talking about things like the weather and the price of cattle. By 8:00 a.m. Henry had said so long and was on his way. He arrived at his farm in less than twenty minutes and was quickly busy with the normal chores that seem never ending around a farm or ranch. About 10:30 that morning, Jim and Martha Wood, a couple who lived nearby, happened by Henry's place and saw him hard at work as was his habit. They saw no one else and had no reason to be alarmed.

Around 5 o'clock that afternoon, Sybil Marshall did become alarmed when her usually punctual husband had not returned home as expected. Knowing that her husband had a history of health problems that included a mild heart attack in September of 1959, she telephoned her brother and asked him to check on Henry. Owens immediately drove out to the ranch and had a quick look around but found nothing. He returned home assuming he had simply missed Henry along the way. When he learned that Henry still had not arrived, Owens, along with Irving Bennett, drove back out to the ranch. They found Henry Marshall lying dead in a back pasture close to his pickup and not far from a cattle feeder. He had died in the dirt of the ranch he loved so much.

Leaving Bennett at the scene, Owens drove back to his home with the dreadful news and then went immediately to the offices of Robertson County Sheriff Howard Stegall to report the death. Sheriff Stegall immediately telephoned Lee Farmer, the elderly local justice of the peace, to inform him that "a man had killed himself." Years later Owens denied having said Marshall killed himself and speculated that Stegall came to that immediate conclusion on his own.

It was about 7:30 p.m. and getting dark by the time Sheriff Stegall and his deputy, E. P. "Sonny" Elliot arrived at the Marshall ranch. They quickly reviewed the scene and noted that the body was lying face up in some grass not far from the pickup. Henry had been shot five times in the lower left chest, apparently with the 22-caliber rifle that lay nearby. It was also obvious that Henry had sustained a severe head wound and his hands were badly scratched. There was no blood on the front of Henry's shirt but the back was fairly saturated. There were no bloodstains on the ground, except around the body, but smears were found on both doors, the hood, and right rear panel of the truck. There was also a six-to eight-inch dent in the lower panel of the passenger door, which had been open when the body was discovered. Inside the truck, Henry's glasses, watch, and pencils had been carefully removed from his shirt pocket and placed neatly on the front seat along with a single edged razor blade. There were no tire marks or human tracks to indicate anyone other than Marshall had been at the scene.

Apparently the lateness of the hour was sufficient motive not to follow accepted investigative practices and take photographs of the scene. The fact that Sheriff Stegall may have had a preconceived notion of suicide perhaps contributed to other investigative procedures being ignored. There were no drawings, diagrams, or measurements made at the scene; neither the fatal weapon nor the pickup were checked for fingerprints and no blood samples were taken from the smears on the truck. The death scene investigation, later called sloppy police work, certainly contributed to the Marshall mystery. Was the front of the victim's shirt pulled up or tucked into the pants when the body was discovered? Was the rifle one, three, or six feet from the body? The key was in the ignition switch but was it in the on or off position? Was there fuel in the gas tank or was it bone dry? Such questions, that normally would be a routine part of any investigation, are still a matter of some speculation in the Marshall case.

Owens, who generally looked after his brother-in-law's place, informed the sheriff that Marshall had no known enemies but that his health had failed of late and he had been acting strangely, often preferring to work alone in the back pasture where his body was found. Based on the physical evidence, the Owens information, and the fact that there were no signs of a robbery attempt, Sheriff Stegall concluded that Henry Marshall had, indeed, died as a result of self-inflicted gunshots even though no suicide note was found. The fact that Henry had been shot five times was, the sheriff decided, of little consequence since the bullets were 22-caliber and thus had very little shocking power when entering the human body. Deputy Elliot reportedly concurred that Henry Marshall had shot himself, so the body was ordered taken to the Callaway-Jones Funeral Home in Bryan, Texas.

The following day, June 4, Sheriff Stegall escorted Justice of the Peace Lee Farmer to the scene for further investigation. After reviewing the evidence and interviewing Owens, Farmer released the truck and Owens drove it back to town and had it washed and waxed. Any evidence the blood smears might have provided vanished down the drain of a car wash. Farmer, meanwhile, visited the funeral home with two of Henry Marshall's physicians. After viewing the body and taking some photographs, all three supposedly agreed that the death was suicide. Later that day Texas Ranger O. L. Luther arrived to investigate the case, but when he was told it was a suicide, he simply left without making any inquiries. In the earliest police report of the incident, dated June 6 and signed by deputy Elliot, the "offense" is listed as suicide. Elliot mentions that Marshall was shot five times by his own gun and that his personal effects were placed neatly on the truck seat. He did not mention other perhaps vital facts such as the massive bruise on the side of the victim's head.

Members of the Marshall family weren't quite so quick to accept the suicide theory. They wondered how the bloodstains had gotten on the truck and what had caused the dent in the door which was not there when Henry left for the ranch. Then there was the matter of the gun. It was well known that the 22-caliber rifle Henry carried in his truck was a bolt action model. That meant each time the gun was fired, the bolt would have to be opened to eject the spent cartridge and then closed to load another bullet in the chamber. For Henry to shoot himself five times with such a rifle would mean he had to point the rifle at himself and fire, then turn the gun around and work the bolt to reload the chamber and then repeat the process four times while pain and shock were rapidly increasing. Family members knowledgeable about firearms doubted that anyone, no matter how bent they were on suicide, could manage such a feat. Because of their doubts, the widow and the victim's brother posted a $2,000 reward for information in the case. The reward was never claimed.

Family members weren't the only ones who questioned the suicide ruling. Manley Jones, who was in charge of getting the body ready for burial, just couldn't believe that the apparently serious head injury and the wounds on the hands were consistent with suicide. Jones telephoned Farmer with his suspicions, but after a heated argument, the justice of the peace refused to consider the new evidence and stuck by his ruling of suicide. Unsatisfied, and perhaps to protect himself in the future, Jones again called in Ranger Luther. After viewing the body, Luther agreed that suicide seemed doubtful but outside of taking some unofficial photographs, there was little the Texas Ranger could do in view of the official ruling.

Henry Marshall was ultimately laid to rest on June 5, 1961 in the Franklin cemetery and the family tried to get on with their lives. A short time after the funeral, Mrs. Marshall visited Farmer and pleaded with him to reverse the ruling and change the cause of death from suicide to homicide. But Farmer was unrelenting and he chose the path of least resistance; the suicide ruling stood. That could have been the end of the Henry Marshall saga but as it turned out, the mystery of the five-shot suicide was far from over.

The next episode in the Marshall case seemed totally unrelated at the time. On March 29, 1962, nine months after Marshall was buried, a certifiable Texas wheeler-dealer named Billie Sol Estes was arrested and jailed in Pecos, Texas after being indicted on fraud charges by a federal grand jury. The arrest of Estes was big news in West Texas. Radio and television stations interrupted regular programing with the dramatic news and newspaper reporters scrambled for more details.

Billie Sol, as he was generally called by most people, always was (and still is) big news in the Lone Star State. He was a personable, outgoing, friendly charmer who had the gift of golden gab. And he was a hustler. In 1939, thirteen-year-old Billie Sol received a lamb for Christmas. In less than two years he had a flock of 100 sheep and was bragging about his ability with sheep, which prompted some to speculate that at least part of the credit should have gone to the ram. He later sold a cow to a neighbor on the promise that the animal would deliver four gallons of milk. When the neighbor complained that the claim was untrue, Estes reportedly pointed out that he hadn't specified over what period of time the milk would be produced.

At age 17, Estes won the national 4H achievement award and a year later boasted of having almost $40,000 in the bank, which was a veritable fortune in the war years of the mid-1940s. But Billie Sol was just getting started, and by age thirty he claimed to be a self-made millionaire. His accomplishments didn't go unnoticed, thanks in part to prompting from Estes himself. When his name came up as a potential nominee of the Pecos

Jaycees for Man of the Year Honors in Texas, Billie Sol didn't get the necessary votes. He did, however, get nominated by a friend on the committee and he ended up being selected one of the ten "Outstanding Young Men" in the United States, an honor Estes proudly bragged on at every opportunity. It was later pointed out, with no small amount of sarcasm, that while Billie Sol was one of the ten most outstanding young men in the nation, he was not one of the most outstanding young men in Pecos, Texas.

As the wheeler-dealer legend spread so did the Estes habit of dropping names. In no time it would appear to the casual observer that his list of associates read like a who's who in Texas. He hosted a giant barbecue for 3,000 people before the 1960 general election, and his friend and powerful democrat Ralph Yarborough was there to make a campaign speech. When Estes heard that former president Harry Truman was coming for a visit, he had an entire addition built onto his mansion to serve as private quarters for Truman's use. Unfortunately, Truman never showed.

Despite outward appearances to the contrary, Billie Sol Estes was actually the most accomplished con man and swindler in Texas history. One of his favorite sayings, "You can sheer a sheep many times, but you can only skin him once," was apparently his philosophy in business. By early 1962, the "good guy" legend of Billie Sol was gone and in its place was "con man, extraordinare."

In the late 1950s and on into the early 1960s, cotton was a big money crop in the United States. So big, in fact, that farmers everywhere scrambled to plant more and more acreage with "white gold." Eventually, the cotton frenzy forced the government to institute an allocation program to control the number of acres being planted in cotton to prevent the market from collapsing. As is so often the case, the allocation program was worthwhile but there was a large loophole in the legislation and it didn't take hustlers like Billie Sol Estes long to find it.

The USDA allocation program dictated that once a cotton allotment was set for a particular piece of land it could not be sold or exchanged. If the land itself was sold, the cotton allotment went with it as part of the sale. The only exception was when a farmer lost his land under the rule of eminent domain. When that happened, the farmer was allowed to transfer his cotton allotment to any new land he purchased within three years, subject to the approval of the state agent for the USDA which, in Texas, was Henry Marshall. The eminent domain rule was the overlooked loophole.

Billie Sol discovered that many farmers in Texas, Oklahoma, Georgia, and Alabama, who had lost their land to eminent domain, were choosing to forgo life on the farm. To take advantage of that situation, Estes devised a complicated plan whereby he would sell those displaced farmers some of his West Texas land for which there was no cotton allotment. The farmers would then apply for the transfer of their allotments and subsequently lease the land back to Estes for $50 an acre.

On the surface, the plan appeared to be a straightforward business proposition, but there was a large catch. The farmers who were supposed to pay for the land in four equal install-ments all secretly agreed with Estes to miss the first payment. Billie Sol would then promptly foreclose on the land with the net result being the farmer got a few dollars in his overalls and Estes got back land that had been enhanced with the valuable allotments. It was later to be determined that using his scheme, Estes received more than one-third of all the cotton allotments issued in the 1961.

Officials of the USDA became suspicious of the scheme and started a quiet investigation. This prompted Billie Sol to try to hedge his bets by exercising whatever influence he had in Washington. When that didn't work he resorted to the oldest trick in the book, bribery. Several members of the Agriculture Department were treated to shopping sprees at Neiman Marcus, trips on Estes' private planes, and a number of other special "perks." His actions may have stalled the inevitable for awhile, but he could not stop the wheels of justice.

Ironically, the first action taken by the USDA was actually favorable to Estes. On October 13, 1960, the Bridgeforth Memorandum was issued which ruled that a contract of sale of land — which would carry with it transfer of the valuable cotton allotment — was in and by itself not sufficient reason for denying the transfer. A second ruling, which was issued on December 20, 1960, was devastating to the Estes plan. The Manwaring Memorandum specifically stated that Estes-type contracts were a "scheme and device" to buy cotton allotments and not to sell land. That memorandum would eventually be the undoing of Billie Sol and would even serve to possibly cast doubt on Henry Marshall.

Two months after U.S. marshals carted Billy Sol Estes off to jail, Orville Freeman, the United States secretary of agriculture, made a stunning announcement. Henry Marshall had been, he reported, a "key figure" in the investigation into the cotton allotment dealings of Billie Sol Estes. An immediate result of the Freeman announcement was the realization that perhaps someone did have a motive for killing Henry Marshall. As if by magic, skeptical eyebrows were raised throughout all of Texas and most of Washington, D.C. at the notion a man could actually shoot himself five times, and with a bolt action rifle at that.

One person who took a special interest in the case was President John F. Kennedy. Although JFK had been in office for little more than a year, he was a political veteran who knew that corruption was like a cancer that could easily destroy careers, power bases, and even lives. Based on initial reports he received, there appeared to be some serious hank-panky going on in the democrat-laden USDA. Then there was the not so small complication that Kennedy's vice president, Lyndon Johnson, was rumored to be somehow connected to Billie Sol Estes. To be on the safe side, John Kennedy asked his brother, Attorney General Robert F. Kennedy, to have the FBI expand their investigation of the Agriculture Department to include the death of Marshall.

Robert Kennedy, who wasn't much of an LBJ fan, quickly complied. FBI director J. Edgar Hoover, who wasn't much of a Kennedy fan, agreed to cooperate because he, like so many others, was questioning the suicide theory. On one report he received supporting the suicide verdict, Hoover scribbled, "I just can't understand how one can fire five shots at himself." Special agent Thomas G. McWilliams, Jr. of Waco was assigned to handle the FBI investigation of the Marshall incident.

Another man who became interested in the coincidence between the Marshall death and the investigation into Estes' affairs was Homer Garrison, then head of the Department of Public Safety and leader of the famed Texas Rangers. Garrison was suspicious of the suicide ruling so he called in the troops. On May 10, 1962, eleven months after Marshall's body had been found, Texas Ranger Captain Clinton Peoples took charge of the investigation to find out once and for all what happened to Henry Marshall.

Captain Peoples and Ranger Johnny Krumnow went immediately to Franklin to begin the investigation. In the weeks that followed, as many as seven Rangers participated in the search for evidence. They interviewed everyone even remotely connected with the case and spent hours at the crime scene sifting sand and looking for physical evidence. Captain Peoples also instructed that family members and anyone else directly connected with the case be given polygraph tests, all of which proved negative.

Ranger Captain Clinton Peoples, right, showing the rifle that killed Henry Marshall to an unidentified man. Captain Peoples later purchased the rifle from the Marshall family and it is currently on display at the Texas Ranger museum in Waco, Texas.

With headlines blazing across Texas and in Washington, Judge John M. Barron of the 85th Judicial District in Texas ordered a grand jury to be convened at Franklin to review all the evidence and rule on a cause of death in the case. Of course, in a small Texas town it was often hard to round up a group of people who weren't either related or at least friendly. Because the judge wanted immediate action, the county officials were desperate for warm bodies — so desperate in fact that three Agriculture Department employees, co-workers with Henry Marshall, were seated on the panel. There was also a rumor, reported in the *Dallas Morning News*, that Sheriff Stegall, a champion of the suicide theory, had placed a cousin on the jury. Stegall denied the report and as it turned out, the person in question, Pryse Metcalf, was not a cousin in the Stegall family. He was, however, married to the sheriff's daughter.

Despite the fact that the jury was possibly "tainted" with a ringer, the panel immediately set to work. First, recognizing that they had been handed a political hot potato, the jury ordered a gag rule on all matters related to the case. Next, they instructed that the body of Henry Marshall be exhumed so an autopsy could be performed by Dr. Joseph A. Jachimczyk (Yuh-him-check) of the Harris County medical examiner's office. When Dr. Joe, as he was commonly called for obvious reasons, arrived at the funeral home in Bryan, he found the place buzzing with gossip and crowded with local law enforcement officers, Texas Rangers, and FBI agents. There was also an army of reporters on hand to chronicle the events for the folks back home. One of those reporters, a young Dan Rather, was frequently on the phone telephoning reports back to the Houston television station where he worked.

The formal autopsy began at 7:00 a.m. on the morning of May 22, 1962. Dr. Joe was assisted by one of his investigators, James L. Turner, and by Dr. Ray Chase of Hearne, Texas. Among those also present were Captain Peoples, Judge Barron, Sheriff Stegall, Dr. James I. Lindsey, Cal Killingsworth, and Charles H. Beardsley, a Texas Department of Public Safety ballistics expert. Manley Jones, the embalmer, was also present to identify the body. After eight grueling hours, the examination was complete and the doctor emerged to face the press. When pressed for a decision, Dr. Joe simply said, "Based on my preliminary examination, I believe that this was not a suicide." That was what everyone expected to hear, but it was not the final verdict which would come from the grand jury. Unfortunately, what the doctor said and what he wrote were slightly but sufficiently different to affect the final outcome.

In his twelve-page report, Dr. Joe concluded that Marshall's death was the result of five gunshot wounds in the chest and abdomen. Of the five, three wounds were classified as "rapidly incapacitating." One shot had severed the aorta and either of the other two would have produced almost immediate paralysis. The two less incapacitating wounds would have required more time to prove fatal. It was the doctor's opinion that Marshall could not have possibly lived for more than thirty minutes after being shot the first time.

The autopsy also revealed other factors that might have contributed to the death. Marshall had a significant bruise on the left side of his head and the blood from his left chest cavity contained a 15 percent saturation of carbon monoxide, which might have been as high as 30 percent at the time of death. A 40 percent saturation is generally fatal. There was also evidence of an old injury to his right arm (Marshall was naturally right-handed) which would have precluded Marshall from extending his right arm sufficiently to pull the trigger of the gun. Although there were five entrance wounds, there were only four exit wounds, which should have meant one bullet was still in the body. Despite extensive x ray and surgical examination, none was found.

Dr. Joe was perplexed by the amount of time that had elapsed since the death occurred and was leery of any complications that time lag might have caused to the case. Those possible complications perhaps inspired conservatism. He wrote, "Being familiar with bizarre gunshot wounds one cannot say . . . on a purely scientific basis that a verdict of suicide is absolutely impossible in this case; most improbable, but not impossible." His official finding was: possible suicide, probable homicide.

Although no one will ever know exactly why, Judge Barron received the official report, promptly ignored the gag order from the grand jury, and made the results public. The shocked members of the jury immediately called upon District Attorney Bryan Russ to subpoena the judge so he could be brought before the panel to explain his actions. Russ refused on the grounds that he could never again try a case in Robertson County if he issued a subpoena to a federal judge.

The grand jury also failed on another critical matter. The Agriculture Department had begun a formal investigation into Billie Sol Estes' allotment scheme a month after Henry Marshall died. The Franklin grand jury members believed the 175-page report of that investigation might shed some light on the Marshall case and issued a subpoena for the full report. Unfortunately, Barefoot Sanders, a former student body president at the University of Texas and close ally of Lyndon Johnson, was a U.S. attorney in Dallas at the time. On Friday May 25, three days after the autopsy, Sanders filed a motion to quash the subpoena on the grounds that the public interest would not be served by a document which wasn't pertinent to the case before the grand jury.

Naturally, there was quite an uproar from Texas. So much so that the following day, Saturday, May 26, Attorney General Robert F. Kennedy relented, a bit, and announced that a 22-page summary of the report, including all references to Henry Marshall, would be provided. The summary was forwarded to Sanders who then took it to the grand jury. It was also rumored that Sanders was instructed to keep the administration informed should the name Lyndon Johnson come up in the case.

Some Texas officials, and a lot of editorial writers in the state, weren't satisfied with the summary. Newspaper stories called out for the entire report to be made available to reduce the mystery and not add to it. Former Texas Lieutenant Governor John Lee Smith wrote a scathing letter to Robert Kennedy informing him that grand jury investigations in Texas are totally secret and thus nothing would be made public. He also informed the attorney general that failure to provide the complete report left the impression that an effort was being made to shield some "prominent personages in the Kennedy Administration." Despite the efforts exerted, the only person who saw the report was Judge Barron, who was allowed to read it under Sander's supervision to satisfy himself that nothing pertinent was being kept from the jury.

Although it wasn't generally known at the time, interest in the case at the Washington level was apparently intense. Years later Judge Barron recalled that John Kennedy personally called him once about the proceedings and that Robert Kennedy called about a dozen times. The judge also said Lyndon Johnson and Clifton Carter, a Johnson aide, had called several times and sent at least one telegram urging a complete investigation. The judge also categorized the Johnson request as "a good act."

Despite being thwarted on a couple of fronts, the Franklin grand jury was able to make progress. Even though grand jury inquests in Texas are supposed to be permanently sealed, in the intervening years since that particular panel met, sufficient details have surfaced to allow for at least a partial reconstruction of some of the testimony.

Apparently the primary points considered by the jury were: the five gunshot wounds; the carbon monoxide in the victim's lungs; the wounds on the head and hands; the neatness with which the victim's personal belongings had been placed in his truck; the victim's mental condition; the restricted use of the victim's right arm; and the fact that no other tracks of any kind had been found at the scene. Evidence such as the blood on the truck, the dent in the truck door, and the lack of blood on the ground was probably discounted by the jurors.

When the grand jury went into formal session, the first witness was Captain Peoples. It was, and is, Peoples' opinion that Marshall was murdered. The Ranger captain believed someone assaulted Marshall with intent to kill him. A struggle ensued and Marshall was hit over the head and dazed. The assailants then attempted to asphyxiate him but he continued to fight. When it became obvious that carbon monoxide poisoning was going to take too long, the assailant turned Marshall's own gun on him and fired five times. It was Peoples' opinion that someone had killed Marshall and then attempted to make it look like a suicide. After presenting his evidence, Judge Barron requested Peoples remain to hear all subsequent testimony.

Dr. Jachimczyk testified as to his autopsy findings and reiterated that the wounds were rapidly incapacitating. However, the doctor also admitted that the shots could have been fired in rapid succession and that perhaps up to thirty minutes might have been required for death to take place. That possibility prompted Sheriff Stegall to concluded that the head and hand wounds had occurred while Marshall was thrashing about on the ground after he had fired the shots. When asked, the sheriff said "yes," he did believe a man could shoot himself five times with a 22 rifle. "I saw a man hit four times once," the sheriff reported, "and walk off."

As to the old injury to Marshall's right arm, the jury members "played" around with the gun for several minutes and apparently satisfied themselves that the shots could have been fired with either hand. A ballistics expert testified that wounds received from a 22-caliber rifle would be quickly closing and the initial pain would resemble that of an accidental ice pick wound.

The matter of the carbon monoxide was a complication. However, several witnesses testified that they believed Marshall had first shot himself and then, upon discovering that he wasn't dead, attempted to asphyxiate himself by forming a sort of tent with his shirt and inhaling exhaust fumes from the truck. That hypotheses was supported by the FBI when they reported that the key in the ignition of Marshall's truck was found in the on position and that the gas tank was empty, indicating the engine had been turned on and run until the gas was exhausted. That testimony was countered, however, by Owens, the man who found the body. He said the key was in the off position and that there was sufficient gas in the truck for him to drive it home the following day.

Concerning a possible motive for suicide, there was considerable testimony that Marshall had been in a depressed state of mind for some time. Pryse Metcalf later reported that Marshall had been "undergoing an extreme amount of pressure" because of the Billie Sol Estes cotton allotment transfers. Others testified that Mrs. Marshall had often called her husband's boss during the final month of his life "crying and talking of Marshall's mental and physical condition." There was additional information that Marshall was taking increased amounts of prescription drugs and tranquilizers, although no such evidence was found in the toxicology report done during the autopsy. As to Marshall's mental state, the Texas Rangers, despite a concentrated effort, found no evidence that Marshall was of the frame of mind to take his own life. As one witness put it, "Marshall had a wife, a young son, land, cattle, and money in the bank. He had no reason to take his life."

Some jurors later expressed the belief that Marshall's motive for suicide was simply that he had gotten caught up in the Billie Sol Estes con and was pressured by higher-ups in the Agriculture Department into doing things he didn't agree with. The result was that Marshall, a good, dedicated public servant, had been sucked into the trap of having written instructions to do one thing and verbal instructions to do something else. As a result he became despondent and took his life.

That theory was totally discounted by Ted Shipper, a private investigator hired by Mrs. Marshall to investigate her husband's death. It was Shipper's testimony that Marshall had uncovered something "unusual" in the USDA and had even made a special trip to Washington to report his findings. Shipper also reported later that the grand jury continually cut him off when he tried to give testimony supporting his position, and that he ultimately started receiving phone calls threatening him and his family.

Deputy Elliot's testimony was damaging to the murder theory. He testified that there were no other tire marks or human tracks in the soft dirt at the scene, which was the most compelling reason to believe Marshall had taken his own life. We have no way to know if Elliot was questioned about how the two men who found the body could have made no tracks or about the possibility that if someone had wanted to make the crime appear to be a suicide, then any tracks might have been purposely obliterated.

The matter of the front of Henry Marshall's shirt was a severe complication. The investigation revealed that there were no bullet holes or nitrate traces on the front, which meant someone, Marshall or his killer, had pulled the shirt up before firing the fatal shots. And according to the FBI, the shirt was tucked neatly into the belt when the body was found. The question then became if Marshall used his shirt as a sort of tent to inhale an almost lethal dose of carbon monoxide after shooting himself five times, how could he have had the presence of mind to tuck in his shirt? It seems clear the jury members opted for the version that the shirt had been pulled up when the body was found.

One Franklin man who testified was Nolan Griffin, a gas station attendant. Griffin said that all the stories in the newspaper had reminded him that a stranger had come into his station about the time of the incident and asked for directions to the Marshall ranch, supposedly to see about a deer lease. The man got his directions and drove off in a 1958 or '59 Plymouth or Dodge station wagon. He returned the following day and said it was the wrong Marshall but that he had gotten a deer lease elsewhere.

Thadd Johnson, a Texas Ranger artist, completed a sketch of the possible suspect and it was distributed to newspapers across Texas. Although one potential suspect was identified as a result of the sketch, the Rangers gave the man a polygraph test and he passed. No other suspects were ever identified.

A total of fifty-five witnesses appeared before the grand jury but none caused more of a stir than Billie Sol Estes, who was out of jail on bond. Even though most of his assets had already been seized by the government, Estes arrived in a two-car caravan of white Cadillacs, one of his trademarks. He was accompanied by family members and his lawyers, state senator W. T. "Bill" Moore and John Cofer of Austin. Although Estes might have cleared up much of the mystery, it never happened. Sources close to the grand jury later reported that the wheeler-dealer refused to answer almost seventy-five questions on the grounds that his answers would tend to incriminate him.

After eleven days of testimony that spanned five weeks, the Henry Marshall case took another strange turn when Judge Barron abruptly and unexpectedly halted the grand jury proceedings without publicly stating any reason. Privately, the judge stated that it was his opinion the grand jury had exhausted its pertinent sources of information and was bogging down. It was also reported that the judge had urged the jury to quickly conclude its work because of the expense involved. The jury had responded by saying they were not in a position, based on the evidence presented, to make a decision one way or the other.

Texas Attorney General Will Wilson, who was running for governor in a field of candidates that included John Connally, sharply disagreed with the judge's decision to disband the panel. Wilson felt the jury was just about to get into the sensitive area of whether or not someone in Washington had ordered Henry Marshall to approve cotton allotments for Estes. That particular area of investigation, Wilson felt, might have lead to a resolution of the case. As to the expense of the jury, Wilson also differed with Barron. "They had one more day of testimony projected," Wilson said. "It would have taken not over two days to make their report. The expense would have been inconsequential in view of the amount already spent." It was reported that several more witnesses had been called to testify but their identities were never disclosed.

Judge Barron responded to accusations that his controversial move had stopped the investigation by saying the grand jury's dismissal did not mean the case was closed. "To the contrary," he said, "it is just entering a new and important phase. Now the Texas Rangers, FBI, and other investigators can really get busy and help us clear this thing up." The judge also said that, in effect, the grand jury was on call and could quickly go back into session if new evidence was uncovered.

Years later two of the jurors, Ralph McKinney and Gaylon Rinehart, said they suspected that someone "got to" the judge. Both men stated that in the beginning of the inquest, they believed that someone wanted the original justice of the peace ruling reversed. Apparently someone else wanted the suicide ruling to stand, and when it became apparent that the last few witnesses might provide a Washington connection and thus a solid murder motive, that unknown person persuaded the judge to halt the proceedings. Despite the beliefs of the two jurors, there was never any official investigation into the actions of the judge nor were there any charges of impropriety.

In another surprise move, Judge Barron privately stated he would not receive a written report from the jury. Of course, by law the judge cannot prevent a grand jury from issuing a written report if the members so choose. And in the case of Henry Marshall, the jury did so choose but time was short. There were reports that Metcalf strongly supported his father-in-law's suicide theory and lobbied other jurors to follow suit, although he denied consciously doing that and rather stated that he strongly believed, based on the evidence, that Henry Marshall had taken his own life.

Whether unduly influenced by Metcalf or not, apparently the members of that 1962 grand jury were dedicated to one simple proposition. Since the original verdict had been suicide, they were looking for absolute proof that it was not suicide. When the sheriff's testimony corroborated the autopsy physician's report that suicide could not be absolutely ruled out, the minds of the jury members were probably set. The jurors were able to discount the evidence that appeared to create reasonable doubt about suicide. By a vote of 10 to 2 the special grand jury concluded, on June 25, 1962, that there was not sufficient evidence to change the verdict to homicide.

While many people were amazed at the ruling, some were elated. Sheriff Stegall undoubtedly felt somewhat vindicated for his snap judgment. Lee Farmer, the justice of peace whom many accused of simply accepting the sheriff's word told a reporter, "When I come to the Pearly Gates, if St. Peter asks me about Henry Marshall, I'll still say it was suicide . . . Nobody told me to write it that way, and nobody bribed me, either."

Such a verdict might have been the end of most cases, but the matter of how Henry Marshall died was far from concluded. Within a month of the final verdict, Dr. Joe received two personal letters, each asking for a different decision. One letter, from Homer Garrison, presented a recap of the evidence gathered by Clinton Peoples and requested the judge reconsider his "possible suicide" ruling. The other letter, incredibly, was from

Pryse Metcalf, the juror, presenting his evidence and the opinion that the official autopsy report should show cause of death as "definite suicide."

On August 17, 1962, the doctor sent a four-page answer to Judge Barron and stated emphatically that, as a result of the information provided by Garrison, he found insufficient evidence to change his ruling but that "the scales are tilted more in favor of homicide than suicide, pending additional investigation."

Dr. Joe found fault with only one point in Garrison's letter, that being a statement that the death could not have been suicide. The doctor stood by his original "possible suicide" ruling. As to Metcalf's letter, the doctor was less than kind. Apparently Metcalf provided a list of the reasons why the grand jury had reached its verdict and the doctor discounted each and every reason, in turn. He disagreed that the head wound could have been sustained while thrashing around in the act of dying and stated that Marshall was struck over the head. He further stated it was physically impossible for Marshall to have used his right hand to fire the gun and that the shirt had not been used as a tent to capture carbon monoxide because absolutely no soot had been found in the fibers.

Jachimczyk concluded, "If, in fact, this is a suicide, it is the most unusual one I have seen during the examination of approximately 15,000 persons." He also stated that as a result of the additional information, "I agree wholeheartedly that the investigation in this case should be continued as a Murder Case." But Dr. Joe still stopped short of changing his ruling to definite homicide.

Judge Barron took no action on the doctor's letter or recommendation and allowed the suicide verdict to stand without comment. The Rangers, however, continued to investigate and Captain Peoples did discover more evidence. He found a strange pattern of broken twigs and branches near the crime scene which seemed to indicate a violent struggle had once occurred. He also located a dusty, black plastic bag that had blown under some brush. Because of the condition of the bag, Peoples was certain it had been in the area for at least a year. It occurred to the Ranger that the bag might have been forced over

Marshall's head and the exhaust pipe of the truck in an effort to make murder look like suicide. Unfortunately, due to the time involved, any traces of carbon monoxide in the bag had long since vanished.

While the Rangers were hard at work in Texas, a special senatorial subcommittee under direction of Senator John McClellen (D-AK) was convened in Washington D.C. to fully investigate the activities of Billie Sol Estes and the Agriculture Department. It appeared a mammoth effort was being launched to get Billie Sol, and in the process, the Marshall death again found its way into the limelight. During the proceedings, McClellen actually demonstrated with a rifle similar to Marshall's how hard it would have been for someone to use such a weapon to kill himself. "It doesn't take many deductions," he said, "to come to the irrevocable conclusion that no man committed suicide by placing this rifle in that awkward position and then firing it and cocking it four times."

During the subcommittee investigation, one special revelation came out that was perhaps significant. In sworn testimony, it was revealed that four months after Marshall had been killed and while the Agriculture Department was looking into the allotment scheme, Billie Sol Estes had tried to pressure the department to cease its investigation. Wilson T. Tucker, deputy director of the cotton department, swore that Estes had told him the allotment matter had already caused one death. Estes supposedly then asked Tucker if he had ever heard of Henry Marshall. Tucker, who did not know Marshall, dismissed the question as idle talk and did not perceive it as a threat.

The McClellen committee pressed on. It was already certain that Estes had penetrated the inner-workings of the Agriculture Department and "gotten to" at least some of the high-ranking officials. In the wake of the committee's investigation, three USDA officials, Dr. James T. Ralph, Emery Jacobs, and William Morris, all resigned after admitting they had accepted bribes from Estes. As McClellen and the senators continued their proceedings, yet another strange twist to the case of Henry Marshall was uncovered.

According to testimony before the committee, Henry Marshall first entered the Estes case in late 1960 when a county-level agriculture department official in Greenville, Texas alerted Marshall that an effort was being made to get allotments, once attached to land used to build the Dallas Iron Bridge Reservoir, transferred to Estes land in West Texas. Marshall requested a signed copy of the contract so action could be taken but, according to testimony, no such contract was provided and no action was taken.

Henry Marshall next entered the case at a Dallas meeting on January 16, 1961, where department officials gathered to determine how Estes-like schemes could be prevented, as mandated by the Manwaring Memorandum. After some discussion, it was decided the best way to thwart Estes' scheme was to require that farmers with allotments actually appear in the county to which they wanted the allotment transferred. That approach, it was reasoned, would prevent Estes from obtaining allotments of absentee farmers. It was probably a good plan but, in the case of Billie Sol Estes, it failed miserably.

It was Henry Marshall's responsibility to see to it that county officials were fully informed on the Manwaring Memorandum and on the proper procedure to be used to assure the ruling was followed. Testimony before the McClellen committee indicated that Marshall did so inform the local committee, and that fact alone presented a major problem. The official records of the USDA clearly showed that all the cotton allotments obtained by Estes were approved after the January meeting when everyone was supposed to be guarding against just such an occurrence. Not only did three thousand acres of allotments pass through the hands of local authorities who supposedly had been notified of the procedure, but they had also passed through Marshall's office. Between January 17, the day after the meeting, and up until the time of his death, Marshall approved 138 different transfers for Estes. The possible implication was that Henry Marshall had been another bribery victim of Billie Sol.

Texas State Attorney General Will Wilson, who was, by then, conducting his own investigation, discounted the bribery possibility. "We find no evidence of bribery involving Marshall,"

Wilson said. "I think Marshall was an honorable man and his career demonstrated a dedication for duty. Then all of a sudden, at the climax of his career, we find him as an active agent in putting through 3,000 acres of illegal allotments."

Wilson also jumped into the mystery of how Marshall died when he said, "The available evidence on Marshall's death shows a more clear motive for suicide than for murder." The innuendo was that Henry had somehow gotten involved with Billie Sol and then when he became alarmed that the USDA investigations might disclose that involvement, he chose to take his own life rather than risk public humiliation. Such a position was, of course, similar to that of the original grand jury. The complication was that Henry Marshall was being credited as the man that prompted the department investigation. The fact that no link between Estes and Marshall had ever been discovered seemed to deal a death blow to the suicide theory.

As for Billie Sol Estes, he had his allotments canceled and was slapped with more than half a million dollars in fines (that were never paid). But Estes, being the consummate con-man, appealed the decision on the grounds that Henry Marshall had not told him of the Manwaring Memorandum. Estes also pointed out that his land contracts had been approved by county officials as well as Henry Marshall himself. The appeal was ultimately denied and it was just as well, since by that time Billie Sol was already distracted by other more pressing legal matters.

When his cotton allotment deal turned sour, Billie Sol branched out into fertilizer. He knew farmers needed fertilizer and that banks were willing to loan money on fertilizer supplies. That simple observation led Estes into his largest scheme. He began borrowing money — lots of money — using what amounted to phantom fertilizer tanks as collateral. Apparently it was Estes' plan to use the money to generate sufficient income to repay the loans. And he might have gotten away with it if not for the efforts of Oscar Griffin, editor of the *Pecos Independent and Enterprise*. Griffin uncovered the fertilizer scheme and wrote about it in his newspaper. As a result of the stories, Oscar Griffin received a Pulitzer Prize and Billie Sol Estes received a twenty-two-year prison sentence which he began serving in 1965 after exhausting all appeals.

With Billie Sol Estes out of the way and reform implemented in the USDA, the Henry Marshall case just sort of slipped out of the limelight. The FBI investigation never amounted to much more than supporting the suicide theory without any significant new information. Senator John McClellan's committee reported, when it finalized its investigation in 1964, that they had never been able to substantiate any connection between Marshall's death and the Estes investigation. Incredibly, after thousands of hours of investigation and a tremendous amount of money spent, the official ruling was still that Henry Marshall had shot himself five times with a bolt action rifle.

By 1965, Billie Sol Estes was in prison, Lyndon Johnson was in the White House, and the United States was being drawn deeper into the Vietnam non-war. There was lots to worry about other than the death of an obscure Agriculture Department employee. While most people may have had trouble believing the suicide story, they managed to get on with their lives. There was one person, however, who refused to ever forget Henry Marshall. Ranger Captain Clinton Peoples was as sure as ever that Henry had been murdered, but it would be almost two decades before he would get the chance to go back to court on the matter.

The next developments in the Marshall case occurred in 1971 but again, at the time of occurrence, the events seemed totally unrelated to Henry Marshall. The first occurred when Malcolm "Mac" Wallace, a forty-nine-year-old former economist for the USDA, died in an automobile accident on a lonely stretch of road near Pittsburg, Texas. Outside a small circle of friends, the death of Wallace held no significance. But the name Malcolm Wallace did have significance for Captain Peoples.

Mac Wallace was a former student body president at the University of Texas in the mid-1940s. Following graduation, Wallace, who was supposedly well connected with many state officials and the Lyndon Johnson family, moved to Washington D.C. and became an economist with the U.S. Agriculture Department. He was still employed at the USDA when he decided to come home to Texas for a vacation in October of 1951. Almost immediately, he became embroiled in domestic troubles with his estranged wife who still resided in Austin. Wallace was convinced his wife was engaged in an extramarital affair and set out to find her lover. On October 22, 1951, Wallace calmly walked into the offices of the Butler Pitch and Putt Golf Course and shot the manager, John Douglas Kiner, five times with a 25-caliber pistol, killing him instantly.

Wallace was subsequently arrested and, thanks to the investigative work of Captain Peoples, among others, he was brought to trial. Incredibly, after convicting Wallace of murder, the jury recommended a five-year "suspended" sentence. That meant that if Wallace kept out of trouble for five years, the verdict would be set aside. The perplexed judge in the case was powerless to change the decision of the jury so Wallace walked out of court a convicted but free man. Members of the jury later telephoned Kiner's parents to apologize for the verdict and to say they had been forced into it because of threats against them and their families.

A few months after the trial, Wallace went to work for Temco, Inc., a government contractor in Garland, Texas. He remained in that position until four months before Marshall's death in 1961 when he transferred to the Anaheim, California offices of Ling-Temco-Vought. Because of the transfer and change in responsibilities, a background check by the navy was required before Wallace could receive a security clearance. During that check, Peoples was interviewed and he stated Wallace should not be given the clearance. Despite the word of a Ranger captain and the fact that he was, technically at least, a convicted murderer, Wallace received the needed security clearance. He was still employed at that job when Marshall was killed, but his actual presence in California was destined to be closely scrutinized.

When Peoples heard of Wallace's death, he was reminded of some unusual aspects of the case. Wallace was supposedly friendly with the Johnson family to the point of dating Josefa, Lyndon's sister. During his trial, Wallace was represented by John Cofer, the same attorney who had represented Lyndon Johnson in the famous "Ballot box 13" voter fraud case in 1948 and who represented none other than Billie Sol Estes in the case of phantom fertilizer tanks. In fact, it had been rumored that Cofer handled the Estes case personally so he could prevent Lyndon Johnson from being dragged into the mess.

So Mac Wallace was a convicted killer who had ties to Lyndon Johnson, Billie Sol Estes, and the USDA and who, despite a criminal record, had managed to get a security clearance from the navy. Naturally, Captain Peoples was intrigued by such coincidences but he had no idea at the time that Wallace might also be connected to Henry Marshall.

The other 1971 event worthy of note occurred shortly after midnight on July 13. John Ernst, a self-styled bounty hunter who operated a business called "Crooked John from El Paso," picked up a friend outside the gates of La Tuna federal prison. When the friend was safely inside the 1962 "souped up" Lincoln Continental, Ernst took off at top speed with a hoard of reporters and photographers in hot pursuit. With the skill of a stock car driver, Ernst maneuvered the Lincoln through the crooked streets of El Paso, and by the time he reached the campus of the University of Texas at El Paso, the pursuing reporters were nowhere in sight. Finally, Ernst's friend and passenger, Billie Sol Estes, could relax and breathe free air. After serving 6 of the 22 years, Estes had been paroled. That parole would begin a slow developing chain of events that would eventually lead to a possible solution to the Henry Marshall case.

There is an old saying in Texas that goes, you can take the boy out of the playground, but you can't take the play out of the boy. For Billie Sol Estes, the play was always another scam, another deal, and there was never a lot of regard for legalities. By 1978, Billie Sol had been indicted, tried, and convicted on new fraud charges. Using clever legal ploys, Estes tried to have the conviction thrown out and get a new trial because he knew his conviction would also constitute parole violation and he might just end up spending the rest of his life in prison.

Parole authorities, however, were well aware of the legal maneuvering and they were ready for Mr. Estes. On August 16, 1979, Clinton Peoples, who had retired from the Rangers to become a U.S. marshal, was in court waiting patiently. The moment U.S. District Judge Robert Hill denied Estes' motion for a new trial, Peoples stepped forward and, to the amazement of all, including the judge, promptly arrested Billie Sol Estes on parole violation charges. The legendary Texas swindler was on his way back to La Tuna. If it hadn't been for the coincidence of Clinton Peoples, perhaps the one man most determined to keep alive the Marshall case, being assigned to arrest Estes, the death of Henry Marshall might never have been revived.

On the trip back to the federal lockup in El Paso, the two men got to talking and Peoples remarked that the Henry Marshall case had always been of great interest to him. Estes said he was aware of that and had, on occasion, almost called Peoples to let him know he was looking in the wrong direction. Peoples asked in what direction he should have been looking, but Estes declined to comment because he was on his way back to prison where other inmates took a dim view of informants.

Peoples pressed on and asked Estes to at least say if Washington D.C. would be the right direction. Estes smiled and replied, "You would then definitely be looking in the right direction." When asked why he had not said more in 1962, Estes replied simply that at the time he was not prepared to die. One thing Estes did do was to promise Peoples that if he was paroled again he would finally put all the pieces of the Henry Marshall puzzle together. It was one promise Billie Sol Estes kept.

On Tuesday, March 20, 1984, Billie Sol Estes again walked into a courtroom in Franklin, Texas after having been paroled from the federal correctional facility at Abilene, Texas. Unlike his first appearance 22 years earlier, Billie Sol was appearing under a grant of total immunity in the Marshall case that would preclude his seeking shelter under the protection of Fifth Amendment rights against self-incrimination. This time, Clinton Peoples knew, Billie Sol Estes finally had to tell the story. And tell it he did. In four and a half hours of testimony, Estes told an incredible tale that implicated Lyndon Johnson, Malcolm Wallace, and Clifton Carter, a political advisor to Johnson, in the death of Henry Marshall.

According to Estes, he had long been a political ally of Johnson and had helped on numerous occasions to raise significant amounts of money for a Johnson slush fund. As a sort of repayment, when Estes developed his cotton allotment scheme, Johnson then used political clout to grease the skids and help assure the allotment transfers would be approved.

In January 1961, the very month Johnson was sworn in as vice president, and the month Henry Marshall was in Dallas discussing how to combat Estes-like scams, Billie Sol Estes learned through his contacts that the USDA was investigating the allotment scheme and that Henry Marshall might end up testifying. The situation was supposedly discussed by Estes, Johnson, and Carter in the backyard of LBJ's Washington home. Johnson was, according to Estes, alarmed that if Marshall started talking it might result in an investigation that would implicate the vice president. At first it was decided to have Marshall transferred to Washington, but when told Marshall had already refused such a relocation, LBJ, according to Estes, said simply, "Then we'll have to get rid of him."

Malcolm Wallace, Estes testified, was recruited to get rid of Marshall. Supposedly Wallace had gone to Franklin a week before the killing to case the surroundings. Estes then described for the jurors how Wallace returned to Franklin with an accomplice and they accosted Henry at his ranch. A struggle ensued and Wallace hit Henry over the head to subdue him. Next Wallace tried to asphyxiate Henry using a plastic bag but when he thought he heard someone coming, he decided to shoot Marshall with his own gun. As far as is known, Estes did not identify the accomplice.

Finally, after all the years, what most people had believed from the beginning was being confirmed. Based only on the unsubstantiated testimony of Billie Sol Estes, the second grand jury officially changed the cause of Henry Marshall's death from suicide to homicide. Since three of the four men implicated in the killing were dead and the fourth was given immunity, the district attorney promptly announced there would be no need for formal indictments since "you can't prosecute dead men." It might have been fitting and proper had Henry Marshall been allowed to rest in peace at that point. Unfortunately, the case was about to become a virtual three-ring circus.

While most of Texas knew Billie Sol was testifying before the second grand jury, what he said was supposed to be a deep, dark secret. It didn't work out that way. Someone actually tape recorded all, or at least a large portion, of Estes testimony. On Friday, March 22, 1984, three days after Estes' appearance in Franklin, the *Dallas Morning News*, the *Bryan-College Station Eagle*, and the *Dallas Times Herald* all reported, accurately, essentially what Estes had said. And to make matters worse, all the papers claimed that they had three different confirmations on their stories. Clearly, as far as the Marshall case was concerned, the finger was out of the dike and a flood of controversy was about to sweep the nation.

Judge Thomas Bartlett, who presided over the grand jury, was madder than a wet hen about the secret testimony appearing on the front pages around the nation. Although he wanted desperately to pursue the matter and prosecute the person who had leaked the information, he had no investigators who could be used to track down the culprits. Newspapers, however, did have plenty of investigators, and reporters all across the state of Texas dove headlong into the controversy searching for any scrap of evidence that might prove or disprove the dramatic Estes tale. Despite the effort, there was little evidence to be found.

One man elated with the verdict was Clinton Peoples. Concerning the suicide theory, the marshal said, "If he could have killed himself with that gun, I'll ride a jackass to the moon." Not everyone shared that sentiment, however. It was widely reported that three federal judges called Peoples "on the carpet" for his involvement in the Estes affair. Supposedly, the three judges were Barefoot Sanders, who was involved in the original case and who served as Johnson's legislative counsel from 1967 to 1969; Robert M. Hill, the judge in whose court Peoples arrested Estes; and Halber O. Woodward of Lubbock. None of the men would confirm the meeting at the time but Peoples, years later in a private interview, did confirm the meeting with at least Sanders.

Opposite page: the Texas Ranger artist's drawing of the mysterious stranger who appeared in Franklin, Texas and inquired about directions to the Marshall ranch.   Above left: Mac Wallace, whom Billie Sol Estes identified as the killer of Henry Marshall.   Above right: A photo of Billie Sol Estes that appeared in several 1962 newspapers. Many people, including Estes' own daughter, pointed out that Billie Sol bore a striking resemblance to the artist's drawing.

An unknown source that was quoted at the time claimed Sanders didn't think it looked good for the marshal to be involved. A spokesman for the U.S. Marshal Service said that while one of the chief jobs of a marshal is to protect federal judges, the marshals do not answer to the judges. Stanley E. Morris, director of the Marshal Service, said in a prepared statement that he saw "no violation of U.S. Marshal Service policies or regulations." The entire matter was perhaps a moot point, because Peoples, using a little foresight, had taken personal leave and paid his own expenses to attend the grand jury. Technically, he was acting as a private citizen. When supposedly told to forget the case, he replied he would do what he damn well pleased on his own time.

Another thorn in the side of Peoples was Tommy G. McWilliams, Jr., the FBI agent who investigated the case. He remained adamant that Marshall had taken his own life and even referred to the testimony of Peoples and Estes as "a bunch of malarkey." He said he believed that if the second grand jury had had the benefit of the original FBI report that they would never have changed the original verdict. He also volunteered to testify if he could have benefit of his original notes.

District Attorney John Pascal, who handled the second grand jury, responded by saying the federal government hadn't cooperated with him one bit. Pascal claimed he was never consulted or given any information by McWilliams, which, according to Peoples, constituted "obstruction of justice."

While all the public bickering was going on, persons close to Lyndon Johnson denounced the whole affair as simply the ramblings of a pathological liar. They claimed LBJ had only met Estes a couple of times and that the two had certainly not had a close relationship. One person who inadvertently denounced the story was former Johnson aide Bobby Baker, who was himself convicted of fraud and tax evasion. In his book, *Wheeling and Dealing: Confessions of a Capitol Hill Operator*, Baker claimed Estes was not an ally of Johnson but that LBJ was nervous about the investigation. Baker also reported that he reassured John Kennedy that Johnson was not connected to Estes because Estes was a close friend of Texas Senator Ralph Yarborough, who had a long-standing feud with LBJ. Another writer, respected Texas historian J. Evert Haley, author of *A Texan Looks at Lyndon*, said he believed the Estes story.

Despite a lot of investigative work, no one ever uncovered a direct link between LBJ and Wallace. There was, however, an indirect link joining Johnson, Estes, and Wallace. That connection was Clifton Crawford Carter, an old friend and close associate of Lyndon Johnson and, according to Estes, one of the four conspirators. Documents were discovered that proved Carter had corresponded on several occasions with Billie Sol, but there little substance in the memos. It was also learned that Carter was acquainted with Wallace, and had, on at least one occasion, accompanied the young man to some Washington functions. The natural suspicion was that Carter, ever the faithful friend, had acted as a political buffer for LBJ so he could take any heat that might arise out of the shady dealings. Absolutely no proof was ever found to substantiate that possible suspicion.

As for Wallace's alleged connection with the Johnson family, no proof was ever found to substantiate the claim. There were, however, some suspicious elements concerning Wallace. The questions about how a low-paid Agriculture Department employee could have afforded a high-priced lawyer for his murder trial was raised. The fact that the lawyer had been associated with both Johnson and Estes did not escape notice and neither did the suspended sentence and the rumors of jury tampering. The natural assumption was that Wallace might have killed Marshall to repay the favor of his suspended sentence.

The most intriguing part of the Wallace case was how a convicted murderer was able to get a job with defense con-tractors. Better yet, how was he able to get a security clearance? Clinton Peoples reported that when the original security clearance was granted, he asked the naval intelligence officer handling the case how such a person could get the clearance. "Politics," the man replied. When Peoples asked who would have that much power, the simple answer was, "the vice president," who at the time was Lyndon Johnson. Years later, after the story broke, that investigator could not recall the conversation with Peoples but he did say no one forced him to write a favorable report. He also added that he wasn't the one that made the decision to grant the clearance. The whole matter might have been solved with a peek at that original report but unfortunately, when the files were checked, that particular report was suspiciously missing. It has never been seen since.

One part of the Wallace mystery that was apparently never discussed publicly is the fact that the golf range manager whom he killed in 1951 was shot five times in the chest, at close range, by a small caliber weapon, which is exactly what happened to Henry Marshall. The similarities of the two deaths may be nothing more than macabre coincidence, but it is somewhat strange that one man would be linked to two five-shot killings.

An aspect of the possible Wallace involvement that was made public was the simple fact that he appeared to be a close match to the composite drawing done of the mysterious Mr. X who had shown up in Franklin looking for the Marshall ranch just prior to the killing. Of course, it was also pointed out that many men with dark wavy hair and black-rimmed glasses would resemble the person in the crude drawing. A lot of people, including Pam Estes, Billie Sol's daughter, noted that the drawing bore an uncanny resemblance to Estes himself.

A bit of intrigue was building around Mac Wallace, but family members steadfastly maintained he was innocent. In support of that position, the *Dallas Times Herald* obtained records which seemed to prove that Wallace was at his job in California two days before Marshall was killed. Other records showed that he was on the job the day the mysterious Mr. X appeared in Franklin. The clear implication was that Wallace was hard at work in California and not part of a murder conspiracy, even though it would have been possible for him to leave the West Coast on Thursday night and be in South Texas a day and a half later to commit the crime.

Perhaps the largest blow to the Wallace theory is that shortly after the killing, he lost his job because he didn't qualify for another security clearance. He ended up in virtual obscurity back in Texas. It seems totally logical that if Wallace had carried out a murder plan on behalf of the vice president of the United States, that he would have been well taken care of for the rest of his life. On the other hand, following the Estes testimony, Clinton Peoples announced that he was going to try to open an investigation into Wallace's death because he felt the fatal head injuries were not consistent with the automobile accident. The investigation never happened.

In an effort to leave no stone unturned, reporters contacted almost everybody still living that had any connection to the Marshall case. Two members of the original grand jury who voted for continuance of the suicide verdict were located and they stuck by their original decision that Henry Marshall took his own life. Another juror, Joe L. Scasta, one of the two who voted against suicide, was located and he, also, stuck by his original decision. "My opinion," he said, "is that it was murder, and I don't give a damn who knows it."

Concerning the infamous 175-page Agriculture Department report, the *Dallas Times Herald* obtained a copy under the Freedom of Information Act. According to a story in that paper, there was some information in the report about Henry Marshall's activities that were curious. One thing that was clear was that Marshall was possibly the most qualified person to decipher the complicated allotment scheme that eventually brought Estes down. Since all such mention of Marshall was supposedly contained in the summary provided to the original grand jury, the only logical assumption as to why the entire report was not made available is that there were hints that high level government officials might be connected to the case.

As for Billie Sol Estes, when the story broke, news hounds went in search of the wheeler dealer to get his reactions and a statement. They found him in, of all places, a Dallas bookstore autographing copies of a newly released book about his life that was written by his daughter Pam. Although Billie Sol expressed shock that the story had been released and said he feared for his life, the immediate suspicion was that he had planned the testimony and purposely had it leaked to perhaps increase book sales. If that was his plan, it didn't work because, although wholesalers reported large orders for the book, they also reported large returns when it didn't sell through at the store level. As to the matter of fearing for his life, several people pointed out that it seemed a waste of time as he was testifying against dead men.

The largest single problem with the Estes story was that he presented absolutely no proof or verification of anything. All he had was his sworn word and most people seemed to believe that if you had the word of Billie Sol and half a buck, all the two combined would get you would be a cup of coffee. Opponents of the provocative tale were quick to condemn the swindler as a total, self-serving liar. It was even pointed out that Estes had used the fact that he was a pathological liar as part of his defense in the 1962 fertilizer trials. Pam Estes, on the other hand, countered those arguments with a simple bit of country philosophy: "Sometimes even liars tell the truth."

There was also another small matter worthy of note. According to the leaked grand jury testimony, the only questions Estes refused to answer were ones about the mysterious deaths of three of his former associates, all of whom had supposedly died of carbon monoxide poisoning within a couple of years of Marshall's death. Estes, who was under immunity only for the Marshall case, refused to comment on the other deaths, supposedly, sources said, because he wouldn't testify to anything that would put him in the penitentiary. The supposition that resulted was that perhaps Estes, not Johnson, had ordered Marshall killed, and the entire story had been fabricated.

Of course, Billie Sol Estes could not let the matter just drop. In several interviews at the time, he implied that his daughter's book had not told the whole story. He intimated that one day he would turn over all his personal notes, diaries, and records and the whole story, along with documented proof, would finally come out in a new book. Were those the ramblings of a pathological liar setting the stage for more book sales, or does he really have the proof that no one else was able to uncover? Only time will tell.

Eventually the fire storm raised by Estes drifted out of the headlines and back into obscurity. In the summer of 1985, the family of Henry Marshall sued the Texas State Bureau of Vital Statistics to set the record straight. On August 13, 1985, State District Judge Peter Lowery of Austin, in consideration of clear and convincing evidence, officially ordered Henry Marshall's death certificate changed to read "Homicide by gunshot wounds."

Perhaps that ruling will signal the end of the saga. But for anyone who has spent any time looking into the Marshall case, there is that unmistakable gnawing deep in the pit of the stomach that suggests the final chapter in the mystery of the death of Henry Marshall has yet to be written.

If you have any information concerning the Marshall case that you would care to share, please send your information to the author at Wordware Publishing, Inc.

The Newton Boys' Lost Loot

by Wallace O. Chariton
Story idea by C. F. Eckhardt

In terms of people killed and publicity, Bonnie Parker and Clyde Barrow were probably the most notorious gangsters the state of Texas has ever produced. But in terms of number of banks robbed, amount of money stolen, diversity of criminal activity, and longevity in the gangster business, Bonnie and Clyde couldn't hold a candle to the famous Newton brothers of Uvalde, Texas.

No one knows positively when the criminal careers of Willie, Willis, Jess, and Joe Newton got started. Although the brothers may have been involved in "chicken larceny" earlier, the first arrest apparently occurred in 1910 when Willis was caught trying to steal something he couldn't eat, couldn't carry, and couldn't sell — a 600-pound bale of cotton. For his trouble, Willis was sentenced to two years in the Texas state penitentiary at Huntsville, Texas. It may have been the first but it certainly wasn't the last time one of the Newtons would hear the clang of a closing steel door.

By 1914, Willis, the acknowledged family leader, was back on the streets and back in the holdup business. One of his first big jobs was to hit the bank in Winters, Texas for about $20,000.

Despite a successful holdup there were problems. An accomplice, Al Inman, was killed by a posse that chased the pair. Willis himself was later captured in Ballinger, but he managed to escape from the local jail.

The complication of having to trust strangers bothered Willis and he decided his criminal activity ought to be a family affair. It apparently took little convincing to get Willie, Joe, and Jess to join right in, because shortly after the Winters job, the family swooped down on Hondo, Texas and hit two banks on the same day, escaping with a reported $150,000. They later hit a bank in New Braunfels for a reported $200,000.

For diversification, the Newtons later struck at the Dallas post office and made off with $38,000 and an undetermined amount of stamps. Not long afterwards, the brothers held up a mail truck in Denison and Katy trains near Bells and Texarkana. As the heat from the law began to build in Texas, the Newtons moved on to banks, trains, and post offices throughout the Midwest, including several train and bank jobs in Kansas and Oklahoma. It has been estimated that during their careers on the wrong side of the law, the Newton boys held up at least 60 banks and an untold number of trains, post offices, and assorted other targets.

So prolific were the Newtons, that by 1924 the effort from assorted law enforcement agencies to capture the gang members was really beginning to build. A total of almost $100,000 in rewards had been posted by Texas authorities, and various members of the family were under federal indictments in Sherman and Winters, Texas, as well as in Kansas and Missouri. Other authorities in Dallas, New Braunfels, and Oklahoma were attempting to get indictments.

As a defense against increased police awareness, the brothers decided they needed an alias. After apparently not much thought, they decided to begin using West rather than Newton. Each of the boys kept his real first name and simply changed his last name, apparently believing that law enforcement officers would never suspect that Willis, Willie, Joe, and Jess West might just actually be Willis, Willie, Joe, and Jess Newton. The boys' choice of an alias may have spoken volumes about the intellectual capabilities of the Newtons. They all had guts, no question about that, but brains? That may have been another story.

To the brothers' credit, they did recognize that, despite the fancy new names, the climate in Texas was getting most unhealthy for aspiring bank robbers. In early 1924, the Newtons packed up and headed for East St. Louis to continue their life of crime. It is doubtful the boys ever considered that they had embarked on a course that would take then straight into the record books of criminal activity.

Not long after their arrival in East St. Louis, the Newtons met and fell in with a couple of fellow Texans named Samuel Grant and Blackie Wilcox. Grant, a convicted killer, and Wilcox, a small-time bank robber, had recently relocated to St. Louis from the Texas state prison at Huntsville. The fact is, had either man waited for a legal release, he would have still been in prison. But the lure of a life of crime had overpowered the pair and they, in turn, overpowered a couple of guards and escaped.

Either Grant or Wilcox, we'll never know which, was acquainted with a notorious character in Chicago named Max Greenberg. Apparently Greenberg got word to his Texas friend that he had a contact inside a railroad in Chicago and was putting together a gang to pull a series of perfect robberies. It's a good bet that the Newtons didn't have to hear the story twice. In a matter of days, the six Texans headed for Chicago, then the world capital of gangster activity.

Greenberg and an accomplice named Walter McComb did have an inside man with the Chicago, Milwaukee, & St. Paul railroad who was willing to supply vital information about certain shipments. The newly formed gang quickly formulated a plan for pulling off their perfect train robberies. To test the plan, the gang hit trains in Harvey, Illinois and Indiana Harbor. Sure enough, the inside information proved totally accurate and the gang decided it was time for the big score.

On Thursday, June 12, 1924, eight armed men stopped a southbound Chicago, Milwaukee, & St. Paul express and mail train near Roundout, Illinois. Unlike the other two holdups, something went wrong. Some people claim Willis Newton disobeyed direct orders from Greenberg, the gang leader. Others say Greenberg simply panicked. Either way, Greenberg opened fire and Willis was hit six times in the jaw, arm, and side.

When the other men heard the shooting, they also opened fire and proceeded to shoot up the train. The guards in the express car panicked and refused to open the door until gang members hurled gas bombs inside. Once the express car was opened, gang members, armed with their inside information, selected the 63 mail sacks they knew contained the most loot. It is doubtful that any of the members of the gang suspected in his wildest dreams that the sacks would yield almost $100,000 in cash and $2,000,000 in negotiable securities. The robbery was destined to be the largest train heist in U.S. history. It was also the last great American train robbery.

The gang members loaded their loot and a very shot-up Willis Newton into four Model T Ford trucks and chugged off into the night in an attempt to make their getaway. Within an hour all the law enforcement authorities in Illinois had been placed on alert and Chief Postal Inspector A. E. Germer had arrived in Roundout to take charge of the investigation and orchestrate an extensive manhunt. He boldly predicted that in a matter of days the crime would be solved and all the gangsters would be in custody. He was correct with that prediction.

Two days after the robbery, Willis Newton, who was more dead than alive, was delivered to an underworld doctor in Chicago. The doc managed to patch Willis up but the gangster was so weak from loss of blood that he couldn't be moved. He was captured without incident later that second day.

By June 16, the postal authorities had gathered enough evidence to know who had pulled the heist and they were watching every road for any sign of the getaway trucks. They got a break when many of the looted mail sacks were discovered near Joliet, Illinois. Authorities managed to follow truck tracks to a hideout and there easily captured three gang members who turned out to be the other Newton boys. The postal authorities then expanded their search and in a matter of days all the gang members were in custody and most of the loot had been recovered.

The story of America's largest train robbery ended when all the participants were convicted and sent to the federal prison at Leavenworth, Kansas. Jess, Willie, and a fully recovered Willis Newton all received 12-year sentences while Joe, the baby of the family, got off with a year and a day.

The Chicago debacle and subsequent prison time might have ended the criminal careers of many hoodlums, but not the Newtons. The fact is, for the next 30 or 40 years, one or another of the brothers continued to try his hand at robbery. The stories of the Newton boys' exploits have become almost legendary in Texas.

In 1962, Willis went to jail for a year in Oklahoma on kidnaping charges. In 1968, 44 years after the great train robbery, Willie got tired of life in a rest home and decided to go out in style. He was later trapped inside the bank at Rowena and, rather than give up, chose to shoot it out with Sheriff Donald Atkins. It wasn't much of a shoot-out and what there was ended when the old man was wrestled to the ground and disarmed. When asked to comment, Sheriff Atkins replied simply, "It's the same old Willie Newton."

In 1973, longtime San Antonio columnist Sam Kendricks caught up with Joe Newton for an interview. When asked if the brothers had finally retired, Joe replied, "Sure, don't you reckon it's time?" As to why they retired, Willis may have said it best in a quote printed in a New York newspaper. "The trouble with this world today," Willis retorted, "is that there are just too many damn laws."

Because the Newton boys' criminal career spanned more than half a century, they touched the lives of many lawmen and there are lots of stories about their exploits. Undoubtedly many of the stories are true and probably just as many would be classified as folklore. The most famous Newton story may very well be nothing but a tall tale since everyone who could verify it has been dead for years. But given the wild nature of the brothers, it may also be absolute fact.

The story was provided by Charlie Eckhardt, a well-known, talented western writer and owner of the Lone Star Barbershop in downtown Seguin, Texas. According to Charlie, back in the

1950s, his family owned a ranch south of San Antonio and one of their hands was a cowboy named Tim Newton who claimed to be a cousin of the famous Newton boys. One night Charlie and some of the boys, including Tim Newton, were sitting around a campfire swapping "true" stories. When it came Tim's turn, he told a tale that fascinated and excited the group. In the more than 30 years since Charlie heard the story firsthand, some of the details have gotten fogged. But enough information remains clear so the story can continue to fascinate and excite anyone with an adventuresome mind.

As the story goes, in the early 1920s, when the Newton boys started their excursions outside of Texas, they ventured first to Kansas where a bank and a train became Newton victims. The boys pulled off the robberies without a hitch and headed back to Texas with a sack full of loot that included somewhere between $15,000 and $25,000 in gold coins.

On their way back to Texas, the boys wanted to go in style, so they brazenly purchased a new Packard touring car and drove it all the way to San Antonio. Once in the Alamo city, the brothers decided to lay low for awhile and let the heat cool off. They collectively decided that the best place to accomplish both laying low and partying would be in one of the San Antonio's "sporting houses" noted for cold running beer and hot running women.

The boys moved into one of the better houses, picked out some female companionship, and embarked on a world-class drinking spree. As Charlie Eckhardt pointed out, while some people get mean when they drink and other people get sad when they drink, the Newton boys got worried when they got drunk. On the second or perhaps third day of their drinking spree, the boys decided that someone might begin to get curious about a bunch of Uvalde boys having so much money, especially with a lot of it in gold. Since all the brothers were, by then, wanted under various federal indictments, one of them suggested the prudent thing to do would be to bury the loot and come back for it later. It must have sounded like a good idea because the boys sent the girls on their way, piled into the Packard, and headed west on one of the many dirt roads that lead out of San Antonio.

When they had driven for awhile, the drunk gangsters stopped beside a field covered with a lot of white flat rocks. The boys selected a nice big rock, turned it over, and began to dig. When they had hollowed out a large enough space, they dumped all the gold and assorted other cash into the hole, covered it over with dirt, and replaced the rock.

Satisfied that their money was safe, the boys were about to leave when one of them asked if they shouldn't mark the spot so it would be easier to find when they returned. That sounded like a good idea but there wasn't anything handy with which to properly mark the spot where the buried treasure was hidden. So the still drunken brothers decided to simply mark the spot by each man relieving himself on the rock. Satisfied that their secret was now protected under the wet rock, the boys returned to the Packard and headed back to San Antonio for more drinking and carousing.

Two or three days later when the money the boys had kept on hand began to run out, they began to sober up. At first there was some confusion about what had happened to the rest of the loot, but as the alcoholic fog began to clear, slowly the memories of the little drive into the country returned. No problem, the boys thought. They decided to get back into the Packard, drive west until they found the field with the white rocks, and turn over every one till they found the right one.

The plan might have worked except for two things. First, when the boys drove to the outskirts of San Antonio they discovered, to their great displeasure, that there were several roads heading west. The then sober Newtons didn't have a clue as to which road they had taken to bury their loot. The boys just picked a road and headed out of town to see what they could find, but they soon discovered something that Charlie Eckhardt may have described best. According to Charlie, in those days if you had tied a thirty-mile-long rope from the flagpole on top of the Alamo and swung it in an arch west of San Antonio, every field that rope would have crossed over would have been covered with large, white, flat rocks.

Despite spending the better part of a day searching, the Newtons were unable to find the wet rock and that was a double catastrophe. Not only were the boys almost broke, but their supply of ready cash was apparently lost for all time. It became apparent very quickly to the boys that they could either spend a lot of time turning over rocks or they could find a bank to rob. It wasn't one of those decisions that had to be pondered long and the Newton brothers were soon back to their wayward ways. Within two or three years they had pulled off the Chicago train heist and taken up residence in Leavenworth. According to cousin Tim, although the boys often talked of the missing loot, they never again even went searching for it.

Over the years, many people have heard the story of the Newton boys' lost loot. This particular tale, like so many other tales of buried treasure, may be nothing more than pure fantasy. On the other hand, this tale, like some other buried treasure tales, may have a basis in fact. There have been reports over the years that several people have searched for the treasure. Perhaps someone found it and kept the find a secret. Or perhaps the loot is today resting beneath the concrete foundation of some building or highway. Then there is also the possibility — admittedly a long shot — that even today the Newton boys' lost loot lies waiting under a large, white, now dry, flat rock somewhere west of San Antonio.

If you have information or stories about the Newton boys, please share them with the author at Wordware Publishing, Inc. If you have solid information about where the buried treasure may be located, the author will be happy to provide shovels, a strong back, and liquid refreshment in return for the opportunity to join in the search and share in the loot.

From Ford's Theater to the Granbury
Opera House
by Kevin R. Young

On April 9, 1865 — 125 years ago — the hardworn veterans of the Army of Northern Virginia watched in silence as their commanding officer rode down the long pike toward Appomattox Court House. In the parlor of the McLean home, Robert E. Lee met with Union Commander U. S. Grant. What followed was to be the climactic act which preserved the Union and sent thousands of African-Americans on the road to freedom. It was also the final act of a dream for the eleven states of the Southern Confederacy; a dream that was to remain only as the memory of "the lost cause." In four years, more Americans had died than in all other conflicts before and after combined.

Even after the surrender of Lee to Grant, the hatred and the bloodshed did not cease. Joe Johnston's Army of Tennessee held on in North Carolina until April 26th; the Trans-Mississippian Confederates in Louisiana and Texas until May. Rip Ford and his Texans fought and won the battle of Palmetto Ranch before disbanding, and Joe Shelby and his handful of holdouts refused to sink their battle flag into the Rio Grande until June. Even after

Appomattox, there were still those who would win a niche in history for their final acts.

One of those acts occurred the night of April 14 — Good Friday — in 1865. It came suddenly and unexpectedly in the bark of a single shot fired from a derringer and the flash of a knife. In a few fleeting moments the act was punctuated with a desperate leap; a spur catching and ripping a decorative treasury flag; the breaking of a leg; and finally with the triumphant cry, "Sic Semper Tyrannis." From the act, one man would emerge as the martyr of a nation and the other as the standard of an assassin. The assassin himself would probably have preferred the parallel of Brutus smiting Caesar but to the eyes of many, it was a Judas betraying a Savior — a concept reinforced by the fact that the act had occurred on Good Friday.

The cut and dry of the deed is simple. John Wilkes Booth, a member of a prominent Shakespearian acting family, killed American President Abraham Lincoln as he sat with his wife watching the play *Our American Cousin* at Ford's Theater in Washington, D.C. In the course of his escape he slashed one of Lincoln's guests in the theater box (Major Henry J. Rathbone who was with his date, Clara Harris), leaped the railing, caught his left spur in one of the decorative flags, landed off balance 12 feet below on the stage, broke his left leg, and then exited the theater to make his escape. Lincoln was carried across the street to a boarding house where he died nine hours later.

Booth's accomplices failed in their attempts to kill Secretary of State Seward (although assassin David Paine did inflict some injury on him and his family). A probable attack against Vice President Andrew Johnson at his hotel also failed due to the lack of nerve of the assassin. One by one the conspirators were arrested.

At around 2:00 p.m. on April 26, Federal cavalry troops surrounded a tobacco barn at the Garrett farm in Virginia. Acting on information that Booth and his accomplice, David Herold, were inside, the Federal officer in charge ordered them to surrender or he would torch the barn. Eventually, Herold did come out and surrender but Booth did not. While the barn was being torched, a shot rang out. The Federals broke into the flaming structure and pulled a wounded man out. With a broken leg already and now a bullet wound in the neck, the dirty, unkempt prisoner soon died. As far as the Federals were concerned, they had John Wilkes Booth.

The subsequent executions of several of Booth's co-conspirators, including the unfortunate boarding house operator, Mary Elizabeth Surratt, and David Herold, and the imprisonment of additional supposed conspirators apparently ended the witch hunts that sent a nation from the joys of military victory into the blackness of mourning. Only Mrs. Surratt's son John escaped the wrath of the federal government. He fled to Canada and then to Europe. Eventually he was captured by U.S. authorities in Egypt and tried in 1867. Unlike his unfortunate mother, he was given a civilian trial, which ended in a deadlock. The federal government dropped the charges.

Nagging questions and gaps in the documentation have produced volumes of concern on the "truth" of the Lincoln Assassination and the motives for the murder. To quote historian Thomas Turner, there has been "voluminous literature" concerning the Lincoln Assassination and its participants. Among the most scholarly works are David Dewitt's *The Judicial Murder of Mary Surratt*; Otto Eisenschinal's *Why Was Lincoln Murdered?*; Stanley Kimmel's *The Mad Booths of Maryland*; Lloyd Lewis' *Myths After Lincoln*; Theadore Roscoe's *The Web of Conspiracy*; George S. Bryan's *The Great American Myth*; and Turner's own *Beware the People Weeping*. A more recent offering is Michael Kauffman's two-part series for *Blue & Grey Magazine* published during the period of the 125th anniversary of the event.

These resources provide invaluable information for anyone wanting to delve into the subject of Lincoln's assassination. The focus of the authors seems to be concentrated on proving or disproving the various conspiracy theories which have surfaced in the last 125 years. Bryan's *The Great American Myth* was a major attempt to set the historical record straight by following the one-man, single-action theory and ending with the fact that Booth was killed at Garrett's. On the whole, these books point and counterpoint each other in the conspiracy department, but all generally accept the fact that Booth was killed in the barn. Only Roscoe in *The Web of Conspiracy* offers the suggestion that Booth may have gotten away.

So the historians really all seem to agree. The career of John Wilkes Booth ended rather abruptly at Garrett's farm in 1865. But some folks don't agree with the historians. They say the story continued to Glen Rose and Granbury, Texas and then on to Enid, Oklahoma.

South of Ft. Worth in the sleepy hills of Central Texas lies the town of Glen Rose. Settled in 1872 and named for the wild roses around Saratoga Springs, Glen Rose is today the quiet county seat of Somervell County. In the 1930s, tracks of dinosaurs were found nearby, causing an instant sensation and arguments between scientists and fundamentalists over evolution versus creation. These days, with the completion of the Comanche Peak nuclear power plant, the scientists argue with the environmentalists. But dinosaurs and nuclear power aren't the only controversies Glen Rose has experienced.

One Glen Rose controversy is actually shared with nearby Granbury. A former resident of Glen Rose, a storekeeper named John St. Helen, fled to Granbury in the 1870s. St. Helen had come to Glen Rose around 1870 and operated a store near the Barnard Mill. What local residents remembered most about him was that he walked with a limp and favored his left leg. One day St. Helen learned that a local girl, Annie Jordon, was going to marry a U.S. marshal named Cliff Scott and that lots of Scott's associates, most of whom carried badges, would be attending the wedding. The news apparently shook St. Helen up considerably because the next day he was packed up and gone.

John St. Helen surfaced in Granbury, a bustling community on the upper Brazos River, just down the road from Glen Rose. Granbury had been a part of the famous "lost cause," and sentiment still ran heavily in favor of the Confederacy when St. Helen arrived. The town itself was named in honor of "The General" — Hiram J. Granbury, commander of Granbury's Texas Brigade and a Confederate officer killed in the 1864 battle of Franklin, Tennessee. The town was also the seat for Hood County, which was named for John Bell Hood, a Confederate general and commander of the famous Texas Brigade. Both men are immortalized today with statues and markers in the town.

Into the pro-Confederacy environment came John St. Helen. He worked for F. J. Gordon in his Black Hawk Saloon — the large rock building on the courthouse square. They say St. Helen was a good bartender — except on April 14 when he drank himself unconscious with whiskey.

One person who apparently knew St. Helen both at Glen Rose and Granbury was a young lawyer named Finis J. Bates. Bates first ran into St. Helen when a client was indicted for selling tobacco and whiskey at Glen Rose without a proper license. Bates' client had formerly operated the store which St. Helen was then running. It became apparent that the federal marshal was confusing Bates' client with St. Helen so Bates approached St. Helen and asked him to travel to Tyler and appear before the federal court to help clear the matter up.

The cabin where John St. Helen lived in Glen Rose, Texas.

While living in Granbury, John St. Helen worked in two different saloons. One of the saloons (top) was located next to the Granbury Opera House and is still a saloon. The other (below) is presently a gift shop opposite the town square.

140

St. Helen politely refused the request. Yes, he told Bates, he was guilty and his client was innocent, but it was impossible for him to make a personal appearance at the federal court. Eventually, St. Helen retained Bates as his lawyer and then informed him that his true name was not John St. Helen. With the federal courts presiding over the South and officered by persons generally connected with the federal army and government, the risk for St. Helen would have been too great. In the end, St. Helen arranged to pay all of Bates' clients expenses and the matter was dropped.

The relationship between Bates and St. Helen continued. At one point Bates attended a Fourth of July celebration at Glen Rose, where he was "greatly surprised at the stage presence and consummate ease of manner and reassuring appearance of St. Helen, who was easily the center of attraction and the commanding personality present." Bates would later note that St. Helen seemed not too terribly occupied with his business matters, but he at all times appeared to have more money than was warranted by his stock in trade. One of his favorite occupations was reading, or rather reciting, Shakespeare's plays.

After St. Helen's relocation to Granbury, Bates kept in contact. Then one night Bates was called to St. Helen's bedside. He was, he thought, dying and he asked to speak to Bates privately. St. Helen, who was so weak that he could only speak in broken, whispered words, informed Bates that his true identity was John Wilkes Booth and that he had assassinated Abraham Lincoln. He asked that a picture of himself be removed from under his pillow for further identification and that his brother, Edwin Booth of New York City, be notified.

John Wilkes Booth, the famous actor and infamous assassin, alive (just barely) and living in Texas? Bates was understandably shaken by what he heard. As for St. Helen, he lasted the night and began to improve. After a few short weeks of bed rest, he was fully recovered. Bates thought nothing more of the story, assuming, perhaps, that the admission had been the ramblings of a man delirious with fever. Bates' opinion changed, however, when a fully recovered St. Helen stopped by his office one day and asked him to take a walk. There, on the rolling prairie, sitting on some rocks under a live oak, John St. Helen told Finis Bates a most incredible story. He renewed his presumed deathbed admission — he claimed to be John Wilkes Booth.

John St. Helen left Granbury soon after telling the story and never returned. Bates was intrigued by what he heard and gathered documentation from various sources which confirmed, or at least strongly suggested, that St. Helen really was the famous Booth. One piece of possible evidence was found by F. J. Gordon. Acting on a tip St. Helen had given Bates during his presumed deathbed confession, Gordon searched St. Helen's quarters after his hasty departure and found what has been described as a 41-caliber Southern derringer of steel octagon barrel manufacture. The hidden gun was found wrapped in a yellowed newspaper which dated to 1865 — an edition reporting the Lincoln Assassination.

After John St. Helen's admission that he was John Wilkes Booth, he hastily left Granbury, Texas. Following his departure, this gun was discovered in his room wrapped in a newspaper announcing the death of Abraham Lincoln.

Bates continued to gather any information he could find and finally, in 1900, he felt he had built a convincing enough case to support the proposition that St. Helen was, indeed, John Wilkes Booth. Bates wrote to the War Department to see if they would be interested in information concerning Booth's possible escape. The judge advocate's office replied simply that, "they weren't interested."

Undaunted, Bates continued to work on the mystery. In 1903, he learned that a house painter in Enid, Oklahoma named David George had committed suicide on January 14 by a self-administered dose of strychnine. Apparently George was an alcoholic and possible drug addict. The old man had been in convulsions when found and was dead before the doctors could save him. Ten days after George's death, a Mrs. E. C. Harper swore an affidavit stating that George had confessed to her, while a resident in El Reno, Oklahoma during the year 1900, that he was, in fact, John Wilkes Booth.

Bates immediately headed for Oklahoma where, after viewing the remains of David George, announced that he had known the man as John St. Helen. Then, after having the undertaker arrange the dead man's hair in the style Booth wore, Bates compared the body with photos of Booth and supposedly one of St. Helen. He was convinced; David George was John St. Helen who was actually John Wilkes Booth.

Both of the aliases supposedly used by John Wilkes Booth may actually offer some insight into the mystery. David George is, after all, the two first names of a pair of Booth's accomplices. As for John St. Helen, the John is obvious and the St. Helen is the Anglicization of St. Helena, the isolated island home of the exiled Napoleon Bonaparte. Booth may very well have seen himself in a Napoleonic light and considered his escape to Texas as a sort of forced exile.

Since no one was interested in the body of David George, Bates had it embalmed and shipped to his home in Memphis. He offered it to officials of the federal government, for a share of the original reward, but they were not interested. So instead, he published his own book on the subject in 1907 and sold 70,000 copies. That book, *The Escape and Suicide of John Wilkes*

Booth caused a minor sensation and was quickly pounced on by most Lincoln historians. The body of the Enid house painter was mummified and Bates entered into an agreement with William Evans, a carnival promoter, who took the remains on tour. Oddly enough, it traveled close to Granbury, showing at Waco's Cotton Palace in 1920. When Bates died in 1923, his widow sold the mummy and it continued on tour as the true corpse of John Wilkes Booth, causing as much controversy as Bates' book. At various times, the mummy was even stolen, survived a train wreck, and endured several owners. At one point, in Big Spring, Texas its owners were arrested and charged with transporting a corpse without a license. One ingenious promoter obtained an incorporation in the state of Texas and traveled under the name of the American Historical Research Society.

Hogwash? A sorry attempt by a shifty lawyer to defraud the public and the federal government? Just one more Texas tall tale? Maybe or maybe not.

Folks in Granbury believed and still believe the story. There was a John St. Helen who had lived at Glen Rose and later at Granbury. People knew him. He did take off rather suddenly never to return. And he had confessed at least once to being John Wilkes Booth. He even had a picture taken — a copy of it is in the museum at Glen Rose. When you compare the photo with a picture of Booth, they are rather similar, considering at least ten years had passed between the times when the pictures were taken. But what of St. Helen's confession to Bates? Does it hold up?

The problem with the St. Helen account as recorded by Finis Bates is, quite simply, Bates himself. To proceed on at this point, one must either elect to accept the published account as verbatim or that Bates embellished what St. Helen had told him.

The gist of the published version is as follows. John Wilkes Booth had planned to kidnap Abraham Lincoln and spirit him away to Richmond where he would be used as a war hostage for the Confederacy. Booth and David Herold arrived at Washington on April 14 (the day of the murder) via the East Potomac River Bridge and were held there from 11:00 a.m. to

The body of David George in a death pose. The photo was staged so that George would be holding a copy of a newspaper announcing the death of Abraham Lincoln. The body was later mummified and has since disappeared.

2:00 p.m. for lack of identification. While being detained, they learned of Lee's surrender at Appomattox.

When they were released from the bridge, the pair traveled to the Kirkwood Hotel where all of the various conspirators met. The group included Vice President Andrew Johnson. Booth called on Johnson at 3:00 p.m. Owing to the collapse of the Confederate cause, Johnson told Booth the best course to protect the South from misrule and confiscation of landed estates of individual citizens was to kill Lincoln and allow Johnson, who was a Southerner, to ascend to the presidency. Johnson had arranged to make sure that General Grant and his wife would not attend the theater with the Lincolns which would allow for lax security. He also gave Booth a special password to use when crossing the bridge to escape. With all the details worked out and Booth convinced that Lincoln's death was the only true course, the tragic events of that evening took place. Booth entered Lincoln's theater box at Ford's, shot the president in the back of the head, jumped to the stage, broke his right shin bone when landing, exited the theater, mounted up with David Herold holding his horse, and took off.

Using the password at the bridge, Booth and Herold continued on. After having his leg set at Doctor Samuel Mudd's, the pair were aided by several former Confederates including a man named Ruddy or Roby. At one point, Booth realized that he had dropped his diary and some private papers in a wagon. Roby offered to go back and get them. Booth and Herold moved on to Garrett's farm, where they stayed for a while. Allies appeared, finding Booth alone, and informed him that Federal cavalry troops were nearby. Booth took to the woods and continued on. It was his later opinion that Ruddy or Roby had returned that night with Herold and was caught in the barn. It was he who was shot and, because of Booth's personal papers, was identified as Booth.

Regardless of which direction you take, it is very easy to punch holes into the St. Helen-Bates account. To begin with, it is stated in the Bates book that Booth and Herold arrived in Washington on April 14. However, documentation supports the fact that Booth checked into the National Hotel on April 8. On the 10th, Wiechmann found him at the Surratt Home (Mary Surratt's boardinghouse in Washington which Booth and several of his accomplices used). On the 11th, according to co-conspirator Lewis Paine (who would fail on the assassination night to kill Secretary of State Seward), he and Booth were in the crowd listening to Lincoln's speech that night. The next morning, Booth appeared at Deery's Billiard Saloon and repeated the visit on the 13th. On the day of the assassination, Booth, John Surratt (who was the son of the boardinghouse widow and a Confederate agent), and Michael O'Laughlin were at the Booker and Stewart Barbershop between 9:00 and 10:00 a.m. Booth returned to his hotel around 10:30 a.m. At noon, he went to Ford's Theater where he found out that Lincoln would be in attendance that night. Booth was back at the National Hotel at around 2:00 p.m. From there he visited the Kirkwood Hotel where he left a rather disturbing note of inquiry to Andrew Johnson. After that, it was off to the evening's bloody work.

Bates' account also stated that Booth and Herold learned of Lee's surrender at Appomattox while they were being held at the bridge on April 14. Lewis Paine's testimony stated that he and Booth were at the formal celebration of the surrender and listened to Lincoln speak on April 11.

Further discrepancies can be found. The Bates account states that it was during the meeting with Andrew Johnson on April 14 that the idea of actually murdering Lincoln was first discussed and decided upon. Yet, according to Paine, Booth tried to get Paine to actually shoot Lincoln on the spot during the April 11 speech. Booth was said to have remarked, "That is the last speech he will ever make." Booth biographer Francis Wilson feels that Lincoln's reference to granting Negroes the right to vote pushed Booth over the edge. However, Lincoln historian Lloyd Lewis points out a story reported in the *Chicago Journal* of April 15, 1865, in which it is reported that while Booth had been performing at the McVickers theater in that city during May, 1863, he remarked to some acquaintances, "What a glorious opportunity there is for a man to immortalize himself by killing Lincoln."

As to the meeting with Andrew Johnson, Booth did make an appearance at the Kirkwood Hotel at 3:30 p.m. on April 14. He asked to see Johnson and was told he was out. So Booth left a note, "Don't wish to disturb you. Are you at home?" The meaning of the note is still most uncertain, although many historians feel that Booth was either trying to throw a false trail to the authorities or confirm that Johnson was at home so an assigned assassin could be assured his target was available. Or was there more?

The issue of the broken leg is also a factor. Remember that the Bates account said that Booth broke his right shin bone when jumping from the presidential box to the stage. The problems with this statement are interesting. First of all, Booth broke his left leg. Second, no eyewitness mentions the leg until after the supposed death of Booth. Michael Kauffman brings this most interesting point out in his *Blue & Grey* article. As he notes, while Booth's diary states that he broke the leg while jumping, Herold stated that Booth had broken it in a horse fall. Booth himself told several people, including the unfortunate Doctor Samuel Mudd, that his horse had folded on him, apparently between the Navy Bridge and Surrattsville. Sergeant Cobb, manning the north end of the bridge, made no observation of Booth being in pain. Everyone past Surrattsville did. Booth managed to mount a skittish mare behind Ford's with most of his weight thrown on the left leg; but he could not dismount on his own at Mudd's. And Mudd's farmhand reported that Booth's horse had a swollen left front shoulder and a fresh cut on its leg. Kauffman's point is extremely well made. Or could Booth have pulled himself up across the saddle despite the skittish mare?

And what about St. Helen's purported claim that Herold was holding the horse? Documentation shows that Booth had asked stage carpenter Ned Spangler to hold his horse. He had work to finish, so Spangler passed the animal on to Joseph "Peanut John" Burroughs, a boy who did odd jobs around the theater.

When Booth returned after fleeing the theater, he took the horse back from Peanut John, mounted on his own, and sped off into the night.

As far as the man in the barn being "Ruddy or Roby," Both Wilson and Kimmel, in their biographical studies of Booth, denounce the idea, citing that a Garrett neighbor named Franklin A. Robey died in December, 1896. But is this actually the same person? They believe so.

There are several possible conclusions that might be made at this point. One is that John St. Helen told a very big, very bad lie to Finis Bates one day in Granbury, Texas. Or perhaps Finis Bates did an absolutely horrible job trying to provide the facts to support St. Helen's claim. Or that Lewis Paine lied all the way to the gallows for Booth as did David Herold. And that the message to Andrew Johnson was a signal that all was well and ready to go.

One very strong point for Bates is his accounting of the password at the bridge. Johnson supposedly told Booth to give the signal "T.B." and counter with "T.B. Road." When stopped at the Navy Bridge, Booth was asked where he was going. He responded, "T.B." The guard asked again where, and Booth replied, "T.B. Road." The guard then called for assistance to help raise the gate and Booth urged his horse on at full speed. Herold apparently used the same system.

Sgt. Silas Cobb of the 3rd Massachusetts was the senior soldier on duty at the bridge that night. Cobb had no idea of what had happened (he wouldn't until after his watch was over). His account of Booth's approach is, naturally, different. The bridge was closed to traffic by orders. When Booth arrived, Cobb asked who he was. Booth gave his full, correct name. He stated that he was returning to Charles County near Beantown but had waited until the moon was up so he would have better light to travel by. Cobb didn't sense anything wrong with Booth so, using his own judgment, let him pass. David Herold, using the alias Smith, was also allowed to pass. In Cobb's mind, the orders were designed to keep people from coming into the city, not from leaving. And after all, peace was at hand.

But F. A. Demond, who Bates claimed to have interviewed in 1916, was supposed to have been one of the sentries on the bridge. Demond stated that he and a soldier named Drake were at one end of the bridge while Cobb was at the other. A

Lieutenant Dana rode up and told them not to let anyone through without a password. Demond claimed it was the first time they had ever issued a password at the bridge. The password was "T.B." with the countersign, "T.B. Road." While this counters what Cobb stated, it certainly confirms what St. Helen is supposed to have told Bates.

There is, perhaps, one possible way to confirm or disprove St. Helen's claim.

After the incident at Garrett's farm and after the body of Booth was brought back to Washington, didn't the federal government take great steps to make a positive identification? The answer is no, and yet most historians are eager to accept the official 1865 government version of the capture of Booth, his death, and the identification of his body.

Lieutenant Luther Baker and Lieutenant Colonel Everton Conger of the Secret Service stated they were sure the body was, indeed, that of John Wilkes Booth. Others weren't so sure. Sgt. Wilson Kenzie and trooper George Zisjen later stated that they informed Baker that the man pulled from the barn was not Booth.

They pointed out that the body was freckled and had red hair. Booth had no freckles and was black haired. They knew this for certain because they had seen Booth when he performed in New Orleans and he had visited their barracks there on several occasions. Booth had in fact, played the St. Charles Theater in New Orleans from March 14 to April 3, 1864.

Otto Einenschiml, in his book *Why Was Lincoln Murdered?*, brings up an interesting point. Apparently, the photograph being used by the Federals searching for Booth was not a picture of John Wilkes, but rather his brother Edwin. "Exhibit 1. — Photograph of John Wilkes Booth" that was used not only at the conspirators' trial but which was also presented to Doctor Mudd when he was first questioned, was a card-d-viste of Edwin Booth. Einenschiml makes the supposition that if the detectives talking to Dr. Mudd had the wrong photo (and believed that it was a true likeness of John Wilkes), then perhaps all the pursuers were armed with the wrong image of their suspect. In Mudd's case, the incredible mistake was tragic —

when shown the image and asked if it was the man he had treated, Mudd said he did not recognize him. Oddly enough, over twenty people identified the image as John Wilkes Booth during the trial. And despite the fact that John Wilkes Booth had shaved his mustache at Mudd's, Edwin still did not bear that much of a resemblance to his famous brother.

The body of the man Baker believed to be Booth was brought back to Washington. According to Baker, Booth had been alive, but mortally wounded, when taken from the burning barn. He never truly identified himself as Booth, despite Baker's attempts to lead him on. David Herold, who had surrendered before the barn had been fired, also never identified Booth until after the party was on their way to Washington. The wounded man died before dawn on the porch of the Garrett home.

Baker's cousin Colonel Lafayette Baker (who was heading up the investigation) was careful to bring the body back in secret. Secretary of War Stanton wanted it that way. The body was placed aboard the gunboat *Montauk* but was "changing rapidly." At least six persons were brought aboard the gunboat by Baker to identify the body. All did — as Booth. Historians take a lot of stock in their testimony, particularly that of Charles Dawson (the clerk from the National Hotel) who noted the initials JWB pricked in ink on the corpse's right hand (there is some confusion as to the location of the tattoo either being on the hand or arm). Another was a Dr. Merrill, who had supposedly done dental work on Booth in recent years. He noted two fillings in the corpse's mouth.

Then came Dr. J. F. May. He had removed a lump from Booth's neck — a wound which later reopened and left a noticeable scar. In 1887, the good doctor remembered that when he first saw the body, it bore no resemblance to Booth. But then he asked if there was a scar on the neck. May described it to the federal surgeon present, who confirmed its presence on the body. May took a look himself. He saw the scar.

The on-the-spot record of May's visit mentions his remark that the body presented to him had freckles. It matches what the two troopers noticed at Garrett's. The original document has had sections crossed out and rewritten. A modern court-of-law would have thrown such evidence out of court today. But in May, 1865 the federal government and Secretary of War Stanton were in a hurry to conclude the business. May also never, in either account, located the scar with any real professional accuracy. He simply said it was there. And he makes no mention of a 44-caliber bullet that had entered the neck. As quickly as May identified the body as that of Booth, the army doctors removed two "spinal spools." If there was a bullet wound, it was now gone forever.

One thing that could have helped was that Alexander Gardner and Timothy O'Sullivan, noted photographers, were also on hand. They took several images of the corpse for future reference. The photos never saw the light of day. One can note that Stanton wanted no one to make a hero out of Booth. For a while the sale of his images was illegal. Also, Stanton had photographs taken of Lincoln lying in state in New York confiscated and destroyed. A copy survived. But the photos of the body on the *Montauk* were not so lucky.

One other item concerning Doctor May. After pointing out so positively the scar on the neck, he noted that the right leg of the body was broken. Booth had broken the lower bone of his left leg.

Others are believed or referenced to having viewed or identified the body. The record of their visits are missing but none of those who came to the federal government's inquest were actors, conspirators, or members of Booth's own family. So the people who really knew him the best were never called forward. Perhaps they were scared that if the body was Booth's, they would lie and say it wasn't. Or maybe they would tell the truth. Lafayette Baker, Conger, and the rest all had very good reasons for wanting the body to be Booth's. There was, after all, a little matter of the reward.

In secret again, the body was transported down the east branch of the Potomac. Everyone thought it was dumped in a marsh where dead animals were often disposed of. It wasn't. Instead, it was placed in an army crate and buried in the floor of the arsenal. There it remained until 1869 when the federal government allowed the Booth family to have it.

So one unembalmed body, which had been laying in the sun and "changing rapidly" before it was buried, was dug up four years later. An inquest of sorts was held at a Washington funeral home. Needless to say, the remains were in rather poor shape. The head had completely detached itself from the body. Joseph Booth, the brother who had vowed never to speak his brother's name again and wanted the family shame laid to rest forever, told the undertaker that if it had one plugged tooth, the body was John's. A dental chart of some sort was produced, and there was the single plugged tooth.

Edwin Booth, the sorrowful yet loving brother, never looked at the body. Neither did adoring sister Asia. And so it went to the Greenmount cemetery in Baltimore were it lies today. There is a family stone with John's name on it, but the individual grave is not marked, by Edwin's request. Historians accept the second inquest story as eagerly as they do the first. It really doesn't seem to matter that they contradict each other. The 1865 inquest says two plugged teeth. The 1869 version says only one.

Basil Moxley, who had served many years as the stage doorkeeper at Ford's Theater, stated that he, John Ford, Sam Glenn, and Charles Bishop were pallbearers at the June 26, 1869 interment in Baltimore. He noted that the body received by the family and carried to grave by himself and the others was that of a redheaded man. He claimed that no two things in this world ever resembled each other less than that body and John Wilkes Booth. Apparently, Moxley and his fellows knew it was a mock funeral and played along.

And so we come back to Granbury, Texas and John St. Helen. Ashley Crockett, whose grandfather died at the Alamo (and is an unsolved mystery of his own), knew John St. Helen — "a man of culture, breeding and accomplishment" — as a man who had a slight limp, about 5' 7" tall with curly black hair and a black mustache. Crockett was the editor of the *Granbury Vidette* and certainly in a position to know the man. F. M. Pevler knew St. Helen and remembered he was "a man who attracted attention by reason of his unique appearance." James Doyle also remembered him as "a very unique character" with "an arched eyebrow and a slight limp in his walk."

Central Texas has been a hot bed of people claiming to be famous. On December 27, 1950, a man named Ollie L. "Brushy Bill" Roberts died in front of the post office in Hico, Texas. At the time of his death, he was attempting to prove that he was actually the legendary outlaw Billy the Kid. Today, more than forty years later, many people still believe Brushy Bill was, in fact, the Kid.

On August 15, 1951, a man who claimed to be the famous outlaw Jesse James died in Granbury. He is buried in the local cemetery with a proper grave marker which includes the notation "Supposedly killed in 1882."

According to a deposition taken by Finis Bates, Mr. M. W. Connolly, editor of a Ft. Worth paper, knew St. Helen in 1883, or at least knew him by sight. Once while standing in the bar at the Pickwick Hotel in Ft. Worth with former Confederate General Albert Pike, Mayor Tom Powell, and the famous Temple Houston, Connolly noticed St. Helen walking through the door. When Pike saw him, he became alarmed. The old Confederate threw his arms up and exclaimed, "My God! John Wilkes Booth!" St. Helen made a fast getaway.

For folks in Granbury, the story of St. Helen lingered on. Some attention came in 1931 when the current owner of the mummy, Mrs. Agnes Black, had a team of specialists in Chicago x ray the remains. The specialists included, according to an Associated Press article, Dr. Edward Milisoavich, a Milwaukee pathologist; Dr. Orlando F. Scott, former expert of the Cook County coroner's staff; and Dr. Herman Budesen, the Chicago Health Commissioner. They concluded that the mummified remains of David George were that of Booth. Their evidence came from the discovery of anatomical deformities on the mummy which matched those reported on Booth, evidence of a fracture on the left leg, a scar on the neck, a deformed thumb and an elevated eyebrow. To add icing to the cake, a signet ring was removed from the mummy's stomach which was inscribed with the initial "B" in a scroll. A minor controversy arose when it was reported that the mummy's right leg was fractured. Lincoln historians quickly pointed out Booth broke his left leg. Dr. Scott quickly reported that the reports concerning the right leg were wrong and the x ray, in fact, showed a deformity of the fibula of the left leg. Scott himself was convinced that the mummy was Booth, but added "it is up to history to prove it." So, according to Bates' claim, the remains were also those of St. Helen.

Reporters for *Harper's* came to Granbury in 1929 and gathered information. The result of their investigation, reported by William G. Shepherd in the November, 1924 issue, was not so much that the Granbury/St. Helen story was wrong, but rather that the Enid/George story was a fake. Shepherd compared samples of George's handwriting with Booth's and they did not, in his mind, match. F. L. Black, writing for the *Dearborn Independent* in 1925, also compiled information concerning both St. Helen and George and came to the conclusion that Bates' claims were false. In modern times, ABC Television's "20/20" rolled into Glen Rose and Granbury to do features on St. Helen which Barbara Walters called "interesting."

Then came the Texas Sesquicentennial. Like most communities in the Lone Star State, Granbury was looking for something unique to help celebrate the 150th anniversary of Texas independence. Since Granbury wasn't around in 1836 when the Texas Revolution occurred, some creative thinking was required.

Jo Ann Miller, who ran (and still runs) the impressively restored Granbury Opera House on the town square, is multi-talented when it comes to creativity. A native Texan and longtime resident of Granbury, she had often heard the story of John St. Helen. As a matter of fact, one of the bars he operated is located next door to the Opera House. Wheels began to turn. Jo Ann, with the help of lawyer John Sims, started developing an idea for a play about St. Helen. They spent lots of time researching not only St. Helen but the Lincoln Assassination. Like everyone else who has dug into the story, they quickly realized that things were not quite as simple as some history books make them out to be. In the end, the pair co-authored a play called *John Wilkes Booth — The Myth and the Mummy*. The well-done play had a very successful run at the Granbury Opera House.

The play is, at the very least, thought provoking, as a historian "with all the facts" debates the mummy of David George. The script takes the view that Booth, St. Helen, and George were all one and the same. By the time it is over, the audience realizes that the historian didn't have all the facts after all, and the mummy is either the real thing or a very carefully designed fraud.

Jo Ann Miller didn't put a lot of credence into the St. Helen story at first. But after researching material for the play and four years of studying, she is convinced that St. Helen was Booth and David George was St. Helen.

And so the mystery continues, even after 125 years. There are oddities indeed, enough to make some things certain: official cover-ups existed in the investigation of the Lincoln Assassination; the proof positive confirming that the man shot at Garrett's farm was John Wilkes Booth is somewhat lacking in completeness; despite lawyer Finis Bates attempts to cash in on some poorly documented stories about David George and John St. Helen, we are left with the fact that there was a man who lived in Texas who claimed to be John Wilkes Booth and that his mummified body, supposedly identified in 1931 as Booth, is still around — somewhere. One thing is absolutely certain — there was a barkeeper in Granbury, Texas named John St. Helen who claimed to be the famous Booth as well. Compare the pictures and see what you think.

In 1887, a Madam Lorita Velazquez published her memoirs and recalled her visit with Lafayette Baker, the man who had spearheaded the hunt for Booth and held the inquest on the identification of the body. Baker remarked, "I intended to have his body dead or alive or a mighty good substitute for it." It should be noted that Velazquez also claimed to be a Confederate spy. Stewart Sifakis, author of *Who Was Who in the Civil War* suggests that while there may be some truth to her wartime claims, her memories should be considered "a case of exaggeration with a hidden element of truth." If the alleged Baker statement was one of those hidden moments of truth, then further doubt could be placed on his "official" account.

Lloyd Lewis, in his 1929 book, *Myths After Lincoln*, denounces the St. Helen/George story as he did the identification of the mummy in 1931. But he leaves one in doubt about whether or not the body brought out of the Garrett barn was actually Booth. Michael Kauffman states that the body of Booth "was meticulously identified." Since his article had just come out at the time of this writing, the deluge of arguments against this blanket statement had yet to hit the editors. "Meticulously identified"? Otto Eisenschmil sums it up perhaps the best, "If the cripple in the barn had been taken alive, his pursuers would have escaped all criticism, and one of the riddles of history would have been answered: Who was shot at Garrett's farm on the night of April 26, 1865?"

In an effort to provide a visual comparison between Booth and St. Helen, Jo Ann Miller of Granbury conducted an interesting experiment. She obtained pictures of St. Helen and Booth and had them reduced to the same size. Next, she had an artist create exact tracings of the photographs which were then turned into transparencies. The drawing at top is John Wilkes Booth and below is John St. Helen. Once the drawings were completed, the transparencies were overlaid and it appears the facial structure of the two men is exactly the same. The photograph on the opposite page is the composite of the two transparencies.

The mystery continues and the question remains unanswered. Did John Wilkes Booth escape and find his way to Texas? From this vantage point, the answer is undoubtedly yes. John Wilkes Booth fired his way into the history books with a blast of his pistol, jumped with a cry about the fate of tyrants into the infernal regions of infamy, and spiritually survived the entire affair. His actions, like those of the character Brutus he had so often played on stage, have been repeated one too many times in our history. It is perhaps, his lasting legacy.

If you have any information about the mystery of John St. Helen that you would care to share, please write to the author at Wordware Publishing. Also, the author and many other people are interested in learning anything that may be known of the present whereabouts of the John St. Helen/David George mummy that has been missing for many years.

The Election That Will Not Die

by Wallace O. Chariton

It was the most famous election in the history of Texas. A tall, lanky, energetic congressman from Gillespie County named Lyndon Baines Johnson was pitted against the quiet, unassuming Texas governor named "Calculating" Coke Stevenson for a seat in the United States Senate. "Landslide" Lyndon won by 87 votes and for most people there isn't much of a mystery about how he did it — LBJ flat stole that election and went on to become president of the United States.

More printers ink was expended on the 1948 senatorial election than on all other Texas elections combined, but through it all one thing was always missing — no one had absolute proof of what really happened. For more than forty years it has been assumed that the proof went up in the smoke of a trash fire in Jim Wells County. That may be exactly what happened, but there is also a chance that the proof which eluded so many is still out there resting comfortably in the private Texanna collection of a Houston physician.

The story of the 1948 election actually began seven years earlier on April 9, 1941, when Texas Senator Morris Sheppard suddenly died in office. Sheppard's unexpected death presented then governor W. Lee "Pappy" O'Daniel with a difficult decision. As governor, O'Daniel either had to appoint a successor or call a special election to fill the vacancy. O'Daniel coveted the senatorship for himself but did not want to step down as governor to run for the office.

After giving the matter some thought, the governor decided on a bold course and he appointed the elderly Andrew Jackson Houston, last remaining son of Sam Houston, to the senate post. It was widely speculated that O'Daniel secretly hoped the senile old Houston could somehow manage to hang on and finish out the term. Because of his age and poor health, Houston surely would not have run in a regular election and the door would be open for O'Daniel.

If that was the plan, Andrew J. Houston did not cooperate. His health continued to falter and he passed away on June 26, 1941. After two men had died in office, the governor opted for a special election and announced he would be a candidate. He wasn't alone.

A total of twenty-five candidates signed up for the election, including Attorney General Gerald Mann, Congressman Martin Dies, and another young representative from the 10th district named Lyndon Johnson. When the smoke cleared, O'Daniel and Johnson emerged as victors and a runoff election was held to determine the winner. By a margin of 1,311 votes (out of a total of 575,131) "Pappy" O'Daniel was given the green light to vacate the governor's mansion and head for Washington as a senator.

It was a bitter defeat for Lyndon B. Johnson. He actually claimed the election had been stolen by a group of O'Daniel supporters that included Lieutenant Governor Coke Stevenson, who naturally became governor with the exit of O'Daniel. It was rumored that Stevenson had used his considerable influence to sway the vote totals coming out of East Texas, something that was not at all uncommon in early political contests. The irony of the entire election was that had Lyndon Johnson garnered more than ten percent of the vote in his home county he would have won the election.

The cards were probably stacked against LBJ for a number of reasons, not the least of which was that O'Daniel was not well liked as governor. Some political historians have speculated that many influential Texans wanted O'Daniel out of the governor's mansion. Thus they worked hard to send him to Washington where, it was believed, he would be out of the way and could not do much harm. If that was the motive, it continued in 1944 when O'Daniel was elected to a full term.

After more than seven years in the senate, a lot of Texans decided they had had enough of "Pappy" O'Daniel, and the search for a suitable replacement was launched. On January 1, 1948, from the sidelines of the Cotton Bowl game between SMU and Penn State, Coke Stevenson quietly announced he would be a candidate. A few days later a Houston attorney named George Peddy announced he would also run for the office. Many political observers predicted Lyndon Johnson would quickly follow suit, but it did not work out that way.

LBJ was perplexed by his political fortunes. He felt certain the 1941 election had been stolen, primarily by Stevenson working on behalf of O'Daniel, and that loss had damaged his reputation. Texans, he knew, had always supported winners. He knew also that if he mounted another campaign and lost, it would be the end of his chance to go to the senate. The prospect of losing certainly had to be considered, because Stevenson had been a popular governor and had considerable support.

Johnson, however, also had his political allies and they urged him to run. For several months Johnson declined the invitation, probably opting to wait for a more winable election. LBJ's supporters tried everything from sweet-talking to taunting, but nothing worked until they threatened to run a longtime Johnson friend named John Connally instead. That threat pushed LBJ over the brink, and he called a news conference in mid-May to announce he would again seek the Democratic nomination for the senate which, in Texas during the 1940s, was tantamount to being elected, since no Republican ever even came close to winning. Johnson set the tone for the campaign by announcing he would have won in 1941 if the election had not been stolen from him.

Although a total of eleven candidates were on the ballot for the Democratic primary of July 28, 1948, it was actually a two-man race between Stevenson and Johnson. When the ballots were counted, Stevenson lead Johnson by more than 71,000 votes but he was unable to get a majority. A runoff election was scheduled between the two men for August 9 and the stage was set for history to be made.

The Stevenson margin of victory in the primary led many people to assume he would be elected to the senate. The candidate himself was apparently of the same opinion. He traveled to Washington to begin laying the groundwork for his term in office and even had his picture taken next to the chair he would occupy once the small matter of the runoff was completed. That stunt turned out to be a classic case of putting the cart before the horse.

Lyndon Johnson knew his political future would come down to one election against one opponent and he was determined to do anything possible to increase his chances of victory. He became the first candidate ever to use a newfangled invention called the helicopter for campaigning. While "Calculating" Coke traveled the state in his old, beat up Plymouth, LBJ whisked about in his 'copter, nicknamed the Johnson City Windmill. He would hover over a town and use a public address system to announce, "It's Lyndon Johnson, your next United States senator." He would land, shake as many hands as possible, and then take off for the next destination. He covered a lot of ground, sometimes as many as twenty cities in a day; shook a lot of hands; kissed a lot of babies; and campaigned for all he was worth.

Using the helicopter as a gimmick was working for LBJ; so well, in fact, that Stevenson aides attempted to get their man into the air. The candidate refused, however, claiming he preferred to keep his campaign "down to earth." It may have been a critical mistake because Johnson was able to cover more than twice the ground as Stevenson and thus increased the public awareness of his presence. For a lot of Texans, especially those in rural areas, the first time in their life that they saw an actual helicopter, Lyndon Johnson was inside, and that experience almost certainly was transformed into some votes when election day rolled around.

Lyndon Johnson, left, and Sam Rayburn, right. The photo was taken during a 1948 campaign stop in Dallas.

Lyndon Johnson used this helicopter, dubbed the Johnson City Windmill, to increase his area of coverage during the 1948 election. Using a specially mounted loudspeaker, LBJ would announce his candidacy prior to landing.

After announcing he was coming, LBJ would land, spend a few moments shaking hands and asking for votes, then quickly take off for the next town.

The campaigning that hot, steamy August was fierce. Both sides made accusations and then answered the other's charges. Johnson, very much aware of a simmering cold war with Russia, stressed his opponent's lack of knowledge on international affairs. Stevenson countered that LBJ was spending money "like water" and that it was coming from suspicious sources. He also alleged that the helicopter may have been an improper gift. Johnson claimed Stevenson had hoof-in-mouth disease and Stevenson countered that Johnson was out of touch with the farm community which, in 1948, comprised the single largest voter block in the state. If Stevenson, a farmer himself, could get the rural community in his corner, he would win no matter what Johnson preached about the evils of communism.

While all the political mud slinging was going on, a man in Duval County named George Parr was quietly watching the campaign with particular interest. He was the heir to the vast Parr political machine orchestrated by his father Archer Parr, the Duke of Duval. For generations, Archer Parr had controlled the people and the politics of South Texas. He had built an influential machine that was well oiled with the trust, admiration, and votes of the Mexican-Americans in the area.

Parr had risen to power in 1911 when he assured the Mexican population that two Anglos would be tried for killing three Mexicans in what has become known as the Election Day Massacre. True to his words, the men were tried and promptly found not guilty since, at the time, it was unheard of for any Anglo to be found guilty of killing a Mexican. However, it was also unheard of for the Anglos to even be tried so Parr, by carrying through on his promise of a trial, earned the undying respect of the Mexican population. He later became a master in converting that respect into ballots on election day. For several generations that followed, only Parr men got elected and since Parr controlled the elections, he also controlled the county.

Parr's corrupt machine operated above the law and well outside the bounds of ethical practices. Money was unlawfully appropriated from county funds, building contracts came complete with appropriate kickbacks, and enemies simply vanished without a trace. While the economy of the area remained depressed, the Parr family lived like royalty.

There were attempts to clean up Duval County but they generally failed miserably. In one case, a grand jury was impaneled to examine the books and Parr simply walked into the "secret" proceedings, snatched the books from the jurors, and stormed out. Without books, the jurors had nothing to investigate so the panel was released. In the rare case when an investigation did make progress, Parr simply had one of "his" judges declare the proceedings illegal. In another case, when the state supreme court (something Parr could not control) sent in auditors to examine the books, the courthouse mysteriously caught fire and all records were destroyed.

In 1914 Archer Parr had himself elected to the state senate and embarked on a most uneventful twenty-two-year political career. He never gave a major speech and about his only accomplishment was to support Jim Ferguson during and after Ferguson's impeachment as governor. Despite his poor record, Parr did use his presence in Austin to extend his circle of supposed friends and political allies. Parr would eventually claim an association with such men as John Nance Garner, a future U.S. vice president; Robert Kleberg, a U.S. representative and owner of the vast King Ranch; J. Frank Dobie, a popular Texas folklorist; and James V. Allred, a future Texas governor.

As old age began to creep up on Archer Parr, he decided to turn over his empire to his son George. While the boy had been schooled well in the fine art of running a political machine, he never quite had the power of his father. But he did maintain control over Duval County and, to some extent, in neighboring Jim Wells and Zapata counties. He might have built an even bigger empire if he had not had to face the one enemy the Parr's could not beat — the Internal Revenue Service.

When an IRS agent showed up one day unexpectedly and demanded to see all the records, George Parr promptly refused and told the agent, in effect, to go straight to hell. Parr would later recall that after that incident, the IRS got real "hos-tile" and he was eventually indicted for income tax evasion on March 9, 1932. Although he first pleaded not guilty, George changed his mind when the evidence was overwhelming and struck a deal for probation in return for a guilty plea.

Back in Duval County, the elderly Archer Parr was also experiencing the wrath of the IRS. It seemed Archer had neglected to report a $25,000 kickback from a corrupt contractor. Although he never did any hard time, Archer Parr was defeated in the next election and retired to Duval County where he lived in relative peace until he died in 1942.

George Parr wasn't so lucky, thanks to his temper. Although he had many narrow escapes from a charge of parole violation, he could not escape from charges he assaulted state Congressman Joe Canalas, a longtime political rival. On May 13, 1936, eight days before his parole term would have ended, George Parr was sent to prison. He served until April 8, 1937, when he was paroled and returned to Duval County to take up the reins of his father's machine and resume the usual corrupt activities associated with the power of the Parr family.

One legacy George Parr continued was making political associations and one of the politicians he befriended was Coke Stevenson. Parr supported Stevenson in his bid for lieutenant governor, went along with Stevenson in the O'Daniel election, and continued the support in Stevenson's bid for a full term as governor.

All the political dealings of the Parr family were based on the simple principal of we'll scratch the other fellow's back and then expect him to scratch ours if it ever starts itching. In the case of Coke Stevenson, the mutual back-scratching scheme did not work out. When George Parr wanted his man, Jim Kazen, appointed as district attorney in Webb County, Stevenson refused to play along. Parr was livid and privately swore to get even the first chance he got. That chance came in the 1948 senatorial election.

Almost one million Texans went to the polls on August 28, 1948 to select a new United States senator. As soon as the polls closed at 7:00 p.m. some of the most creative vote counting in history began. Under the Texas election laws in force at the time, precinct judges had to count the votes and report the totals to the county chairman within seventy-two hours. By midnight on the 28th, the early returns from the county chairmen showed Stevenson leading by 1,894, but already some of the governor's staff were becoming concerned about possible improprieties.

A Stevenson aide reported that a Johnson supporter in the Panhandle had asked if a few vote totals could be changed if necessary. Alarmed by such reports, Stevenson sent some of his top aides to South Texas to try to prevent any similar illegal activities from occurring. It was a noble effort but it failed miserably.

By mid-afternoon on Sunday, August 29, the Stevenson lead had shrunk to 315 and alarm bells were being sounded around the state by Stevenson supporters. The candidate himself hurriedly left his ranch where he was preparing a victory speech so he could get to Austin and do anything possible to prevent the election from being stolen. Stevenson was in Austin by the time some "late" returns came in from Parr country which gave Johnson a lead of 693 votes. There were still 10,000 votes to be counted so the election clearly hung in the balance.

Stevenson had regained the lead by 119 votes on the morning of August 30. Supporters in both camps spent hour after hour pouring over election returns looking for obvious errors and some were found. In Dallas, considered a Stevenson stronghold, figures from one box had been transposed and the total from another box had not even been counted. It appeared Johnson was in trouble so his supporters, it was claimed, stepped up their efforts to find some votes. Someone called a San Antonio sheriff to ask for some votes to be changed but he refused since Bexar County was using voting machines and thus the ballots could not be altered. By morning on Tuesday, August 31, LBJ was in danger of losing the election he could not lose.

Exactly what happened on August 31 to change the course of history is uncertain. Some claim there was a secret meeting in George Parr's office near Alice, Texas and that LBJ personally attended. Johnson supposedly told Parr that with 200 more votes he could win. Longtime Johnson supporters discount that story because there is no evidence LBJ was away from his campaign headquarters at the Driskill Hotel in Austin long enough to make such a trip, even using the helicopter. The more popular theory is that the meeting was held somewhere near San Antonio and that a Johnson aide handled the details.

Whatever the truth is, George Parr had a problem. He had already used up his poll tax and tally sheets in the missing ballots that were reported from Duval County so there was nothing more to be done from that area. Thanks to the widespread influence of the Duke of Duval, Parr turned to associates in Jim Wells County and asked for more votes for Lyndon Johnson.

On September 1, 1948, the election bureau reported that Stevenson was in the lead by 349 votes with only 40 left to count. However, the bureau also advised they were checking and rechecking all ballots closely to make sure no mistakes had been made in such a tight election. Both candidates watched the counting closely to try to be certain no dead men or horses were showing up in the polls. The following day the complete, but unofficial, count showed Stevenson the winner by 362 votes. That was not the end of the story.

As the official canvas of the vote totals continued, the Stevenson lead began to shrink dramatically. By the morning of September 3, the lead was down to 255 and before nightfall it was a scant 113 votes. If LBJ did make the prediction about 200 votes needed to win the election, he was right on the money, and George Parr was just the man to deliver the needed ballots.

Exactly one week after the runoff primary vote, officials in Jim Wells County reported a correction in the returns from precinct 13. The total for Lyndon Johnson was changed from 767 to 967, exactly 200 more votes and a sufficient number to put LBJ in the lead by 17 votes. Coke Stevenson cried foul and claimed he had been beaten by a stuffed ballot box and that he could prove it. The fight was on.

The checking of election returns was escalated and the numbers continued to change. On Sunday, September 5, the Johnson lead rose to 181 votes but it quickly started falling again. The political jousting was quickly stepped up with Stevenson hollering and Johnson counter-hollering. LBJ called for a full investigation by the FBI and many of the state's largest newspapers, including the *Dallas Morning News*, echoed that sentiment. Everyone it seemed wanted to get to the bottom of the voter fraud issue quickly. They might as well have been wishing for a ride on a unicorn.

Sensing the election slipping away, the usually reserved Stevenson went on the offensive. He and several members of his staff went to Alice to confer with officials from Jim Wells County. Although they did get some information about 200 votes that were added to the tally in alphabetical order and in the same color ink, they were refused permission to look at the tally sheet or the ballots. In desperation, Stevenson called in the Texas Rangers. To be specific, one Ranger, the legendary Frank Hamer, was summoned to see if he could open the vault and bring the ballots into the light of day.

Hamer, one of the most famous Rangers of all time and the man who tracked down Bonnie and Clyde, was an old friend of Governor Stevenson and he immediately dropped everything and headed south out of Austin to go to his friend's aid. He arrived on the morning of September 8 and found the entrance to the First State Bank of Alice, where the election materials were held, blocked by two groups of Winchester-toting George Parr henchmen all prepared for a Texas-sized shootout.

The Ranger's reputation preceded him, as it always did. As he, Stevenson, and two assistants approached the bank, Hamer simply said "git" to the first group and the men stepped aside. "Fall back," Hamer ordered of the men in the second group and they withdrew without even attempting to fire a shot. Stevenson and his men entered the bank and demanded to see the voting material.

Tom Donald, the Parr man in charge, agreed so long as they honored a court ruling by a Parr judge that no notes could be taken, since they had no court order to allow them access to the ballots. The Stevenson men had predetermined to memorize as many names as possible and quickly started reading the list. Donald was called away for a phone call and when he returned, he grabbed the tally sheets and proclaimed "that's it." He promptly put the sheets back in the vault and locked the door.

The meeting was over but Stevenson had seen enough to convince him the votes were fraudulent.

Knowing something and proving it are often two entirely different propositions. In the case of the ballot box 13, Stevenson faced an uphill battle. Jim Wells officials, George Parr, and the courts refused to cooperate. Lyndon Johnson ridiculed his opponent by claiming that Stevenson and his pistol-packing pal had violated the law by demanding to see the tally sheets. Although Johnson never said it in so many words, he implied that if the ballots were later checked and found to be improper, then it would have been because of Stevenson and Hamer changing things when they were in the vault. Stevenson continued to claim he had been "rascalled" out of the election and vowed to see justice done. It was not that easy.

Stevenson filed an affidavit with Jim Wells County officials charging a mistake had been made in the count of precinct 13. In effect, the charge would have forced the opening of the box for public inspection. Just one hour before the opening, Johnson obtained a restraining order preventing Stevenson or anyone else from opening that box. Once again, Calculating Coke was rebuffed in his efforts to gain control of what was to become the most famous ballot box in Texas history.

When all other maneuvers failed, Stevenson decided to take his case to the executive committee of the state Democratic convention that convened on September 13. Shortly after noon, above the loud objections of pro-Stevenson candidates, Vann Kennedy, the state secretary, announced the results of the official vote canvas — Johnson 494,191 to Stevenson 494,104. Lyndon Johnson had won by the whopping total of 87 votes.

Stevenson was down but hardly out. He continued his fight to try to keep Johnson from receiving the nomination on the grounds of voter fraud and improper election returns. That motion failed twice, by the vote of 29 to 28. Johnson was cleared to have his name on the ballot as the Democratic candidate in the October general election, which meant he was on his way to Washington as a senator.

When it appeared Stevenson had lost, he sealed his own fate with a complete reversal of accepted Democratic policy in Texas when he actually endorsed Jack Porter, the Republican who would be running against Johnson. The bold move angered many Stevenson supporters who felt that any Democrat, even one who stole an election, would be better than a Republican.

The unexpected move did not stop the election investigation and the federal authorities eventually became involved. When that happened, the entire case took a dramatic turn for the worse as far as Stevenson was concerned. On October 27, 1948, less than a week before the general election that would send Lyndon Johnson on his political way, federal investigators discovered that the famous ballots and tally sheets from box 13 had been destroyed.

According to the story, when officials were preparing for the general election, they needed some empty ballot boxes, so Epifiano Betacourt, the 65-year-old courthouse janitor, had, on his own initiative, removed all the voting material from the run-off election and burned it in a wire trash can in a vacant lot. Naturally, officials in Jim Wells and Duval counties were sure sorry for what happened but it was just one of those unfortunate accidents that seemed to happen whenever federal officials wanted to investigate South Texas.

Even though investigators uncovered evidence that a similar ballot burning had taken place in 1919 when Archer Parr faced an investigation, there was little anyone could do with the evidence reduced to ashes. Some investigations continued but Lyndon Johnson's name was allowed on the ballot and he won handily despite Stevenson working for the opposition. Because of the widespread publicity on the election, one of the best Texas trivia questions of all time was born. Who did LBJ defeat in the 1948 senatorial election? Most people remember the battle with Stevenson and that is their answer which is not correct. The battle with Stevenson was in the primary; Jack Porter was the man actually defeated for the senate seat.

That 1948 senate election also spawned a legendary political joke that, it has been said, even LBJ enjoyed telling. It seems a small Mexican boy was discovered sitting on a street curb crying his little eyes out. "What's the matter?" asked a friend.

"My daddy was in town yesterday and he did not come to see me," the boy said between sobs.

"But son," the friend replied, "you know your father died five years ago."

"I know," the boy replied, "but he was in town yesterday to vote for Lyndon Johnson and he didn't even come to see me."

After the election Coke Stevenson retired from public life. He died in 1975 and a historical marker in Junction honors his contributions to Texas. George Parr eventually got into more trouble with the IRS. He was twice convicted of income tax evasion and suffered through a traumatic bankruptcy, which was evidence that the Parr empire had collapsed. On April Fool's Day 1975, George Parr drove out to the back of his ranch and ended his life with a bullet to the head.

Lyndon Johnson's political star was launched with the 1948 election and he quickly rose in stature and power. He was considered for the presidency in 1960, which is perhaps testimony to how quick voters can forget. He settled for vice president running with John Kennedy. Following Kennedy's assassination in Dallas in 1963, LBJ became president. He was elected to a full term in 1964 and retired in 1968 following a stormy administration during the escalation of the Vietnam war. He died of a heart attack at his beloved Texas ranch in 1973.

For most people the story of the 1948 election is not much of a mystery — Lyndon B. Johnson stole the senate seat, pure and simple. But there is still the matter of proof. While a few people claimed to have specific knowledge of the events and a very few others were allowed to see the actual ballots, most of them are gone now. The actual proof to substantiate the claims supposedly vanished in the janitor's trash fire. There is, however, a small possibility that the ballots and tally sheet with the infamous 200 names of people who supposedly voted for LBJ in alphabetical order were not destroyed.

In 1968, twenty years after the famous election, Lyndon Johnson announced he would not seek reelection to another term as president, which was probably just as well since his popularity had been reduced proportionally with the escalation of the Vietnam non-war. Although seemingly unrelated, 1968 was also the year that San Antonio celebrated its 250th anniversary with a gala world-fair-like celebration called Hemisfair.

One of the pavilions at the Hemisfair was an oldtime saloon sponsored by the Falstaff Brewing Company. It was a popular watering hole for anyone seeking to beat the Texas heat that summer and it was a good place to meet friends. One late afternoon in the middle of August, a college student home for the summer walked into the pavilion and took a seat at the only open table. He ordered a beer but changed to Dr Pepper when the waitress asked for identification. He settled in to wait for friends that were due in about half an hour.

At the table next to the kid sat a man who appeared to be a tourist. He was tall, well-tanned, dressed in walking shorts and a lightweight shirt, and idly fondling a glass of beer. He appeared to be waiting for someone and the kid assumed the man's family would be along shortly. Instead, a smartly dressed, dark-skinned Mexican gentleman appeared and took a seat.

The student did not intentionally listen in on the conversation between the two men but he was so close he could not help but hear some of what was said. The tourist was actually a physician out of Houston and he had come to San Antonio specifically to meet the other gentleman who was named Sanches or Salinas or something similar. After some small talk about the weather and the fair, the men got down to the issue at hand.

"So, Mr. Sanches," the doctor said, "tell me of these documents you mentioned on the phone."

"Yes, señor," the Mexican replied, "as you were informed I have some sensitive papers that are now available to collectors such as yourself."

"Describe the papers."

"Of course. There are ballots and tally sheets listing all the persons who voted in precinct 13 of Jim Wells County in the notorious 1948 election for the United States senate. As you know, señor, Mr. Lyndon Johnson was the eventual winner."

"Yes and I know the materials you speak of were supposedly destroyed, uh, I think they were burned by some janitor."

"Sí, señor, that is what everyone believes. . . ."

"But you say it is not true."

"I can say the famous ballots were supposed to be destroyed with all the others but they were not. Someone whose name I am not at liberty to disclose removed the box 13 materials before the janitor set the fire."

"That someone would be George Parr, I suppose."

The Mexican smiled. "No sir, not Señor Parr. Someone close to Mr. Parr, perhaps, but not the famous Parr himself."

The doctor hesitated a moment, thinking. After a sip of his beer, he continued, "If what you say is true, why weren't the materials burned?"

"It is simple, señor. If you had proof that a United States senator had won his election by fraud, would you allow the proof to be destroyed?"

"Senator, hell. Lyndon Johnson was president and a damn good one."

"Of course, but that was not known in 1948. He was then a senator and as such was in a position to possibly offer some assistance to anyone holding the ballots should the need arise."

"You're trying to tell me someone blackmailed Lyndon Johnson. You're full of . . . . "

"No, señor, I said nothing of the kind," the gentleman continued. "I merely implied that someone took the precaution of preserving the documents so they would be available should they be needed. I do not mean to imply that they were ever actually used. As far as I know, President Johnson, along with the rest of the world, believes the documents were destroyed."

The doctor finished his beer. "So why are you trying to sell the documents now?"

Sanches smiled. "Señor, while it was theoretically possible that the documents could have caused President Johnson serious discomfort in the area of public relations, now that he has announced his retirement from the public eye, the useful value of the document has fallen dramatically. In fact, the papers now have little value other than as significant historical documents."

"So why did you call me?"

"Señor, it is known that you are a collector of rare and valuable documents that may or may not come with a proper bill of sale. It is also known that you are a strong supporter of Mr. Johnson. Therefore, the person holding the documents suggested I offer you the opportunity to own an important part of history."

The doctor sat quietly listening to the man's words. In a moment, he continued, "What you are saying, sir, is that perhaps you are trying to blackmail me. You know I am closely aligned with the Democratic party and with Lyndon Johnson. As such, I naturally would not want the documents made public because of the embarrassment it would cause the Johnson family. My supposition is that if I decline your offer, you will threaten to sell the papers to the press. Am I correct?"

"Señor," Sanches replied, "my mission is to sell the documents. We believed you might be interested and have made the contact. If you are not, we will naturally seek other buyers. That is only natural, yes."

"Will you go to the press?"

"I cannot say we will or we won't. We simply want to arrange a buyer, that is all."

The doctor again hesitated, thinking. "If I am interested, how do I know the papers are legitimate? And what price are you asking?"

"I can make samples of the documents available for your inspection at any moment. Assuming you approve, the asking price is $5,000."

The doctor stood up abruptly. "Have the material in my room in one hour. If the papers are authentic, we'll talk." He walked out of the saloon and the Mexican quickly followed.

The conversation was reconstructed from information provided by the student. At the time, he didn't think much about the incident and assumed it was some sort of gag. In fact, about all the kid knew of Lyndon Johnson was that the president had arranged a ticket to Vietnam for any college student whose grades slipped. The young man's friends arrived and the entire group left to enjoy the fair. The college student thought no more about the conversation he overheard for several years.

Ten years later, in 1978, that same young man had graduated college and embarked on a business career. He had also become an amateur Texas memorabilia collector. In May of that year he was in Houston on business and happened to visit an antique show. As was his custom, he asked every dealer for anything related to Texas. One dealer, a short, rotund cowboy from South Texas had a surprising answer to the inquiry.

The dealer said he did have some Texas items but that he always sold such material to a collector in the Houston area. He said the man was a doctor who happened to have some of the rarest pieces of privately held Texanna. Intrigued, the young collector asked about the collection. To his amazement, the dealer offered that the doctor's collection included some rare documents from the 1948 senatorial election.

Pressing for more information, the collector said he thought that all the election materials from 1948 had been destroyed in a fire. Not so, the dealer replied and he even said that he was one of the fortunate ones to have actually seen the material. When asked if the material was for sale, the dealer said no way, that the doctor wouldn't even allow most people to see the documents. When asked, the dealer refused to disclose the name of the doctor.

Strange as it is, the story was relayed by the college kid turned collector who asked that his name not be used. He said the facts were presented exactly as they occurred and that nothing was left out or made up. The largest problem with the story is that no one else has ever even implied that the ballots from box 13 were not destroyed. While it makes logical sense that evidence against a United States senator might have been kept, it seems to stretch the limits of believability that the secret could have been kept from so many for so long. An effort was made to locate the mysterious Houston doctor without results. There simply have been too many doctors in that town to hope to trace one without even so much as a last name. The dealer who claimed to be a supplier to the doctor was also not found, although some people believed he might have been a man who died a few years ago.

Several Texas historians and some Texanna document dealers were canvassed to see if anyone had ever heard the story of the box 13 documents being saved from the garbage fire. Only the late John Jenkins of Austin said he had heard something about the papers in the early 1970s but that he had assumed the report was either a rumor or a scheme to sell fake documents.

It appears the tale told by the former college student cannot be verified, which may or may not mean it is false. Perhaps the documents from box 13 do still exist and are today locked away in some vault in Houston waiting for a devout Democrat to pass on. It is just as possible that the Mexican gentleman in the Hemisfair saloon was nothing but a con man out to make a fast five grand with forged documents. Unless the papers are ultimately found, it may never be possible to learn exactly who the 200 phantom Texans were that managed to vote alphabetically and send a former school teacher on his way to the White House.

If you have any information about the possible whereabouts of the documents from ballot box 13, please contact the author at Wordware Publishing, Inc.

The Great Stagecoach Inn Caper

by Wallace O. Chariton

By 1860, Texas Governor Sam Houston was a troubled, beleaguered, virtually broken man. For almost thirty years he had been perhaps the most loved and respected man in the state and the republic that preceded it. But as the Civil War clouds gathered across the South, the crusty old general fell from grace for the simple reason that he could not support the cause of the Confederacy.

While the vast majority of Texans were almost looking forward to spilling some Yankee blood, Houston believed, correctly, that a united South could never defeat the well-trained, properly supplied northern army. There would be blood spilled, Houston predicted, but in the end most of it would be on grey uniforms. The last thing on earth Houston wanted was for a lot of those rebel grey outfits to be filled with Texans.

As a fighter, Houston had squared off against Indians, the British, and the Mexicans and always walked away victorious. But in 1860, as governor, he faced his most lethal opponent, an army of Texans ready to go to war. His mission was to try to save the state he helped forge from what he felt would be certain destruction — he had to keep Texas from joining the Confederacy and seceding from the Union. On January 1, 1861,

Governor Houston embarked on a brief speaking tour of central Texas communities in an effort to bolster support for his opinion. He did not have much success.

Houston's speech in Waco on New Year's Day was not well received; in fact, some members of the audience hurled small stones at the speaker in protest of his uncomplimentary remarks about the southern cause. Four days later in Belton the mood of the crowd was so volatile that the governor took the precaution of strapping on a pistol belt before appearing. Houston did not have to use the guns but he also did not convince many that it would be disastrous to join the Confederacy.

Houston's next stop was at the Shady Villa Hotel along the banks of the Salado Creek. Once again, the crowd had all the warmth of a Texas blue norther, but Houston must have perceived the people to be less prone to violence. When he stepped out on the wooden floor of the balcony that morning, Houston was not wearing a pistol belt under the leopard skin vest that had been given him by Chief Bowl, an old and trusted friend. Although Houston considered the vest to be a sort of lucky charm, it did not work any magic that day because the audience was just as set on secession as all the others.

Despite a cold reception, Houston was at least able to use some of his famous quick wit at Salado. At one point the eloquence of his speech was rudely interrupted by the snorting and kicking of a horse trying to break free from a harness. The commotion caused Houston to pause, and when the horse's owner attempted to get control, the governor remarked, "Let him alone, he's trying a little practical secession." The crowd smiled politely and Houston was about to resume his speech when the horse finally choked himself down. The teamster stepped forward, beat the poor animal, got it to its feet, and then struggled to replace the broken harness. Houston could not resist. "See how it works!" he said. "See what a fix he is in when he is brought back into the Union." The crowd laughed and applauded but it was out of admiration for the wit and not for the anti-secession position.

The balcony from which Sam Houston delivered his famous anti-secession speech. Although the Stagecoach Inn has undergone many changes, much of the original hotel still exists exactly as it did in 1860.

The rest is history, of course. Houston was not successful in his campaign, and just over a month after he left Salado, Texans overwhelmingly voted to join the Confederacy. Houston refused to take the oath of allegiance and was removed from office. The war was on.

When Sam Houston left the Shady Villa Hotel that chilly January day in 1861, the words of his speech were quickly forgotten, but he inadvertently did two things that were remembered. First, he became part of an unofficial fraternity of famous guests who stayed at the hotel and second, he became an unknowing participant in a future unsolved Texas mystery — he left behind his signature in the hotel guest register.

The area near where Sam Houston gave his major anti-secession speech has been a popular spot in Texas for centuries. The cooling shade of the numerous oak and pecan trees have acted as a magnet for everyone from explorers to tourists. The sparkling mineral water that seeps up from underground springs provides soothing, almost medicinal refreshment.

In the 1700s, Spanish explorers favored the location and even named the small stream Salado, which means salt, because of the high mineral content of the water. There is also a persistent legend that one Spanish expedition was overloaded with gold and silver bounty and decided to lighten their load after camping near the Salado. Supposedly, the Spaniards carefully secreted their treasure in a hidden cave below the present day inn. The spot was chosen because it would be easy to locate when the explorers returned for their treasure. The Spaniards never returned and a lot of people believe the treasure lies today in the cave waiting to be discovered. Many treasure hunters have searched for the secret cache but none, as far as it is known, has ever found so much as a single piece of gold.

The cool shade and salty mineral water was as much an attraction to wild animals as it was to men. In the early 1800s, one thing was almost certain in Texas; where there was abundant game, there were Indians. The area around Salado Creek became a popular camping and hunting ground for the Comanche and other tribes. They feasted on buffalo, deer, and antelope and always had plenty to drink when the hunting was finished.

White men also discovered the pleasant spot when searching for game. The huge herds of buffalo that frequented the area naturally attracted the buffalo hunters. The slaughter often commenced with hunters firing from the security of cover in the trees. The Salado Creek camp and hunting grounds were so attractive to the buffalo hunters that some of them actually constructed a permanent log cabin in the area in the 1840s.

By the 1850s, the Republic of Texas had become one of the United States and settlement in the region began to increase. One of the early settlers was W. B. Armstrong, who became infatuated with the area around Salado Creek. He decided to make his home in the area and to take advantage of the frequent travelers who passed through. He built a sturdy hotel with thick beams fashioned from nearby oak trees and a strong fireplace built from rocks picked up along the creek. The Shady Villa Hotel was finished and open for business when Sam Houston passed through the area on his filibustering campaign.

When war did come, many volunteers from South and Southwest Texas passed through Salado and stopped at the Shady Villa before heading into battle. Entire volunteer companies often camped in the woods along the creek and the officers stayed in the hotel. When Sam Houston's prediction of certain defeat came true, many of the soldiers who managed to survive passed back through Salado on their way home to try to rebuild a life.

Shortly after the Confederate defeat, the United States established a reconstruction government in Texas and dispatched a golden haired boy wonder of a general named George Armstrong Custer to head up the military operations. During his year-long stay in the Lone Star State, Custer and his wife Libby were interested tourists, and on at least one occasion they stayed in the comfortable, inviting Shady Villa Hotel.

The loss in the Civil War was a bitter pill to swallow for most Texans but they were comforted, to some extent, by an unexpected set of circumstances that would eventually help bolster the prosperity of Texas. While most of the men were away fighting in the war, the large herds of longhorn cattle started by the Spanish were left unattended and they did what cattle do best, they multiplied. By the end of the war in 1865, literally millions of longhorns were roaming the wide open expanse of Texas.

The enormous excess of cattle in Texas just happened to coincide with an unprecedented demand for beef in the northern states where most of the supplies had been exhausted by the war effort. The only problem was the cows were in Texas and the market was in the North. To resolve that problem, enterprising Texans organized cattle drives to take the herds north to the nearest rail line so the animals could be shipped to any destination in the country.

One of the most popular cattle trails ran north from South Texas through Salado. The abundance of wood, fuel, and water for the animals made Salado a popular stop on the drive north. Untold numbers of cowboys spent their last comfortable night in the Shady Villa before heading north to Kansas or Colorado or Nebraska. Cattle barons like Shanghai Pierce and Charles Goodnight occasionally came to Salado to conduct their business, and like all the other patrons of the Shady Villa, they left behind their signature in the guest register.

With increased prosperity came increased progress. The Butterfield Stage Line passed through Salado and established the Shady Villa Hotel as an official stop on the line. Literally hundreds of passengers traveling south from Dallas toward Austin and San Antonio stopped off at Salado. Some only stayed long enough for food and refreshment and others stayed overnight. Either way, the hospitality of the Shady Villa was a welcome change from the dusty trail.

There was also a dark side of the hotel being used as stage depot. Stagecoaches often carried valuable cargoes and passengers frequently had their entire cash savings in a pocket or purse. This meant the crude, uncomfortable, and easy-to-stop vehicles were a favorite prey of early desperados. It is believed that men like Frank and Jesse James, members of the Dalton gang, and the famous Texas gunfighter Sam Bass all stayed at the Shady Villa at one time or another while planning a stage holdup.

The hotel's reputation for genuine Texas hospitality and an outstanding bill of fare continued to grow into the 20th century. Travelers were known to stray miles off course just for the chance to stay at the Shady Villa. The list of famous names in the hotel register also continued to grow. In 1914, when the United States dispatched Captain Robert E. Lee, son of the famous Civil War general, to participate in the search for Mexican bandit Pancho Villa, he stopped at the Shady Villa on his way to the border.

When the horse and stage were replaced by the automobile and the Chisholm Trail was covered in concrete to become Interstate 35, the Shady Villa continued to prosper. Located almost exactly halfway between Dallas and San Antonio, the hotel became a favorite stop of tourists heading south to see the Alamo or heading north to place a bet at Arlington Downs horse racetrack.

The hotel's reputation for friendliness and good food never wavered but its physical condition did deteriorate. For a while it appeared the hotel, which had been converted into a motor lodge, would eventually become a forgotten relic of the past. Then in 1940, Mr. and Mrs. Dion Van Bibber purchased the establishment and had the buildings renovated. The Van Bibbers were careful to preserve as much as possible of the original hotel structure. The beamed ceilings, wooden plank floors, stone fireplace and original walls were left intact and became part of the renamed Stagecoach Inn. Van Bibber also redid the menu and created delicacies that are still served today in the famous inn.

Van Bibber did, however, make one critical mistake — he trusted his fellow man. He was fiercely proud of the hotel's heritage and felt strongly that the precious register ought to be on display for all the world to see. He had a small display stand erected in the lobby of the new hotel and placed the book where any guest could spend a few leisurely moments literally leafing through the pages of history. It was a wonderful gesture that enchanted many guests until the generosity backfired.

In 1944, during the height of World War II, some unknown guest of the hotel did more than read the names in the register.

He or she carefully closed the large book, slipped it under a coat, walked boldly out of the Stagecoach Inn, and disappeared. The famous register which had amazed Texans for almost one hundred years was suddenly gone.

Van Bibber was crushed by the brazen theft. Friends who knew him claim he never could understand how anyone could stoop so low as to steal a piece of history and deprive future generations of the pleasure of seeing it. But for all his grief, Van Bibber did not even report the theft to local or county authorities or to the Texas Rangers. Van Bibber was a proud man who disliked adverse publicity of any kind and thus he simply accepted the fact that the priceless book was gone and went on about his business of running one of the finest inns in all of Texas.

Because the heinous crime was never reported, no official investigation was ever carried out. No one bothered to make a list of the guests at the hotel that day so they could be checked to see if perhaps some known thief was among the group. No one was ever questioned about the theft and certainly no one was ever given a polygraph test. The crook inadvertently pulled off the perfect crime because there was never any sort of effort to find the perpetrator. The book simply vanished and that was that.

What happened to the famous Shady Villa guest register remains an unsolved Texas mystery almost fifty years after the fact. Some have speculated that the thief was an early autograph collector and may have cut up the register to save only the more famous autographs. That is, of course, one possible explanation. However, in the mid-1940s autograph collecting was not the popular hobby it is today so perhaps the book was stolen simply for the historical value. If that is what happened, there is a chance, albeit slim, that the book might yet be found. Unfortunately, there is a significant obstacle that will have to be overcome.

In the early days of hotels in Texas, many establishments, like the Shady Villa, used generic hotel ledger sheets as pages in their guest registers. Therefore, the Shady Villa register will appear simply as pages of names, dates, and numbers and it will be difficult to identify the book as the actual Shady Villa register. If the book was found intact, about the only method of identification would be to verify that such names as Sam Houston, Robert E. Lee, George Custer, and Sam Bass are included.

Like Von Bibber, a lot of Texans have trouble understanding why such a crime was ever committed. In 1944 the potential rewards from the sale of autographs would have been a mere pittance when compared to the historical value of the book. Because the register is gone, we will never know exactly who stayed at the hotel and when. A lot of genealogists would like to know if their ancestors happened to have stayed at the hotel at the same time as Houston or Custer or any of the others. The opportunity to find out vanished in 1944.

It would be entirely too optimistic to predict that the book would ever be returned or that it is even still intact. About the only chance will be if someone actually took the book in a weak moment as a souvenir and today it is packed away in an old family trunk. Perhaps the thief is long since dead and his relatives have some odd book full of names and they have no idea that it came from the famous hotel. Unfortunately, even if that were the case, the chances that the book will be returned appear slim since to do that would mean admitting that a relative was a common thief.

Without the book, we are left with only sketchy memories of who actually stayed in the hotel. The list may actually include numerous Civil War soldiers, famous cowboys, politicians, authors, and the like. Military men like George Patton, Dwight Eisenhower, Chester Nimitz and even Douglas MacArthur may have stayed at the hotel because they all were in Texas at one time or another. Unless the book is recovered, we'll never really know exactly who stayed at the Shady Villa Hotel.

There is always the slim chance that some good Samaritan will discover the register and return it to its rightful place at the hotel. If that were to happen, anyone with even the slightest bit of Texas in his heart would be much obliged. With or without the register, the Stagecoach Inn remains a popular stopping place on Interstate 35 south. If you have been there, you know of the charm and grace; if you haven't been there you ought to go.

Before you go, check the attic to be sure there is not some dusty old book full of signatures that might be the long lost register.

If you have any information about what might have happened to the famous register or if you know of other names that were in the book, please contact the author at Wordware Publishing, Inc.

The Mystery Lady of the San Bernard

by C. F. Eckhardt

Down in the southeastern part of Texas, not far west of Galveston Bay, a small river empties into what is now a lake. The river is called the San Bernard, and if you bother to ask why the name is half Spanish and half English, somebody'll tell you "because that's the way it's always been."

The truth is, it hasn't always been that way. Once, when the river was called El Rio de San Bernardo, it emptied not into a lake but into the Gulf of Mexico. A forest of huge, spreading live oaks surrounded the river's mouth. It became, between about 1810 and 1840 or so, the location for one of the strangest mysteries not just in Texas, but in North America and maybe the world.

Sometime around 1810, an English-speaking white man came to the mouth of the San Bernard, where he established himself as a hermit. We don't have any idea who he was or where he came from, but he was apparently an educated man and he had some teaching ability. We may guess, no more, at why he chose to live in isolation at the lonely river mouth. If it had not been for a very peculiar chain of circumstances, we wouldn't even know this man had ever existed.

The Indians who hunted the mouth of the San Bernard — and most of the upper Texas coast — were Karankawa. Modern revisionist historians make noises that claim the best-remembered feature of the Karankawa is no more than a myth — that they were not, after all, cannibalistic. Enough memoirs and eyewitness accounts, most of them glossed over or deliberately ignored by these revisionists, speak loudly to the contrary. The Karankawa practiced at least ritual cannibalism. Whether or not they ate folks 'cause they figured they were good eatin' — as the Tonkawa apparently did, from some of their own statements — we don't know.

Our hermit brought himself into downright dangerous country at the mouth of the San Bernard. The Karankawa had no use for white men because the Indians and the pirates of Galveston Island got off to a bad start years before, when the pirates snatched some Karankawa girls for the usual reasons and the Karankawa snatched some pirates for dinner. The two groups had a working relationship — when Karankawa and pirate met, whoever got to a weapon first lived.

For various reasons, none of which we're entirely sure of, the Karankawa thought the hermit was crazy. This was definitely to the hermit's advantage. All American Indian tribes seem to have had a ritual prohibition against harming the insane. One explanation, given by various authorities, has to do with the idea that the Indians felt something, either some god or a demon, had taken possession of the body of an insane person, and that if someone were so foolish as to harm or kill the one so possessed, the demon or whatever would then possess the person who harmed or killed its previous host. True or not, a great many people, when attacked or surrounded by Indians, managed to escape alive by behaving in a "crazy" manner.

It was apparently not forbidden to make the acquaintance of or even to befriend one so possessed. Around 1810, a young Karankawa brave, probably no more than a boy, did make friends with the hermit. The white man taught the young Indian to converse fluently in English — not the "Me heap Injun, you gimme 'backy, white man" pidgin of the movies, but complete and complex sentences with proper structure.

The young Karankawa who had learned English from the mysterious hermit of the San Bernard first came to the attention of Stephen F. Austin's colonists when they settled in Karankawa domain in the 1820s. By then the young Indian brave was a mature warrior. Like most Karankawas he was fairly tall, around six feet; "splendidly muscled," or so the old memoirs say; relatively handsome even by white-man standards; and "highly intelligent." He was probably considered to be highly intelligent because he spoke excellent English.

He was also noted for wearing a peculiar headdress made of the antlers of deer — a headdress that, once the long-rifle-armed white men moved into the area, might have been a little risky in the woods. If he was like most other Karankawa warriors, about the only garment he wore besides his headdress was a buckskin jockstrap. His feet were huge, flat, and wide (other Indians called the Karankawa "Big Feet" when they weren't calling them things like "Eaters of Men") and he packed a bow about six feet or so long, a handful of bamboo arrows, and a big knife. He also stunk to high heaven, since the Karankawa, year-round on the coast, wore a home-made mosquito repellent, some of the more appetizing ingredients of which were pennyroyal and rancid sharks' liver oil.

Besides the fact that this particular Karankawa could speak excellent English and often served the Austin colonists as an interpreter, he had another distinguishing characteristic. He wore around his neck a large gold locket — a woman's jewel. Inside the locket, so said those he allowed a look, was a miniature painting of a handsome young man and a small boy. Engraved across the back of the locket was a single word, THEODOSIA.

Our Karankawa was, of course, asked where he got the locket. It was given to him, he said, by his white wife. Where did he get a white wife? He was given her by the Great Storm, and the gods — or something — quickly took her away.

There have been a lot of storms along the Texas coast. The 1900 hurricane that devastated Galveston, the 1919 storm that all but destroyed Corpus Christi, Hurricanes Carla, Beulah, and not a few others come to mind. To an historian of old Texas, though, there is but one Great Storm. It is the storm of 1816.

The 1816 storm may have been the hardest blow ever to hit the Texas coast, and it was certainly the hardest one to hit it in at least three hundred years before 1816. It put at least fifteen feet of water over Galveston Island, likely considerably more than that. Jean Lafitte, at the height of the storm, sailed a ship drawing twelve feet of water completely across the island and snagged nothing. As late as the 1830s, high-water marks and flood debris as much as twenty feet high in trees as far as ten miles inland were seen. Spanish records tell us that there was an abundant forest of ancient live oak trees at the mouth of the San Bernard prior to the 1816 storm, but Anglo records beginning in the 1820s describe that stretch of coast as low, desolate, and almost treeless.

According to the Karankawa, his people survived the storm, as they always had, by climbing the sturdy but flexible salt cedars and tying themselves to the trees to keep from being blown away. The salt cedars, being deep-rooted and willowy, would bend with the wind but remain rooted and upright.

Sometime after the storm blew itself out and the waters receded which, to judge by recent experience, might have been anywhere from two to three weeks after the wind stopped, the surviving Indians climbed down from their salt cedars and our Karankawa decided to wander down to the mouth of the river to see what he could see. Mostly, he said, he was looking to see how his white man had done.

The white man hadn't done well. When the wind began to blow and the water began to rise, he had, by visible evidence, at least, climbed to the crown of a massive, spreading live oak and tied himself in the branches. Of all the trees to climb in such a situation, a live oak has to be the worst. For all its huge size, ancient age, and spreading crown, a live oak is, in fact, extremely vulnerable to high wind, especially when the wind is accompanied by torrential rain. The wind itself is capable of snapping huge branches like matchsticks, but when the rain falls, the surrounding earth loses its grip on the shallow roots of the oak. Once the ground is saturated and soupy, even a fairly mild blow is capable of toppling a three-hundred-year-old live oak.

The white hermit hadn't known this, which tells us pretty clearly that he probably wasn't a coastal Southerner by birth. Live oaks — called 'water oaks' farther east — are pretty common throughout the South, and their peculiar vulnerability to wind and rain has been well-known since the 1600s. The hermit climbed up a huge oak and tied himself to the branches. When the tree came down he was either killed in the fall or drowned by the high water. He was, in any case, dead.

There was, however, something far more immediately interesting than a dead hermit at the mouth of the San Bernard. Lying half-in, half-out of the riverbed, her keel snapped, was a seagoing sailing ship.

Shipwrecks, particularly during storms, were by no means uncommon along the Texas coast, and the Karankawa had been taking advantage of the bounty brought by storms since at least the 16th century and maybe earlier. Our Karankawa warrior climbed aboard and began to explore.

His description of the ship may have been muddled by retelling over the years, but it seems that it was large enough to have a noticeable sterncastle, which means it was a pretty-good-sized ship. According to some of the retellers, the Karankawa said it had a "wigwam" at the back, which he almost certainly didn't say since "wigwam" is not a Karankawa word. It is, however, "generic Indian," like "squaw" for woman, "papoose" for child, and "canoe" for light boat. Apparently the first few Indians the Anglo settlers encountered on the East Coast said "wigwam" for place of dwelling so that word became "Indian" for house. Whatever the Karankawa said, he got the point across — the boat had a noticeable raised structure on its hind end, which in nautical terms is called a sterncastle.

He found lots of useful rope on the decks and the by-now-certainly-useless bodies of several men in various states of decomposition or chewed on by varmints lying around the place. These he apparently ignored, except to note their presence.

Eventually he made his way into the sterncastle, where, to his great surprise, he heard a weak, high-pitched, woman-like voice calling for help in English. He followed the sound to its source and found, in a cabin, a small but fully mature white woman, completely naked except for a gold locket — the one he now wore — around her neck and chained by one ankle to a bulkhead. She called out in English, he answered, she saw him and fainted dead away.

Exactly how he got her loose from the bulkhead we don't know, but if just half the stories of the muscle development and physical strength of Karankawa warriors are true, he might well have simply grabbed the chain in both hands, set himself back, and jerked it loose. However he did it, he picked up the woman, carried her off the ship to the bank of the river, laid her on the sand, and began to bathe her face in river-water. She shortly revived, and he gave her water in a shell to drink.

The fact that he spoke English must have given her some hope, for she asked him to take her where there were white men who spoke this language. Unfortunately, so far as the Karankawa knew for sure at the time, there were two people still alive out of the only three in all the world who spoke that language — he and the woman.

At that, said the Karankawa, or so the storytellers have him saying, she appeared to lose all hope. She then began to tell him a story. She was, she said, the daughter of a great chief of the white men, but a great chief badly misunderstood by his people. She was the wife of another great, but somewhat lesser, chief. A long time before — perhaps three winters, perhaps more — she got on a great boat very similar to the one that now lay wrecked, in order to go and visit her father. The first boat was attacked by another boat which was the one now wrecked on the beach. Her boat was burned, and all aboard it save her were murdered. She had been kept, naked and chained, as a slave to the crew of the wrecked boat ever since. Then, he said, she gave him the gold locket and told him that if he ever met white men who spoke this language, he must show it to them and tell them the story.

At that, so said the Karankawa, she lay down to sleep and "as she slept the Great Spirit built the white wigwam around her, and so she died." This latter comment, which appears in the first printed retellings of this tale as collected by the Texas Folklore Society in the 1920s, is probably some romantic's addition to the story. At any rate she died. He dug a grave, put her in it, put either a door or a hatch-cover over her body, and covered her up. Oh, yes, he also said she told him there was a vast treasure aboard the ship, but having no use for a white man's treasure he didn't bother to look for it.

The Karankawa was real. He's mentioned in the memoirs of some of Austin's colonists. The locket and the story behind it have been a part of the oral history of Austin's Colony since its founding. The 1816 storm was all too real. The vast live oak forest the Spanish wrote about at the mouth of the Rio San Bernardo wasn't there by the time the settlers renamed the river the San Bernard. High water marks were plainly visible, traceable, at least in Indian memory, directly to the great blow of 1816. Coast Indians, for as long as the coast Indians remained, dated things not from the coming of Austin's colonists, but from the Great Storm. Considering the number of storms they must have weathered along the Texas coast over the countless generations they'd inhabited it, for them to consider one particular storm The Great Storm must mean it was, in truth, a great storm.

The ship was, and to some extent still is, real. Although he didn't say anything about the Karankawa and his necklace, Noah Smithwick, in *Evolution of a State*, specifically mentions going down to the mouth of the San Bernard to scavenge iron from the old shipwreck there to use in his blacksmithing business. Twentieth century archaeological records have confirmed the existence of not one but several shipwrecks at the mouth of the San Bernard, and at least two or three of them are of the approximate right vintage to be the one that brought the Karankawa his "white wife."

But who was the lady?

On December 25, 1813, the coasting-barque *Patriot* cleared Charleston harbor's bar en route up the Atlantic coast to New York. Two of her passengers were Mrs. Joseph Allston, wife of South Carolina's governor, Joseph Allston, and Governor and Mrs. Allston's infant son. The boy was being taken to New York to meet his maternal grandfather. Mrs. Allston was the former

Theodosia Burr, only daughter — and only legitimate offspring — of former vice president of the United States Aaron Burr.

When *Patriot* sailed across the bar at Charleston harbor and into the Atlantic, she also sailed out of mortal ken. From that day to this, no officially acknowledged trace of *Patriot* or any of her passengers, crew, or cargo has ever been found. In some rather questionable references, *Patriot* is listed as a "victim" of the widely publicized but mostly fictional "Bermuda Triangle."

Some thirty years after *Patriot* vanished, a rum-soaked, consumptive old derelict, dying in a Sailor's Home, "confessed" that he had been a crewman aboard *Patriot* on her final recorded voyage. So said he, there was a forecastle plot to mutiny, and as soon as *Patriot* dropped land astern, the crew captured the ship, forced all passengers and officers to walk the plank — including Theodosia Burr Allston, who died with her infant son in her arms — and then went a-pirating on the Spanish Main. For any number of reasons the story was, and is, doubted, but it is the only acknowledged indication of *Patriot*'s fate ever to surface.

Aaron Burr was definitely a "great chief." He was also, if ever a man was, badly misunderstood by his people. Joseph Allston was also a "great chief," though a lesser one than his father-in-law. Theodosia Burr Allston did, in fact, board a boat to go visit her father. The attack the lady described to the Karankawa was about three years before the Great Storm, or just about 1813, which corresponds with the date of *Patriot*'s last voyage.

Piracy was a fact of life throughout the Caribbean and up the East Coast until the early 1830s. Even as the lady was telling her tale and dying, one of the largest nests of pirates ever to assemble on the North American continent was trying to put its house back in order just a few miles east of where she lay on the sand.

The tale of the beautiful and aristocratic maiden kidnapped and held as a love slave by a pirate chief is a fictional motif about as old as storytelling. In most such tales, the maiden usually manages, at least in Victorian romances, either to be rescued by her handsome betrothed before the "fate worse than death" befalls her, or she manages to reform her pirate admirer, who is, of course, the once-penniless-but-now-recognized-as-legitimate-but-he-doesn't-know-it-yet sole heir to an ancient

and wealthy peerage. The pirate, true to his aristocratic heritage, refuses to "extract from her the ultimate sacrifice a
maiden may make, save her own life" without recanting his evil
ways so he will be worthy of taking her hand in marriage. If
such stories don't predate Jason's chase after the Golden Fleece,
they don't postdate it long.

The truth is, there were any number of women captured and
held as slaves aboard pirate ships and their lot was not a
romantic one. They were repeatedly and viciously raped, often
beaten, fed scraps and forced to sleep on rags, and in all
likelihood — though even those few official accounts which
acknowledge the existence of such slaves forbear to mention it
— kept naked and chained as was our mystery lady. Should the
ship go down, they were usually left to drown aboard her. They
were no doubt infected with every venereal disease known to
medical science and some neither the early 19th century nor
even we today have identified. For this young woman to have
survived for three years in those conditions indicates she was a
woman of rare courage and fortitude. And if she was, in fact,
Theodosia Burr Allston, and if she inherited her father's character, that probably described her very well.

No, the life of a female slave aboard a pirate ship was
certainly no bed of roses — and no romance novel, either — but
such things did, by documentation, happen. There could very
well have been not just one female slave aboard one pirate ship,
but dozens of such women aboard the many pirate ships then
plying the Caribbean and Gulf of Mexico. We know of the fate
of but a few, and this one only by chance.

What about the treasure? The Indian, remember, said that
there was a great treasure aboard the ship, but, having no use
for white man's treasure himself, he did not hunt for it. Has that
ever surfaced?

Some of the treasure, at least, may very well have been found.
In the 1840s, after Texas became a Republic, yet another peculiar
character showed up in the Austin's Colony area. He was an
old, grey-haired, grey-bearded man dressed in rags and skins.
He also carried a bag of gold coins.

In that bag were coins of many nations, the very sort of thing you'd expect to come from a pirate ship's treasure-trove. They were all dated before 1816. According to his tale, he'd been a prisoner aboard a pirate ship in the Gulf of Mexico when the Great Storm hit. His ship was driven ashore at the mouth of the San Bernard, and her keel was broken. Everybody aboard, except him, of course, was killed. After the storm died and the waters went down, he fled into the swamps. Over the years, he'd gone back and forth to the ship, systematically looting her of her treasure and anything else he could use.

Shortly after he appeared, the old man died, which may have been as a result of old age and whatever, since he'd been hiding out in the swamps, by his own statement, for at least a quarter of a century; or it may have been, as has been rumored from time to time, as a direct consequence of his refusal to show several local hardcases where he'd hidden the rest of the treasure. At any rate, the archaeologists didn't find any huge golden treasure on any of the various ships they identified at the mouth of the San Bernard.

The only thing missing here is the locket, and it's gone for good. It was still on the neck of the Indian brave when the Karankawa tribe left the Texas coast and themselves vanished from mortal ken. How that happened is the subject of several stories, one of which Noah Smithwick tells. According to his story, the Karankawa, not understanding the war between the Mexicans and the Texicans, greeted a group of Mexican soldiers by telling them that they were great friends of the Texicans. The survivors then licked their wounds, and, chancing upon another group of white men greeted them with "Viva Mejico!" This time it was Texicans they met, and this time there were no survivors.

A more likely tale has them being invited to leave the Texas coast for healthier climes, the invitation being attached to the muzzles of any number of long rifles. In Frank Cheavens' novel of the Karankawa, *Arrow Lie Still*, we are given a last view of the few surviving Karankawa as they paddle their dugout canoes dispiritedly down the coast while a storm rises above the Gulf and the onshore wind freshens. We are given to understand that they all drowned.

Truth told, we really don't know what happened to the Karankawa, except that by about 1838 they — and the brave with the necklace — were gone and nobody knows for sure where. Without the one missing piece — the necklace — it will be almost impossible to prove that the Mystery Lady of the San Bernard was, in fact, Mrs. Theodosia Burr Allston, only daughter of Aaron Burr, and the other end of what our cousins in South Carolina refer to as The Mystery of the Missing First Lady. Make up your own mind.

If you have or know of any information relating to the Karankawa Indians, the missing Theodosia Burr Allston, or the lost locket, please contact the author at Wordware Publishing, Inc.

The Disappearing Declarations
by Wallace O. Chariton

On March 1, 1836, the icy winds of a fresh norther howled through Washington, Texas, a crude, insignificant frontier settlement located near a gentle bend of the Brazos River. Down on Main Street, near the intersection of Ferry Street, elected delegates to the Texas constitutional convention gathered inside a newly constructed but unfinished clapboard building that had been rented for three months from Noah T. Byars and Peter M. Mercer. In less trying times the Texans might have postponed their convention until the weather faired up but there was no thought of delay; it was time for Texas to move forward and form a new, independent government. In an effort to combat the frigid conditions, the delegates nailed thin pieces of cloth over the empty window holes and then huddled beneath quilts and buffalo-hide lap robes while they worked.

After the election of permanent officers, the first order of business was the appointment of a committee to write a declaration of independence from Mexican rule. The committee consisted of James Gaines, Edward Conrad, Collin McKinney, Bailey Hardeman, and George C. Childress who was named chairman. Once appointed, the members withdrew to begin what was anticipated to be a long task. Incredibly, in less than

24 hours, the special committee reported back to the convention with a first draft of the declaration.

The swiftness with which those early Texans were able to complete such an important document has been a point of some concern to students of Texas history for generations. How was it possible, those historians wonder, that such a history-making document could have been written in barely over twelve hours? Most historians eventually come to the conclusion that all, or at least a substantial portion, of the declaration had been completed before the convention ever convened. Although the author of the document was never specifically identified, it is generally believed that George Childress did most of the actual writing and, since he arrived in Texas just in time for the convention, he probably did most of his composition work either in Tennessee or while en route. Once the declaration committee was formed, George simply presented his document which was then reviewed and perhaps annotated to some small extent and subsequently offered to the full convention.

If that is what happened, and it almost certainly is, then George did his work well. After the presentation of the document, only Sam Houston offered any sort of rhetorical speech and it was Houston's humble opinion that the declaration of independence ought to be accepted as presented, engrossed, and officially signed. While Houston's motive may have simply been to put the matter at rest quickly, he may have had other more personal reasons. March 2, 1836, the day the declaration was presented and the day Houston urged it be immediately accepted as written, was also Houston's forty-third birthday. What better present for a revolutionary soldier than to have a declaration of independence issued on the anniversary of his birth? And ol' Sam got his wish, almost. While Texans do celebrate March 2 as Independence Day, they are technically incorrect and twenty-four hours too early because only a verbal declaration was made on that day.

The convention delegates, following Sam Houston's lead, did vote to accept the declaration on March 2 and they ordered clerks to prepare an original, final version of the document. Unfortunately, the final version was found to be somewhat lacking in

The famous building where the original Texas Declaration of Independence was signed in 1836.

clerical sufficiency, perhaps owing to the shakiness of the hand holding the quill and trying to write in subfreezing temperatures. The copies were so bad they could hardly be read, so the delegates decided they should not affix signatures to a document with such historical significance until it was absolutely letter perfect. The clerks were sent back to the writing table with instructions to correct the errors and to make five additional good copies. It must have been a long, cold night for the clerks.

On March 3, 1836, the final and correct documents were complete and the fifty-two delegates reassembled to formally sign the Texas Declaration of Independence. Express riders were then dispatched to carry copies of the declaration to San Antonio de Bexar, Goliad, Nacogdoches, Brazoria, and San Felipe. The convention delegates also requested that 1,000 copies of the document be printed in handbill form for distribution throughout Texas and the world.

Once the chore of declaring independence was out of the way, there still remained the complicated matter of a constitution for the newly formed, self-proclaimed Republic. Before the delegates could get back to work, however, a dirt crusted, exhausted express rider on a well-lathered mustang galloped into Washington carrying dramatic news from Lieutenant Colonel William B. Travis. The much feared Mexican army invasion, not expected until the grasses were up in the spring, had already begun. The Alamo was under siege.

There was some sentiment among the delegates to adjourn the convention immediately so any man able to carry a rifle could fly to the aid of Travis and the boys. But clearer heads, Sam Houston's for one, prevailed and work on the vital constitution continued, albeit at a somewhat excited pace for fear the Mexican army might soon be marching on Washington. Seven additional delegates arrived, presented their credentials, and were seated in the convention. Each new arrival asked for and received permission to add his signature to the most important document in Texas history.

On March 17, 1836, the deed was done; the Republic of Texas had a new constitution. Although the convention hall had been leased for three months, incredibly the work had been completed in eighteen days, which is perhaps testimony to how fast politicians can work when they think an enemy might attack at any moment. By the nineteenth day, most of the men in Washington were preparing to either join the army or to join other colonists that were fleeing the expected enemy advance in what has become known as the "runaway scrape." When the delegates departed Washington, they left behind one of the more perplexing mysteries in all the pages of Texas history: What happened to the copies of the Declaration of Independence?

Much of what we know about the signing of the Texas Declaration of Independence is courtesy of William Fairfax Gray, a traveler and land speculator from Virginia who happened to be in Washington, Texas during the convention of 1836. Gray kept careful notes on the proceedings in his personal diary and his keen eye for detail has helped in the recreation of the events of the day. Thanks to Gray we know the original declarations were not correct and had to be redone, that five copies were made, that the signing took place on March 3 and not March 2, and that express riders left on March 3 to carry the copies to various points around the colony. But as valuable as Gray's notes are, they stop far short of explaining what might have happened to the missing copies.

Only one complete copy of the signed Texas Declaration of Independence is known to exist but even the circumstances surrounding that one known copy are somewhat mysterious. And if it were not for a sharp-eyed Texan named Seth Shepard, who served as an associate justice of the Court of Appeals for the District of Columbia, we might not even have one copy.

As late as 1896, it was generally believed that the original copy of the Declaration of Independence went up in smoke when the Texas state capitol burned in 1881. But then in the summer of 1896, Seth Shepard was asked to write the introduction for *A Comprehensive History of Texas* which was edited by Dudley G. Wooten. A Washington D.C. clerk named William H. Phillips mentioned to Shepard that he had seen what appeared to be a copy of the Texas Declaration of Independence in the files of the United States Secretary of State. Shepard

The photographs above and on the opposite page are of the actual signed copy of the Texas Declaration of Independence, now in the Texas State

Archives in Austin. It is assumed that the missing four copies were also signed.

investigated and sure enough, there in a dusty old Washington file was a fully signed copy of the declaration.

Shepard asked Secretary of State Richard Olney for permission to return the document to Texas and the secretary agreed so long as the governor of Texas would issue a receipt. Governor Charles A. Culberson agreed and after an absence of 60 years, the Declaration of Independence came home to Texas. Although the mystery of where the declaration had been all that time was resolved, there still remained the question of how the document got to Washington in the first place.

On the back of the declaration discovered in the nation's capitol was the notation, "Left at the Department of State May 28, 1836, by Mr. Wharton. The original." While such a notation might seem conclusive, there was still a problem. Although William H. Wharton was in Washington on the date indicated, he along with Stephen F. Austin and Branch T. Archer were serving as commissioners from Texas and they had been traveling since December of 1835, so Wharton could not possibly have had the declaration, unless someone gave it to him.

The logical candidate is George Childress, who was commissioned on March 19, 1836 to go to Washington to encourage the United States to formally recognize the existence of the Republic of Texas. It has been speculated that Childress gave the declaration to Wharton for presentation to the secretary of state or perhaps that Childress accompanied Wharton for the presentation and that a clerk simply noted Wharton's name.

A problem with that scenario is that, while in Washington, Childress also published a 24-page handbook containing the Texas Constitution and Declaration of Independence. Apparently Childress used one of the printed handbills for his declaration information because the booklet did not contain all the names of the original signers. It has been argued that if he carried the original, he surely would have included all the names in his publication. Perhaps not. Childress almost certainly carried some of the handbill versions of the declaration to use as working copies. In all probability, he relinquished the original and then relied on the printed copies for any further purpose.

The Washington copy of the declaration also contributed to another Texas legend that was incorrect. When Shepard notified Dudley Wooten that a true copy of the declaration had been discovered, Wooten naturally wanted to include a reproduction in *A Comprehensive History of Texas*. Wooten obtained a photo-engraving of the actual document that was thought to be a complete facsimile copy of the original. Regrettably, someone, probably the photoengraver, omitted the name of Asa Brigham, one of the signers. As a result the Wooten "true" copy of the declaration contained the names of fifty-eight signers rather than the correct fifty-nine names. Generations of Texans came to believe that only fifty-eight men had actually signed the document.

Regardless of the circumstances, one precious copy of the declaration was found in Washington and ultimately returned to Texas. But there are few clues to help solve the mystery of what happened to the other copies.

A perplexing part of the mystery is why didn't the Texas government officials retain one fully signed, original copy for their files? Or if they did retain such a copy, and logic dictates that they must have, what happened to it? There is no specific record indicating such a document was ever captured by the Mexican army or destroyed, unless the true original copy was consumed by the flames of the 1881 fire as many believe.

There is no substantiation that a copy of the Declaration of Independence was in Texas between 1836 and 1896. In fact, there is some evidence indicating such was not the case. In 1842 the *Telegraph and Texas Register* published a list of the signers of the declaration which was provided by Jesse Grimes, one of the participants. Unfortunately, the list is incomplete and inaccurate, so the question becomes, if Texas officials had a copy of the document, why would a newspaper have to rely on an individual for information? Or if an original copy was available, at the very least, why didn't someone correct the editors of the *Telegraph*? It never happened.

An interesting point about the "original" copy is that William F. Gray, in his diary, clearly stated that a "copy" was to be forwarded to Washington. And yet the copy ultimately discovered in the nation's capitol is marked "The original." The

Washington document did contain all fifty-nine signatures, which means it was not one of the copies sent out on March 3 because only fifty-two delegates were present on that date. But would the government officials have truly sent the original to the United States and either retained a copy or nothing at all? It would seem more likely that the true original was retained in Texas and subsequently lost or destroyed. As incredible as it seems, the actual signed, original Declaration of Independence may, indeed, have been stored away in some old dusty Austin file and cremated in the Capitol fire. We will probably never know the truth with any degree of certainty.

Perhaps the most intriguing part of the declaration mystery is what happened to the five copies that were distributed throughout the colony? Since the avowed purpose of the copies was to allow for more rapid dissemination of the great news, how is it possible that all five copies vanished?

We know one copy went to Gail Borden, Jr., then editor of the *Telegraph and Texas Register* at San Felipe. Borden complied with the request from the convention delegates and published the document in its entirety in the *Telegraph* and then printed 200 broadsides for distribution throughout the colonies. Unfortunately, Borden's typesetter committed a dramatic error, when the handbills were printed, by omitting the names of George C. Childress and Sterling C. Robertson. Although the names were correct in the version done for the newspaper, the handbills that were widely distributed did not contain the name of the man thought responsible for authoring the document.

A side note is that Borden only printed 200 broadsides when the convention delegates had requested 1,000. That might indicate that each of the five locations receiving the declaration copies were to print 200 of the handbills so the distribution could be accomplished quicker than if Borden produced all 1,000 in San Felipe and then expressed them to other locations. There is, however, no evidence indicating that other locations actually printed the handbills.

Another mystery about the copies is whether or not they were actually signed by the delegates. Since Borden published a list of all the signers that were present in Washington on

March 3, he must have been provided the names. That means that either each delegate signed all the copies or some clerk prepared five separate lists of names. It would seem a good bet that each delegate signed all the copies because that would have been faster, and a fully signed original document might have

UNANIMOUS

DECLARATION OF INDEPENDENCE,

BY THE

DELEGATES OF THE PEOPLE OF TEXAS,

IN GENERAL CONVENTION,

AT THE TOWN OF WASHINGTON,

ON THE SECOND DAY OF MARCH, 1836.

Reproduction of the printed version of the Declaration of Independence that was produced by Gail Borden in 1836. Of the 200 original copies, less than seven authentic originals are known to exist.

been deemed necessary to convince the people of Texas that independence had, in fact, been declared. If that assumption is correct, then it means, incredibly, that five or six fully signed, original copies of the declaration simply vanished.

The disposition of Gail Borden's copy is possibly the most puzzling. Borden was in Texas and active in the affairs of the Republic for several years following the revolution. However, while he was careful to preserve many valuable Texas documents, a copy of the declaration was never found among his personal papers. The fact that Borden did not, apparently, retain his copy may be an indication that the copies were not actually signed by the delegates and thus were thought to be useless. Unless one of the copies is discovered, we may never know the truth.

As to what happened to the other copies, it is almost anyone's guess. One copy was believed sent to Colonel James W. Fannin at Goliad. In some of the surviving documents written by soldiers in Fannin's command can be found references to an express rider arriving with the news that independence had been declared. Unfortunately, none of the references specifically mention a copy of the actual declaration. However, if the intention of the convention delegates was to remove any doubt about the declaration, they surely would have enclosed a signed document. If that happened, it is not hard to surmise what might have happened to Fannin's copy.

Within two weeks after the fall of the Alamo, Fannin and his army of 400 plus men were on a retrograde movement heading east from Goliad according to the orders of Sam Houston. Following a short march, the Goliad army was discovered and surrounded by the enemy. One day later, after some brief but spirited fighting, Fannin decided he had no choice but to surrender. Given the fact that Fannin had time to plan his actions, he almost certainly would have surmised that the enemy would be greatly angered to discover a copy of a declaration of independence. It seems consistent with frontier military logic that if Fannin had such a copy, he would have destroyed it rather than risk the document falling into enemy hands. It must be noted, however, that there is absolutely no record to indicate Fannin did have and subsequently destroyed a copy of the declaration. All we know with any degree of certainty is that the convention delegates planned to send a copy to Goliad and express riders left carrying the documents. After that, everything is pure speculation.

If in fact other copies of the declaration were dispatched to Brazoria and Nacogdoches, there is no surviving record to authenticate that the information was published or that the handbills were produced as requested. It is possible that the information was published and that no copy of the newspapers containing the information survived. It is also possible that no handbills were produced in either location for fear the government would not be able to pay the printing bill. There is no information whatsoever to indicate what might have happened to the original copies of the declaration.

There is an indication that one copy was supposed to be sent to San Antonio de Bexar. Unfortunately, if an express rider did leave Washington on March 3 with a copy of the declaration for Travis and the boys at the Alamo, that rider would have arrived after the fall and there is no way to know what might have happened to the declaration copy. On the other hand, since the delegates knew the Alamo was under siege, they may have elected to send the fifth copy to some other destination. Either way, the copy is missing.

The declaration of independence mysteries don't end with the handwritten, signed copies of the original. There is also the matter of what happened to the 200 broadsides printed by Gail Borden. Almost certainly, many of the handbills were posted for Texans to read and subsequently fell victim to the elements. But there is evidence that many, if not most, of the documents ended up in private hands, and yet only about five copies, not counting the rash of forgeries that recently were unleashed on the buying public, are known to have survived.

The surprising thing about the low survival rate of the handbills is that the documents surely would have been cherished by whomever got possession of them. We know some copies were mailed or carried out of Texas and were perhaps passed down through families, not cared for properly, and finally rotted away. Other copies may very well have met a tragic end in some flood, fire, or tornado. But given the importance of the declaration and the fact that so many old documents were carefully preserved, it is hard to believe that 95 percent of the copies would have simply vanished. Or did they?

At this late date, there is no trail to follow that might lead to any of the missing declaration copies. Still, it's hard not to speculate that somewhere out there a faded, torn, probably water stained, but nonetheless original signed copy of the Texas Declaration of Independence, or at least an original printed version, might be lurking in the lining of a forgotten old trunk or tucked safely inside a family Bible. Stranger things have happened in this world, and if such a copy still exists, a handsome reward surely awaits the finder. An authentic copy of the printed handbill recently sold for a staggering $75,000. As large a sum as that seems, it would probably be about the amount of tax on the value of an authentic, original signed copy of the Texas Declaration of Independence. While the odds grow smaller each day that any such copy will ever be located, it is always fun to play what if. It is easy to imagine that if an original signed copy were located, its value would probably exceed the total budget of Texas during the entire nine-year period of the Republic. But if you happen to be the finder, don't quit your day job too quickly.

If a supposed copy of the declaration were to turn up, either a handwritten original or one of Borden's printed copies, the first order of business would be to prove authenticity. The burden and cost of establishing that proof would rest squarely with the finder and it won't be a simple or inexpensive proposition. Copies of famous Texas documents have been proven in the past to be skillful forgeries, so something as dramatic as a Declaration of Independence would certainly require authentication from document experts, who do not work cheap.

Even if the found declaration passed all the tests to verify age of paper, type of ink, handwriting, and provenance, any prospective buyer would probably require an ion-diffusion test which verifies, within about fifteen years, when ink was actually placed on paper. Such a test, which can cost $5,000 and up, is unbeatable by the forger and would, therefore, either make or break the document and possibly the finder's pocketbook. Perhaps the ultimate irony would be if someone found a declaration copy and then did not have an idle five grand to risk trying to prove beyond the shadows of doubt that it was one of the missing authentic, signed copies of the greatest document ever written in Texas.

Since copies of the declaration, either the handwritten or printed versions, might be considered treasures, there is some good and bad news for potential treasure hunters. The good news is that multiple copies were produced, so the odds that one or more survived is greater than if only one document was missing. At least four and probably five copies of the handwritten version are still mysteriously missing and perhaps 195 copies of the printed version are unaccounted for. Such numbers might be considered a bright spot in the mystery.

The bad news is that a lot of people have been looking for the missing copies of the Declaration of Independence for many years with few results. In the 1930s and 1940s, a New Jersey oilman named Thomas Streeter spent a considerable amount of time looking for old Texas documents and despite his efforts, he was only able to find one copy of the printed version and no trace of any handwritten copy. Since the early 1960s, collecting Texanna has been a popular sport in Texas and a lot of old documents have been found, but again that harvest has yielded only one additional copy of the printed version.

For Texans, the irony of the lost declarations may be that any remaining copies of the rare documents, especially the printed versions, will not be found in the Lone Star State. It is certain that some of the printed copies were sent back to the United States, and today some few remaining copies may be in private collections with the owner not even realizing the value or importance of the old document.

Regardless of what actually happened in 1836, document collectors and dealers will continue the search. Unfortunately, in view of the lack of results to date, the mystery of the disappearing declarations will probably continue to be unsolved.

If you have any information about what might have happened to the lost copies of the declarations, please contact the author at Wordware Publishing, Inc.

The Lost Papers of the Alamo

By Wallace O. Chariton

It's a story almost as old as Texas itself. On February 23, 1836, approximately 2,000 Mexican troops under the direction of General Antonio Lopez de Santa Anna marched triumphantly into the small village of San Antonio de Bexar. The avowed purpose of Santa Anna was to retake the town which his brother-in-law, Martin Perfecto de Cos, had surrendered to the upstart Texans less than three months earlier.

Opposing the Mexican force was a small band of Texas freedom fighters under the co-command of a young firebrand named William Barrett Travis and a grizzled old veteran and living legend named James Bowie. Because the enemy force had not been expected for several weeks, the Texans were caught completely off guard and had no choice but to fall back into the confines of mission San Antonio de Valero, an ancient old Spanish mission more commonly referred to as the Alamo. The Texans abandoned the village which Santa Anna's forces promptly retook without firing a shot. They would not, however, retake the Alamo quite so easily.

Santa Anna immediately called for the Texans to surrender "at discretion," which meant the men in the Alamo would be at the mercy of the ruthless Mexican dictator. Suspecting that such surrender terms would result in the immediate execution of all his men, Travis opted to stand and fight, a decision which was communicated to the Mexican general with a single shot from a huge eighteen-pound cannon mounted on the Alamo walls. That single shot also signaled the beginning of the siege of the Alamo.

For thirteen days — easily the most famous thirteen-day period in Texas history — Travis and the boys held out against overwhelming odds. The Mexican artillery pounded away at the ancient mission and at times it seemed as if it were raining cannon balls. But the old mission, which was anything but a strong fortress, held fast and amazingly not a single Texas soldier and only one horse was injured by the artillery fire.

Inside the Alamo, the Texans clung to the faint hope that reinforcements would surely arrive at any moment. Travis, who assumed sole command when Bowie's health failed, sent out repeated messengers with urgent pleas for assistance in the form of men and supplies. For the most part, those pleas fell on deaf ears and only a small force of thirty-two men from Gonzales came to the aid of the Alamo. Travis' total force of Texans amounted to something close to two hundred men; the Mexican force was at least ten times larger. But still the Texans vowed the price of retaking the Alamo would be so dear that even if Santa Anna was successful, the victory would seem more a defeat.

Unlike his enemy in the Alamo, Santa Anna did receive reinforcement. On March 3, 1836, the same day Travis received word that no help was coming, almost a thousand new Mexican troops arrived along with more and larger cannons with which to continue the relentless pounding of the mission. The addition of the new firepower and the fact that even more artillery was expected within the week might have given Santa Anna the means to simply blow apart the Alamo without ever attacking. But for Santa Anna, there could be no glory without blood and there could be no blood without a fight.

Just before dawn on Palm Sunday, March 6, 1836, more than 1,800 Mexican troops attacked the Alamo from four sides. Although the Texans fought valiantly, killing or wounding more than 600 of the enemy, the outcome was perhaps inevitable from the moment the first shot was fired that chilly morning. By the first light of day, the incredibly fierce battle was concluded and all the Texans except a precious few were dead. Santa Anna had his victory and his revenge but the price paid did, indeed, make the victory seem more a defeat.

In the decades that have come and gone since that Sunday morning, the Alamo saga has been one of the most studied and written about events in all of American history. Even today, that old mission stands stately in the heart of modern San Antonio casting its mysterious spell over all who enter. For Texans and lovers of freedom around the world, the Alamo grounds are hallowed. For researchers and writers, the Alamo saga is seemingly a bottomless pit of mystery and intrigue. A great deal is known about what happened during the thirteen days to glory and yet there are so many unanswered questions, so many mysteries yet to be solved, that the Alamo will be fodder for the creative mind for generations to come.

One reason the Alamo is such an excellent target for the writer's pen is that the story is never ending. There always seems to be some new twist to the original drama or some different angle to be followed that it is, incredibly, still possible to find many Alamo subjects to explore. A good example might be the haunting question of what happened to the papers of the Alamo? It is certainly not a new question, but rather one that has generally been ignored by the historical community, perhaps because so little is known of the papers. And it appears there is not much of a chance that the knowledge will ever be increased.

As soon as the choking smoke of battle began to dissipate and the Mexican survivors managed to clear the stinging smoke from their eyes, they immediately ransacked the entire Alamo mission, looking for valuables of any sort. They also were looking for any documents that might have some intelligence value. Since the body of every Texan was searched and stripped before being tossed unceremoniously onto Santa Anna's funeral pyre, any documents found, as well as any meager personal belongings, would have been retrieved. The personal quarters of the Texans, including those of William B. Travis;

James Bowie; Amos Pollard, the garrison physician; and Green B. Jameson, the post engineer, were also quickly searched. Any official documents found most certainly would have been retrieved for Santa Anna's personal inspection. The two questions that remain more than 150 years later are: What was included among those papers and what happened to them?

These early drawings depict the Alamo as it appeared shortly after the fall.

Obviously, any answer to the question of what was included among the papers of the Alamo must be pure speculation, since the papers have been missing from the moment the Mexicans overran the mission. However, it is possible to make reasonably educated guesses based on known facts and on the known traits of some of the men who died fighting for Texas independence.

In the case of William B. Travis, we know he was well read and had something of a penchant for writing. For several months, between 1833 and 1834, he kept a detailed personal diary of his activities as well as his actions as a practicing attorney in Texas. He also kept an account book during January and February of 1836 in which he noted expenses made on behalf of the troops in the Alamo. Young Travis was also fond of writing long, fairly detailed letters, several of which were sent out from the Alamo by messenger during the siege. One of Travis' letters, his February 24, 1836 appeal for help that was addressed "To the People of Texas and all Americans *in the World*," is considered by many to be the most patriotic document in American history.

Given his passion for writing, it does not seem totally out of the question to hypothesize that perhaps Travis kept a personal diary of the events that occurred during the siege. If not an actual diary, then perhaps he kept notes, observations, or even fragments of letters he intended to complete if afforded the opportunity. We know the young commander had at least some sense of the historic situation he was in, and it seems entirely possible, and in tune with his character, that he might have wanted some personal records for future reference.

Considering that Travis was in command, there is also the strong probability that he maintained some sort of muster roll with full name, rank, and place of origin of each of the troops in the Alamo garrison. One such muster role was completed by Travis' predecessor, Colonel James C. Neill, and sent to the provincial governor of Texas in January, 1836. Since service in the Texas army entitled soldiers to a land bounty, it would have actually been very strange if Travis, or at least one of his aides, did not maintain some sort of records that could be used to verify service. If such a muster roll could be found, all the questions about who was actually in the Alamo at the time of the fall might finally be answered. Unfortunately, such a document has never been found and there is no positive record that such ever existed. Only logic and common sense seem to indicate a strong likelihood that someone had a record of the men.

Aside from his personal writings, Travis would also have been in charge of any official documents maintained in the garrison. What such a cache of memorandums might include is anyone's guess. We do know, however, that in 1836 Texas, there was no such things as carbon paper or copy machines so the accepted practice was to make a duplicate copy of all correspondence for the local files. If that practice was followed in the Alamo, and it almost certainly was as long as the paper supplies held out, then the official document file would have contained copies of all Alamo correspondence. Of course, if the original was sent out of the Alamo, then there is the strong possibility that it survived. But there is also irrefutable evidence of other documents having been sent out of the Alamo and yet the original is missing. Because the Alamo files are also missing, we have no way to know how many other potentially vital document copies are lost.

There was another Alamo defender who, like Travis, had a knack for writing. He was the famous frontiersman and former U.S. congressman, David Crockett. Davy was so famous, in fact, that shortly after the fall his supposed diary with entries dated right up to the moment of his death appeared in print. As the story went, a Mexican soldier picked up the diary after the final battle and it was later purchased for publication. Although entertaining and surprisingly accurate, scholars generally discount the possibility that it might be genuine. But since Crockett did like to write, there is always the chance that he did keep a genuine written record of his Alamo exploits and that it may one day be discovered.

After Travis and Crockett, the one man who can reasonably be assumed to have had documents was the garrison engineer Green B. Jameson. Based on records that have survived, we know Jameson wrote several long and detailed memorandums. And, being the engineer, he also completed many drawings of the Alamo grounds. He almost certainly would have had notes and sketches from which the drawings were made and he surely would have kept copies to refer back to when needed. There is undeniable evidence that at least one set of documents he sent out of the Alamo was lost, so his copies, if they do exist, will be the only record of what he said and what he drew.

Another possible source of Alamo documents is often over-looked by historians. We know that at least three men, James Butler Bonham, John Smith, and Albert Martin, were sent out of the fortress as messengers and returned. Martin returned with the Gonzales volunteers and died in the fall. Smith left, returned, and left again carrying Travis' last call for aid. He was, at the time of the final attack, on his way back with a small band of volunteers. As for Bonham, he may have left and returned twice, but at least he did go back into the mission on March 3 and there is now evidence that he carried a special letter to Travis which was certainly inside the fort when it fell. Since Bonham carried a special dispatch, there is always the possibility that Smith, Martin, and other messengers that might have gone out and returned were also carrying either official documents or personal letters.

Other than official papers relating to military matters, there is also the strong likelihood that some, possibly most, of the individual soldiers carried personal documents of one sort or another. Mail service in Texas during the war was something less than reliable, so soldiers with letters from back home would have held onto the precious documents for as long as possible. While on the surface it might seem far fetched to believe that the Mexican soldiers would have cared about personal letters, the truth is Santa Anna was specifically looking for evidence that soldiers from the United States were aiding the Texans in the struggle for independence. If personal letters written from the United States of the North were found, they might have been kept as possible supporting evidence for the general's theory.

It seems highly probable that there were a significant number of historically important documents inside the Alamo com-pound at the moment the mission was overrun. If that supposition is correct, the question then becomes, what happened to the papers?

From the standpoint of military logic, it might be assumed that Travis, as commander, would not have wanted any sensitive documents to fall into the hands of the enemy and thus, as the end drew near, he would have cremated the priceless pieces of paper. Or maybe he didn't.

On February 23, the Mexicans were first spotted in a field about eight miles below San Antonio. Although close, the distance did allow time for the Texans to forage through the town looking for stray supplies and still manage to get inside the Alamo before the enemy arrived. During that time Travis would have had the opportunity to destroy all documents if he were of that mind set. He apparently was not. When the Mexicans did finally arrive, they immediately searched the town and, strangely enough, they discovered some documents. Santa Anna's secretary, Juan Nepomuceno Almonte, noted in his diary entry for that date that "many curious papers were found." Much to the chagrin of Alamo historians, the papers were never identified and there is no indication as to why they were labeled "curious." There is always the chance that those papers were the official documents of the garrison and that Travis left them behind in his haste to relocate to the mission.

At any time during the thirteen-day siege, Travis might have opted to destroy any documents inside the fortress, thus robbing historians of the information. However, since Travis apparently expected some sort of reinforcements up until virtually the last moment, he actually would not have had a motive to burn the papers. It seems doubtful that he would have destroyed anything until he was sure the end was near, and that revelation did not come until 5:30 on the morning of March 6 when the assault began. Even though Travis may have suspected the attack would occur that day, he probably did not expect it until after the break of day. Since Santa Anna had his men charge before first light, the Texans were caught off guard and had to scramble to the walls. It would seem to follow that even if Travis wanted to destroy the papers, he suddenly had more important matters to attend to, namely 1,800 charging, angry Mexicans.

Since, by most accounts, Travis was one of the first to fall, it appears doubtful he had time to destroy evidence. A more plausible supposition is that any documents inside the Alamo were captured along with the fortress itself and there is some proof that is exactly what happened.

On March 31, 1836, three weeks after the fall of the Alamo, a Mexican broadside appeared containing the Spanish translation of a most unusual letter. The original document was written in Gonzales, Texas on March 1, 1836 by R. M. "Three Legged Willie" Williamson, who was a noted Texas attorney. The letter, addressed to Williamson's close friend and fellow lawyer, William B. Travis, was carried into the Alamo on March 3 by another attorney, James Butler Bonham.

In the text of the letter, Williamson assured Travis that more than 300 reinforcements were on the way and he pleaded "For God's sake hold out until we can assist you." As history shows, the supposed three hundred volunteers never made it to San Antonio, if they existed in the first place.

Of more importance to the case at hand was the statement, "As to the other letter of the same date, let it pass, you will know what it meant: if the multitude gets hold of it, let them figure it out." Williamson seems to be saying he had written another letter to Travis on March 1 and it was apparently somewhat inflammatory. Whether or not Bonham also carried the other note to Travis is unknown. However, Williamson does say, "I remit to you with major Bonham a communication from the interim governor." That seems conclusive proof that Bonham carried at least two pieces of mail, and yet no record exists of any official correspondence from the governor to Travis, which perhaps means that the governor's letter was highly personal. What potentially valuable information that letter contained has never been discovered.

The significance of the Williamson letter, other than to illustrate that the Alamo messengers did carry dispatches, is that this particular letter was in the Alamo when it fell and yet three weeks later the original was in Mexico where it was translated and printed in broadside format. Is it possible that only one letter was found? Very doubtful, would be the reply from most historians, especially since the printed broadside specifically mentioned at least one and probably two other documents that almost certainly were captured.

Skeptics might counter with a question about why, if other letters were captured, was only this one printed as a broadside. One possible explanation might be that Santa Anna himself ordered the letter published to cover up a glaring mistake. In his official report of the battle of the Alamo, written at about 8:00 on the morning of the final assault, the general boldly announced that about 600 (three times the actual amount) Texans had been killed. He also drastically understated his estimate of Mexican casualties. Unfortunately, the general's efforts to make the battle look more meaningful was somewhat usurped by a few of his own soldiers, who apparently could count. In other reports sent back to Mexico, various other soldiers indicated that perhaps 230 or 250 Texans had been slaughtered. The general, at his scheming best, may have had the Williamson letter printed, with its reference to 300 volunteers, to discredit the body counts of his own men.

Along with the general's official report on the battle, he also sent a flag captured over the Alamo. It was the banner of the New Orleans Grays, which Santa Anna offered as proof that Americans were aiding the Texans. Although it was not specifically stated, there are many historians who believe Santa Anna also sent any captured documents back to Mexico. Even if the general himself was not responsible, the Williamson letter seems conclusive evidence that someone in the Mexican army sent documents back home. Unfortunately, that may have been the worst thing that could have happened.

Any documents sent to Mexico would have ended up in the Mexican National Archives, and frankly they would have been more accessible if they'd been deposited on the dark side of the moon. For reasons known only to Mexican authorities, the vast majority of revolution papers have never been formally declassified and thus are not available to the general public. There is no such thing as an Open Records Act south of the Rio Grande.

There have been isolated instances of researchers being allowed into the archives. At least one person was allowed to photograph the crumbling flag captured at the Alamo. The late Dr. Eugene C. Barker, one of the most noted Texas historians of all time, was allowed limited access to the archives and he was able to "find" the formal surrender terms signed by James Walker Fannin at Goliad. That particular find was somewhat of an embarrassment for the Mexican government because it had always been maintained that Fannin surrendered his men at discretion and thus Santa Anna was within his rights to order them executed. The formal surrender terms, when found, proved that Fannin and his men had been murdered in cold blood.

No researcher, Mexican or Anglo, has ever been granted permission to search the archives for lost Alamo papers. Those historians lucky enough to get a glimpse at the material in the archives have never uncovered any evidence of Alamo papers. On the other hand, they usually report that the archives are in such disarray that it is almost impossible to find anything. The suspicion of most historians is that if any Alamo papers still exist in the archives, they are rotting away in some box somewhere probably destined to never see the light of day again.

Unless some politician happens to get on the bandwagon and attempts to negotiate with the Mexican government for permission to lead an expedition into the archives, the fear that the precious Texas revolution papers locked away in the Mexican city are doomed to oblivion may well come true. Considering that the Mexican government flatly refused to allow the Alamo flag to be brought to Texas for the sesquicentennial celebration in 1986, it might even take a full-scale invasion of Mexico City to free the documents. Since that won't happen, the mystery of what information might be contained in the lost papers of the Alamo will probably, sadly enough, never be solved.

If you have any information concerning the papers that might have been in the Alamo or about any Alamo papers that may still be in Mexico City, please contact the author at Wordware Publishing, Inc.

Raiders of the Lost Archives

by Wallace O. Chariton

Archives might be called the looking glass into the past. Personal letters, official documents, rare books, broadsides, receipts, notes, photographs, maps, drawings — all are the tracks of those who have gone before us. Most people consider archives as state treasures, something to be carefully preserved so future generations can share the legacy of our forefathers. Unfortunately, most is not all.

From the earliest days of the Republic of Texas, at least some effort has been made to preserve the public and private records of what transpired. The effort, though noble, was not always successful. In the early days there was little or no protection from such things as fire, water seepage, paper eating insects, and apathy. A lot of well-intentioned people carefully stored away documents only to find out later that the paper had become so brittle that it disintegrated when touched. Even if the paper survived, the poor ink quality often caused words to fade or bleed through the paper so badly that they could not be read. Time, the elements, and crude manufacturing methods were all enemies of the records of the past.

There was also another more sinister enemy of Texas archives — the raiders. Incredibly, for generations the archive raiders had a virtual free hand to ply their dastardly trade because, while a good effort was made to preserve the documents, there was very little creativity in the security methods used to protect the materials. The prevailing attitude among librarians and archivists was that the documents and artifacts belonged to the people and they had a right to use them. Anyone who wanted to look at a particular document just had to ask. If that person wanted to steal the document, he just had to wait until no one was looking, which was often, then slip the paper into a pocket or briefcase, and walk out. The process was so simple for so many years it is almost amazing that anything is left.

One reason the open season on archives did not produce more devastating losses was that, for many years, very few people outside the libraries cared much about musty smelling, fragile old documents. Other than a relatively small number of writers, researchers, and historians, not many people even cared that there were such things as archives. That general lack of interest meant that there was very little market value for materials that are today considered priceless. Without an easy market, the thieves had little incentive to pursue their clandestine operations.

William B. Travis' famous letter from the Alamo to "The People of Texas and all Americans *in the World*" is a perfect example of lack of interest and value. Today that letter is considered by many to be the most patriotic document in American history and it would surely be worth hundreds of thousands of dollars if it were in private hands. Only a small miracle kept that from happening.

The heirloom document ended up in the possession of John G. Davidson, Travis' great-grandson. In May of 1893, Davidson fell on hard times and offered to sell the letter to the state of Texas for $250, even though he claimed he had been offered $500 by another party. Almost unbelievably, state officials hesitated and even haggled over the price. On May 24, 1893, Davidson actually lowered his price to $85, and five days later, after more deliberation, a purchase warrant was issued for the document. It may be the best bargain the state ever got, and fortunately that letter was secured so no one could steal it.

Another example of apathy toward archives on the part of early Texans is the story of Thomas Streeter, the New Jersey oilman who came to Texas often on business during the 1920s and 1930s. He became infatuated with Texas history and began collecting documents (by purchasing them rather than by stealing them) and in twenty years or so he was able to amass the largest private collection of Texanna in history. Thanks to a little research, a lot of leg work, and a fair amount of luck, Streeter was able to obtain a large number of rare, one-of-a-kind documents for his collection. Even when he could not locate an actual document, he compiled research about the contents that would later prove extremely valuable to researchers and historians.

By the mid-1950s, Streeter's health was beginning to fail and he decided to try to sell his collection to the University of Texas in Austin. UT officials passed on the offer and Streeter went looking for another buyer. In 1957 he found one, and the greatest collection of Texanna ever assembled was purchased by Yale University. Several years later, when the collection had been indexed and cataloged, the University of Texas was one of the first institutions to purchase microfilm copies.

In the early 1960s, things began to change. The state of Texas was in the beginning stages of a twenty-year period of incredible growth and prosperity. Interest in Texas artifacts began to soar, and specialty shops sprang up selling rare, unusual, and very collectible items of Texanna. Collecting Texas became a popular hobby for many and a lucrative business for some. Unfortunately, as the interest in Texanna rose, so did the values, and higher prices meant increased interest by the archive raiders.

Raiders of lost archives actually come in many varieties. Occasionally, he (or she) is nothing but a common thief bent on the personal gain received from selling documents to unsuspecting or misguided private collectors. At other times, the archive raider is the collector himself who wants to cut out the middleman. In some instances, the raider was out to get a copy of a rare printed document so he could skillfully produce forged copies and sell them as originals. Of course, there were other cases where the forger simply created a fake document and sold it as an original. No matter what the method, the forger deprived archives of scarce operating funds that could have been used for the purchase of legitimate artifacts.

Perhaps the most fiendish archive raider is, thankfully, becoming an endangered species. For a lot of years, people who collected autographs and signatures of famous persons were primarily interested only in the person's name. It has been widely speculated that some raiders appropriated precious documents and then cut off the signature for sale to a collector. The remainder of the document — the real meat — was then discarded so the theft could never be traced to the raider. No one knows how much valuable information may have been lost to such schemes, but the worst may be over. In recent years, the value of signed documents has soared far beyond that of simply a signature, so at least the material in the stolen papers is not lost forever.

While most of the archive raiders are inspired by criminal intent, some are actually acting out of ignorance. There have been many instances where archive-quality, irreplaceable material was unceremoniously pitched in some trash can to save space in a file cabinet. Old newspaper photographs have frequently been lost because someone had to make space. In 1980 one San Antonio newspaper threw away a fifty-year collection of pictures, and early in 1990 a passerby noticed several boxes full of photographs in a trash bin behind a Dallas newspaper. The public library was notified and archivists managed to get to the trash before the trash man. Several years earlier, a lady in Houston threw away three trunks full of irreplaceable material from the 1936 Texas Centennial. In that case, the trash man won.

A final class of archive raider is the person who innocently gains control of documents for whatever reason and simply neglects to return or preserve the papers. In the old days, it was common practice for original letters to be sent to newspapers and printers for reproduction and distribution. Regretably, a lot of the originals, probably including the missing copies of the

Texas Declaration of Independence discussed earlier, have vanished.

Throughout the long and colorful history of Texas, many valuable archives have disappeared for one reason or another. Sadly, most of them are probably lost forever, but there is always the chance that someone, somewhere may actually have a document or photograph or book and not fully understand its historical importance. While it would be impossible to list all such missing material in one volume, here is a potpourri of some of the more famous archive items that, one way or another, have been raided:

****

In early January of 1836, a newly appointed lieutenant colonel of the cavalry named William B. Travis was ordered to San Antonio. He was given the whopping sum of $100 with which he was supposed to outfit as many as 100 volunteers. As it turned out, $100 wouldn't even supply 30 men, much less 100.

Between January 21 and February 17, 1836, Travis carefully recorded his expenditures in a small, blank morocco-bound book that included his name. Six days after the last entry, the Mexicans arrived; thirteen days later, Travis and all the other men of the Alamo were dead. Exactly how the account book survived without falling into enemy hands is not known, but it is speculated that one of the many messengers carried the book out of the fortress a few days before the fall.

Travis' account book next surfaced in December of 1837 when John R. Jones, the executor of Travis' will, quoted from the book in a claim against the Republic of Texas for $143, the amount shown to have been spent. The account book and several related documents ended up in a single file that has vanished. In 1930 a graduate student at the University of Texas named Ruby Mixon did her thesis on Travis. Her official papers, in the Barker Texas History Center on the UT campus in Austin, contain a typed transcript of the Jones letter which includes details of the expenditures in the Travis book. Apparently the original file was gone by 1930 and since then all traces, even the copies, have vanished. If not for Ruby Mixon, we would not even know of the account book. Because the book is missing, we also do not know what other information it might contain. Jones was, after all, only interested in expenditures so he might very well have neglected to mention any sort of diary entries that could have been included. Unless the book is recovered, we may never know what Travis really had to say.

****

Another potentially important Travis document is missing and in this case little is known about the contents. In 1856 a man named Henderson Yoakum completed a two-volume history of Texas which covered the period from the first settlement in 1685 to annexation into the United States in 1845. On page 59 of volume two, Yoakum briefly references a letter written from Travis to Sam Houston. Supposedly, Travis talked of the militia not being prepared to garrison a town and that money would be required to support a regular army.

The sketchy details provided by Yoakum are intriguing to many historians. In seems that Travis was against using volunteers and local militia to defend towns and he may very well have included some of his reasoning as a way of explanation. If the entire letter was available, it might be one of the most historically important letters of the Alamo period. We know Travis did not want to go to San Antonio, and the letter cited by Yoakum might offer more clues as to why he did not want to make that trip.

The mention by Yoakum is all that is known of the letter. We do not know if the document was a part of any official collection or if it was in private hands. All we can be sure of is that Yoakum saw the letter in 1856. What happened to it after that remains a mystery.

****

And there is one more Travis mystery. When his famous letter calling for help and pledging "victory or death" reached San

Felipe, the printing firm owned by Joseph Baker and Gail Borden was instructed to print 200 hundred copies of the message in broadside form for distribution among the people of Texas. The broadside proved so popular that several more printings were completed and a total of 1,000 copies were eventually distributed.

As popular and dramatic as the printed plea was, it would seem probable that many copies might have survived as mementos or keepsakes. It did not happen. Only two original copies of the printed version are known to have survived. One was purchased by Thomas Streeter and ended up in the Yale Library with the rest of his collection. The other known copy was in a well-known Texas library until a black-hearted thief stole it for the express purpose of making exact forged copies for sale to interested collectors.

The forgeries were of excellent quality and several prominent collectors and library archivists were taken in. Eventually, however, the scheme was uncovered and most purchasers were able to get their money back. The stolen original copy used as a model for the fakes has never been recovered.

****

Another Alamo defender, James Butler Bonham, wrote a letter to Sam Houston on the last day of 1835 recommending William S. Blount of North Carolina for a position in the Texas Calvary. The original of the letter ended up in the state archives where, in the 1920s, a typed transcript was completed. Regretably, by the 1980s both the original and the transcript had vanished. Someone probably stole the document and the copy in an effort to remove all trace that the letter ever existed. Fortunately, when the transcript was originally made, a copy was provided to the Daughters of the Republic of Texas library at the Alamo, so at least historians know what the letter contained.

There is a good possibility that the Bonham letter was stolen by someone looking only for the signature. Bonham, unlike Travis, was not prone to taking up the quill and putting words on paper. Only a very few documents are known to have been written by Bonham so his signature is extremely rare. Since his letter to Houston was not of any particular historical significance, the signature may have been removed and the letter discarded.

****

Sam Houston led the outnumbered Texas army across the plain of San Jacinto on the afternoon of April 21, 1836 in a surprise attack against Santa Anna's superior forces. In eighteen minutes, victory was won and independence from Mexican rule became a reality. During the brief battle, Sam Houston received a musket ball to the ankle and became one of few Texans to sustain a wound. Although painful, the injury was not considered life threatening, and Houston was still able to receive Santa Anna when the Mexican general was captured the following day.

Once the battle and the prisoners were secure, Houston was removed and sent to New Orleans for treatment of the gunshot wound. Upon his arrival in Louisiana, the general had the original copy of his official report on the battle given to a local newspaper to be printed and distributed. Although several copies of the printed report still exist, the original document was never seen again.

****

As the smoke began to clear from the San Jacinto battlefield, a Texas soldier named Anson Jones, a future president of the Republic, found a curious book lying on the ground. It turned out to be the private diary of Juan Nepomuceno Almonte, Santa Anna's interpreter during the war, who was captured after the battle. Almonte either lost the book while fighting or threw it away hoping it would get lost in the excitement.

Jones realized two things immediately. First, the diary was a valuable book and second, there was a possibility that other Mexican forces would soon attack. In an effort to be certain the book did not fall back into Mexican hands, Jones bundled it up and had it sent to James Gordon Bennett, then publisher of the *New York Herald*. The *Herald* was probably selected because that paper was known to be sympathetic to the Texas cause.

Bennett received the book, had it translated into English, and published the material in six parts, beginning in June of 1836. He did, however, omit some valuable information. In his book Almonte had identified by name some influential Americans who were more sympathetic to the Mexican cause than to Texas and who had apparently given aid to Mexico. Bennett believed the people were too well-known to risk using their names, so they were left out of the printed version. That omission removed any chance of learning the names because the original diary vanished. Some people believe the book was returned to Jones in Texas and then lost, but the most popular theory is that Bennett either purposely lost or destroyed the book so the names would never be disclosed. Either way, the book has been missing for more than 150 years.

****

The original copy of the Constitution of the Republic of Texas has not been seen publicly since it was hurriedly completed on March 17, 1836. At the time, the Mexican army had destroyed the Alamo garrison and was thought to be marching toward Washington on the Brazos where the constitutional convention was meeting.

As soon as the document was completed, the convention adjourned and most of the men hurried off to join the war effort. The original of the constitution was sent to Nashville, Tennessee so it could be printed and distributed well out of the reach of the Mexican army. It has never been seen since. There are some bits and pieces of a few sections of the document in the state archives but they are mostly working drafts. To construct a complete document, archivists in the 19th century had to piece the constitution together based on various newspaper reports.

The original document would not be hard to identify, so it is strange that something as obvious and important as a constitution could be lost, but that may be what happened. Some people believe the actual document was returned to Texas after the war and subsequently lost when the state capitol burned in 1881. One person believes the original was lost in a Nashville fire and another believes that a sort of lien was attached to the document because the printing bill was never paid. Unless the fire story is accurate, there is a good chance the original is still out there somewhere waiting to be discovered.

****

Photographs are among the most prized of all archives because they provide actual images of the persons and the events described in the words of the history books. Unfortunately, rare and valuable pictures are also a favorite target of archive raiders.

In the old days, before photocopy machines were invented and before archives routinely copied most pictures, the loss of a vintage photograph was particularly devastating. Although someone might have had a description of the photo, without a copy it was extremely difficult to know which picture had been in which archive. In many instances, the pictures were not recorded or inventoried, so if one was stolen, the archive never even knew it was missing. Of course, even if there was a record or an inventory, once the photograph was stolen, it was still just as gone.

In one collection donated to the Texas State Archives in Austin, an early inventory notes that there are two daguerreotypes of Sam Houston. One of the pictures is the famous pose of Houston dressed in a western-style duster with what appears to be a bandanna tied around his neck. It is considered one of the best Houston pictures of all time. There is a chance the other picture would be just as interesting but we'll probably never know for sure. It is missing and presumed stolen.

****

This photograph showing Sam Houston in a western-style duster and bandana is considered one of the best ever made of the old general. Another picture of Houston was donated to the Texas State Archives at the same time as this picture, but the second one has disappeared.

The most devastating case of an archive collection being raided was actually carried out on purpose. Although no one knows exactly when it happened, it was sometime after 1873, possibly around 1903 or 1904. It's one of the saddest stories in the annals of Texas history.

The story actually began in 1857 when the editors of the *Galveston Daily News* decided to publish an annual recap of life in the Lone Star State to be entitled the *Texas Almanac*. Between 1857 and 1873, the *Almanac* was published each year except 1866. A total of sixteen issues were produced and today the original copies are expensive collectors items.

In 1873, George B. Dealey took over as manager of the A. H. Belo company which operated the *Galveston News*. For reasons that have been lost to history, Dealey decided to suspend publication of the *Almanac*. It has been speculated that Dealey was a businessman concerned with bottom line profits and that the *Almanac* publication was suspended because that book was not paying its own way.

In 1885 Dealey was an integral part of another dramatic decision. The *Galveston News* was struggling to get copies of its daily paper to various distribution points around the state and it was feared that other competing papers would be formed to fill the void. To resolve the situation and to strengthen its position in the market place, A. H. Belo decided to try a revolutionary new idea and establish a branch paper in another area. He planned to utilize the new telegraph and "ship the news by wire" to the second location. George Dealey was assigned the chore of finding a suitable location and he selected Dallas. The first issue of the new *Dallas Morning News* rolled off the press in 1885.

Again for reasons lost to the passage of time, it was decided to resurrect the old *Almanac* in 1904 and print the books out of Dallas as a project of the *Morning News*. When that decision was made, there was no longer any need for *Almanac* files in Galveston and the unthinkable happened. Someone ordered the files purged and, incredibly, a significant amount of vital Texas material was discarded. According to most accounts, everything associated with the old *Almanacs*, including original copies of stories and irreplaceable photographs, was boxed up and carted off to the local city dump.

In addition to publishing the state's vital statistics, the early issues of the *Almanac* also included interesting stories about Texas history. Perhaps the most famous story appeared in the final Galveston edition in 1873. It was written by an historian named William P. Zuber, and he told the famous story of how Louis or Moses Rose had actually escaped from the Alamo and lived to tell about it. The Zuber tale also included the first (and only) details of William B. Travis supposedly drawing the famous line in the dirt.

Thanks to that one story, generations of Texans have believed the line incident really happened, and the tale has become so intertwined in legend that it can never be removed. Serious historians, on the other hand, have challenged the story almost from the moment it was published. So intense were the challenges that Zuber spent considerable time defending the validity of his tale. At one point, he made a startling announcement when he admitted that a small part of the story was, indeed, fiction, but that he had included it because it made the story complete and that it fit the spirit of Travis the man.

Unfortunately, Zuber did not say which portion of the story was fiction. He did, however, offer a valuable clue. Zuber maintained that when he sent the original story to the editors of the *Almanac*, he bracketed the fiction part, supposedly so the editors could decide for themselves whether or not it should be included. The editors decided the fiction part should be included and printed the story as Zuber had written it but without the famous brackets. There isn't a single Texas historian who wouldn't give his eye teeth for a peek at that original handwritten copy of the Zuber story. But apparently it is gone forever, thrown out with the rest of the *Almanac* files.

Another valuable Alamo document may also have gone out with the trash. The 1860 edition of the *Almanac* included the first and only translation of a report done by Francis Antonio Ruiz, the man assigned by Santa Anna to oversee the burning of the bodies of the Texans who fell at the Alamo. While the report provided some valuable information, there are some inconsistencies, especially concerning where Davy Crockett fell, and many historians believe that perhaps an error was made in the translation. Although many people have searched for the original, it has never been found, leading to speculation that it might have been a victim of the great *Texas Almanac* file purge.

Despite the disastrous results of the *Almanac* files being discarded, there may be a glimmer of hope. Many years ago a rumor circulated that some of the people assigned to throw away the files actually went through the documents and kept certain items for souvenirs. One man, whose family lived in Galveston for generations, said his grandfather had always claimed that he had packed up two boxes full of the precious archives for a member of the paper's management staff. Unfortunately, the man did not recall his grandfather ever mentioning the name. Based on such slim evidence, there is a chance that at least part of the *Texas Almanac* files did survive and will one day surface. For historians, a slim chance is considerably better than no chance.

There are probably hundreds more stories of lost or stolen archives. Fortunately, most of them are old stories because many of the libraries of today have become fortress-like and the precious Texas archives are considerably more secure than ever before. Most libraries require patrons to register, and such things as briefcases, notebooks, and jackets — perfect hiding places for stolen documents — are expressly prohibited. Patrons are never allowed in secure areas and usually only one file at a time can be reviewed. There is also a continuing effort to increase security. The Alamo library recently spent more than $40,000 to enlarge the vault, increase shelving, and to beef up individual security. No cameras, notebooks, or pens are allowed. The libraries have, however, given in to one modern invention and most archive repositories allow lap-top computers.

The new and strenuous security measures are a constant hassle for any researcher who has to use the archives extensively while doing research for a particular project. The hassle is, however, a small price to pay when you consider that the alternative might be to not have any access at all to the files and records. The raiders are still out there, you can be sure, and without strong security measures, the libraries would have no choice but to seal their files, and that would be devastating.

There is, perhaps, a final point that should be made. For most missing documents, the mystery of what happened to them and where they are today continues. For a surprising number of artifacts, however, the mystery has actually been solved, in an odd sort of way. There are many cases of archivists knowing exactly where their missing documents are located — locked away in some private collection.

The popularity of Texanna collecting which was spawned in the 1960s continues unabated today. Numerous people around the state and the nation have significant collections that are not available to the general public. Some of the documents in those collections were stolen from archives. In most cases, the collector was not the guilty party but rather a victim of the thief. The documents may have actually passed through several hands on their way to the collector, but that does not change the fact that the materials are stolen goods. Unfortunately, in the case of archive material, there is a large difference between knowing something is stolen and proving it sufficiently to effect a return.

During the past 100 years or so, a mammoth amount of material has been donated to archives around the state. In the days before sophisticated computers, it was often difficult to keep track of who gave what to whom and when. Such a record, which would ordinarily become part of the provenance of a particular document, is often hard to find, which means it is equally difficult for an archivists to prove a particular letter or photograph was stolen. In the case of the missing photograph of Sam Houston, there is no description or copy of the original so there is little chance the picture can ever be recovered. As for the copy of the Travis broadside that was taken by the forger, the archive will not only have to find it but then prove that the copy is the one stolen, and that is a difficult proposition.

There are still opportunities to recover some material but it will take time and money. Michael Green, reference archivist for the Texas State Library estimated that as much as forty or fifty thousand dollars might be required to go through the entire state records and establish the provenance for all materials in that repository's holdings. In these times of budget cuts and skyrocketing taxes, the chances that such sums will be made available are slim and none, and slim is saddling up to leave town.

If you have any information concerning lost or stolen archives, please contact the author at Wordware Publishing, Inc.

Sources

Books:

Chariton, Wallace O. *100 Days in Texas, The Alamo Letters*. Plano, Texas: Wordware Publishing, Inc. 1989.

_____. *Exploring the Alamo Legends*. Plano, Texas: Wordware Publishing, Inc. 1989.

Day, James M. Captain. *Clinton Peoples, Texas Ranger*. Waco, Texas: Texian Press, 1980.

Fowler, Mike and Jack Maguire. *The Capitol Story, Statehouse in Texas*. Austin: Eakin Press, 1988.

Gray, William F. *From Virginia to Texas*. Houston: privately published, 1909.

Jenkins, John H., General Editor. *The Papers of the Texas Revolution, 1835-1836, 10 Volumes*. Austin: Presidial Press, 1973.

Kahl, Mary. *Ballot Box 13*. Jefferson, N. C.: McFarland and Company, 1983.

Kemp, Louis W. *The Signers of the Texas Declaration of Independence*. Houston: The Anson Jones Press, 1944.

O'Brien, H. V., Jr. *The Story of Old Rip*. Cisco, Texas: The Longhorn Press, 1965.

Ruff, Ann. *A Guide to Historic Texas Inns and Hotels*. Houston: Lone Star Books, 1982.

Smith, Roy Lee. *Eastland County, Gateway to the West*. Eastland, Texas: Eastland County Book Committee, 1989.

Streeter, Thomas W. *A Bibliography of Texas*. Portland, Maine: Anthoesen Press, 1955.

Stehling, Arthur. *L.B.J.'s Climb to the White House*. Chicago: Adams Press, 1987.

Syers, Ed. *Ghost Stories of Texas*. Waco, Texas: Texian Press, 1981.

Webb, Walter P., Editor-in-Chief. *The Handbook of Texas*, 3 volumes. Austin: Texas State Historical Association, 1952-1976.

Welch, June Rayfield. *All Hail the Mighty State*. Waco, Texas: Texian Press, 1979.

_____. *Going Great in the Lone Star State*. Dallas: G.L.A. Press, 1976.

Yoakum, Henderson. *History of Texas From Its First Settlement in 1685 to Its Annexation to the United States in 1846*, 2 volumes. New York: Redfield, 1856.

Newspapers: Various issues of the following:

Austin American Statesman
Dallas Morning News
Dallas Times Herald
Houston Post
Paris News

Magazines:

Texas Monthly, March, 1989
Texas Observer, November 7, 1986
Time, July, 1974

Personal Interviews:

U.S. Marshal Clinton Peoples, retired
Mr. Charlie Eckhardt, Seguin, Texas
Mrs. Dorothy Vaughan, Paris, Texas
SFC James H. Baker, Paris, Texas
LTC Daniel E. Wisely, Paris, Texas
Roy Lee Smith, Eastland, Texas
James Dabney, Eastland, Texas

Unpublished:

Mixon, Ruby. *William Barret Travis, His Life and His Letters*, Masters Thesis, University of Texas, 1930.

Peoples, Clinton. His personal papers in the Dallas/Texas History Collection of the Dallas Public Library. Reviewed with permission.

Sources for: From Ford's Theater to the Granbury Opera House

Books:

Bates, Finis L. *Escape and Suicide of John Wilkes Booth.* Memphis: Bates Publishing Company, 1907.

Eisenschinal, Otto. *Why Was Lincoln Murdered?* New York: Halcyon House, 1937.

Kimmel, Stanley. *The Mad Booths of Maryland*. Indianapolis: The Bobbs-Merrill Company, 1937.

Lewis, Lloyd. *Myths After Lincoln*. New York: Blue Ribbon Books, 1929.

Roscoe, Theodore. *The Web of Conspiracy*. Englewood Cliffs, New Jersey: Prentice-Hall, Inc., 1959.

Sifakis, Stewart. *Who Was Who in the Civil War*. New York: Facts on File Publications, 1980.

Bryan, George S. *The Great American Myth*. New York: Carrick and Evans, 1940.

Baker, Lafayette. *History of the United States Secret Service*. Philadelphia: privately published, 1867.

Turner, Thomas Reed. *Beware the People Weeping*. Baton Rouge, Louisiana: Louisiana State University Press, 1982.

Velazquez, Lorita J. *Women in the War*. Richmond, Virginia: privately published, 1876.

Samples, Gordon. *Lust For Fame: The Stage Career of John Wilkes Booth*. Jefferson, N.C. McFarland and Company, 1980.

Magazines, Periodicals, and Newspapers:

Blue & Grey Magazine, April/June 1990 issues.
Cattleman Magazine, August 1968.
Dearborn Independent, March 21, April 4, April 11, May 2, June 6, 1925.
Harper's Magazine, November 1924.
Pie Magazine, September 2, 1941.
San Antonio Express, December 18, 19, and 20, 1931.
Chicago Westerners Brand Book, March-April 1978.

Personal Interview:

Jo Ann Miller, Granbury, Texas, May 30, 1990.

Play Script:

Miller, Jo Ann and John Sims. *John Wilkes Booth — The Myth and The Mummy*. Granbury, Texas: privately published, 1986.

Photo Credits

The following are sources for the photographs used in this book. In all cases, the photos were used with permission.

pg. 10   *Houston Chronicle*
pg. 17-18   *Paris News*
pg. 27-28   Author's collection
pg. 29-30   Author's collection
pg. 31-32   Author's collection
pg. 45   Author's collection
pg. 59   State Comptroller's office
pg. 60   Austin History Center, Austin Public Library
pg. 72-73   Roy Lee Smith
pg. 77   *Dallas Morning News*
pg. 81   Author's collection
pg. 81   Roy Lee Smith
pg. 83   Author's collection
pg. 100   From the Clinton Peoples collection in the Texas/Dallas History and Archives Division, Dallas Public Library.
pg. 120-121   Texas Observer
pg. 120   *Waco Tribune Herald*
pg. 139   Author's collection
pg. 142   Jo Ann Miller
pg. 140   Author's collection
pg. 145   Jo Ann Miller
pg. 154   Author's collection
pg. 158-159   Jo Ann Miller
pg. 165   Texas/Dallas History and Archives Division, Dallas Public Library.
pg. 166-167   Texas/Dallas History and Archives Division, Dallas Public Library.
pg. 185   Author's collection
pg. 207   Barker Texas History Center, University of Texas, Austin
pg. 210-211   Texas State Archives
pg. 215   Author's collection
pg. 224   DRT Library at the Alamo
pg. 243   Texas State Archives

Index